D0592935

Pola Negri

POLA NEGRI

HOLLYWOOD'S FIRST
FEMME FATALE

Mariusz Kotowski

UNIVERSITY PRESS OF KENTUCKY

Published by the University Press of Kentucky,
scholarly publisher for the Commonwealth,
serving Bellarmine University, Berea College, Centre College of Kentucky,
Eastern Kentucky University, The Filson Historical Society, Georgetown College,
Kentucky Historical Society, Kentucky State University, Morehead State
University, Murray State University, Northern Kentucky University, Transylvania
University, University of Kentucky, University of Louisville, and Western
Kentucky University.
All rights reserved.

Editorial and Sales Offices: The University Press of Kentucky
663 South Limestone Street, Lexington, Kentucky 40508-4008
www.kentuckypress.com

Unless otherwise noted, photographs are from the author's collection.

Library of Congress Cataloging-in-Publication Data

Kotowski, Mariusz.
  Pola Negri : Hollywood's first femme fatale / Mariusz Kotowski.
     pages cm
  Includes bibliographical references and index.
  ISBN 978-0-8131-4488-7 (hardcover : alk. paper) —
  ISBN 978-0-8131-4490-0 (pdf) — ISBN 978-0-8131-4489-4 (epub)
  1. Negri, Pola, 1899–1987. 2. Actors—United States—Biography. 3. Actors—
Poland—Biography. I. Title.
  PN2287.N35K68 2014
  791.4302'8092—dc23
  [B]   2013045085

This book is printed on acid-free paper meeting the requirements of the
American National Standard for Permanence in Paper for Printed Library
Materials.

∞

Manufactured in the United States of America.

Member of the Association of
American University Presses

To my wife, Heidi,
and to my parents, Marianna and Henry Kotowski.
Thank you for your love and support—
they have inspired me every day.

Contents

Illustrations follow pages 86 and 150

Foreword

When Mariusz Kotowski approached me in 2006 about showing his documentary, *Pola Negri: Life Is a Dream in Cinema*, at the Museum of Modern Art, I was well aware (as a film historian) of Negri's place as one of the major stars of the silent period. I came to be surprised, however, by the fact that she seemed to have been forgotten by so many people. This made the showing of Mariusz's film and a small Negri retrospective seem all the more urgent. The story Mariusz tells in his film and in this biography is so full of twists and turns and surprises that it would probably have been rejected as the basis for a film or a novel as too implausible.

Born Barbara Apolonia Chałupec, Negri rose from humble Polish origins to wed nobility and become world famous. First becoming a film star in Poland and then in Berlin, Negri fell under the tutelage of Max Reinhardt's protégé Ernst Lubitsch, one of cinema's most creative directors in the period encompassing the two world wars. She was brought to Hollywood, blazing a trail for later European imports such as Greta Garbo and Marlene Dietrich. She had affairs with Charlie Chaplin and Rudolph Valentino, two of Hollywood's most illustrious personalities. With the advent of talking pictures, when the sound of her Polish accent caused a crisis in her career, she returned to Europe. Eventually, she resurfaced in Germany. The Third Reich had seen to it that all her Jewish friends and colleagues were gone, and Hitler himself, reportedly, was her biggest fan after seeing her first German talkie, *Mazurka*, in 1935. She managed to escape Germany before America's entry into World War II and, improbably, spent the rest of her life deep in the heart of Texas. She was able to squeeze in a few novelty roles in American films and write an autobiography before her passing.

Negri's life was one of contradiction and possibly even confusion. She flourished as a glamorous vamp in many of her major roles, but she aspired to the kind of artistic recognition afforded to Chaplin and Garbo. Her Svengali, Lubitsch, made only one Hollywood film with her, *Forbidden Paradise*, gravitating to actresses with a more subtle touch than Negri: actresses like Marie Prevost, a former Mack Sennett bathing beauty, and Irene Rich, who played naturalistic roles opposite Will Rogers. Negri played Catherine the Great in *Forbidden Paradise,* but her performance was co-opted and eclipsed a decade later by Dietrich in Josef Von Sternberg's masterpiece *The Scarlet Empress.* Throughout the 1920s Negri was generally directed by second-raters like George Fitzmaurice and Dimitri Buchowetzki. Her brand of exotica began to wear thin, despite occasional flashes of a truly accomplished actress. It is hard to know what direction Negri's career might have taken if the microphone had not intruded.

I was personally amazed by Mariusz Kotowski's exuberance and energy in the cause of reviving Negri's memory. The Polish cultural community in New York is very active, and Mariusz managed to galvanize this group into supporting two overflow screenings of his documentary at the museum. The event was covered by Polish television, which interviewed me, and I experienced, in Andy Warhol's phrase, my fifteen minutes of fame. Polish cable television stations all over North America broadcast the report, and I begin to receive phone calls from unlikely places asking how to contact Mr. Kotowski. I now have many Polish friends. I am personally highly gratified that Mariusz Kotowski's film has received so much attention and that Pola Negri is being celebrated in her native country.

Charles Silver
Associate Curator, Department of Film
The Museum of Modern Art, New York City

Introduction

When I was growing up in Poland, Pola Negri was a household name. My mother introduced me to her at a very young age, even though we were not able to see any of her films. At the time, during the 1960s and 1970s, Polish people did not have access to American films, which is where Negri really made her name, and none of her German works were available either. She was a countrywoman who had made good in the magical, far-away land called Hollywood. How did she do it?

Books about Hollywood stars were banned in postwar Poland, where I grew up on the other side of the Iron Curtain. The Communist rulers felt they needed to protect the people from the moral decay of the glamorous, decadent West. To a young man like me, that made the allure of the great stars even stronger. I had never seen a Pola Negri film, but I grew up hearing stories about her—stories that were always told with a sense of pride. The Polish people would never forget their beloved Pola, the Warsaw ballerina who became the Hollywood megastar of her day and graced film screens and stages all over the world.

When I was ten years old, I was so inspired by the art of filmmaking that I vowed to make movies in America someday. I left Poland to pursue a career in dance and choreography that took me, eventually, to America and the life in film that I had imagined as a boy. Busy with film school and directing, I hadn't thought about Pola Negri in some time. Then one night in 1998, I walked into Joe Allen's restaurant in New York and came face to face with a magnificent photograph of Pola, gazing out at the world with sensuality and command. I couldn't help but think she was looking straight at me, perhaps even challenging me.

My next Negri moment occurred on a 2002 visit to Grauman's Chinese Theatre in Los Angeles. I looked down and found that I was standing almost on top of Negri's square on the Walk of Stars—the one she contributed in 1928 when she was at the pinnacle of her film career at Paramount. "Dear Sid, I love your theatre," she wrote. She was the eleventh person to add her star to the walk; she and her ex-fiancé Charlie

Chaplin (star number 10) were the only stars invited to add squares that year. How could the world remember the Little Tramp and forget about Negri? Looking down at her dainty handprints and shoeprints, I resolved to do what I could to revive the memory of this fascinating woman.

I started traveling around the country, interviewing people who still remembered Negri or had insights into her place in film history. Those interviews became the basis of my 2006 documentary, *Pola Negri: Life Is a Dream in Cinema.* I visited the Pola Negri archives in San Antonio and started collecting photos, clippings, reviews, and memorabilia that helped me weave together the threads of her life. *Pola Negri: Legenda Hollywood,* my 2011 Polish-language biography of Pola, was named Book of the Year in Poland. The response to both works showed me that the Negri mystique is as strong as ever and that people are hungry to learn more about her. What is it about this mysterious beauty that fascinates us a hundred years after she began her career in Poland? Why is her story so little known—shrouded in mystery and filled with misperceptions?

Negri was a diva in the true sense of the word. Before there was Greta Garbo, there was Pola Negri. Before there was Marlene Dietrich, there was Pola Negri. She was the first actress brought to Hollywood from Europe and featured in starring roles during the period of an exceptional boom in the art of making movies. The first talking film in 1927 was still years ahead, and silent movies required acting that was larger than life—one of the reasons why both producers and audiences loved Negri so much. Born in Poland and discovered in German cinema, she had classical training in acting and dancing—useful in the pantomimes of the silent-movie era—as well as the ability to speak and sing in five languages.

Gifted with an expressive face, an eloquent body, and an indomitable will that helped her transcend a chaotic and impoverished childhood, Pola Negri made more than sixty movies in America and Europe. She is credited with creating the cinematic femme fatale. Her lifestyle was fabulous, glamorous, and discussed almost daily in gossip columns worldwide. She was a friend and lover to some of Hollywood's most enduring legends: fiancée of Charlie Chaplin, engaged to "dark lover" Rudolph Valentino just before his untimely death, wife of Prince Serge Mdivani. She was Adolf Hitler's favorite actress, although they never met in person. Her films made him cry, however. Her fortunes reversed many times in her life—from being the highest-paid star in Hollywood to escaping Nazi Germany with what she could carry in a suitcase. Her life story is a rich and complex one, and it could only have happened in the silent era.

Because we do not hear their voices, silent stars speak only from our own imaginations. In our minds, we attribute to them the most lyrical speech patterns and the most exquisite emotions. They transmit their good and evil actions directly to us, undisguised by dialogue. A silent star could not make a case for herself other than what she said with a look or a gesture.

Silent stars also show us what drives characters' emotions, what triggers their desire or despair. Pola Negri was like a human volcano, dynamic and expressive, bubbling with energy that could not be tamed. Comfortable in any role, she could play a vain, opportunistic woman or Catherine the Great as easily as a gypsy dancer or a bandit queen. She could effortlessly convey utter joy as well as heart-breaking despair—emotions that, to her, were just a normal part of human life. A 1987 Combined News Services obituary stated: "All sources agree that Negri was one of the first women in Hollywood to rate the accolade 'star.'" Later in the obituary Negri is quoted as saying: "I was the first and I was the best."[1]

From a young age, Pola Negri knew she was meant to succeed, and she thoroughly enjoyed the pleasures of stardom and the exalted view once she got there. Her determination sustained her in a career that reached some of Hollywood's highest heights. "Pola Negri is a star and she intends to play that role as long as she lives," declared Marjorie Clapp.[2] She presented the image of a spectacular and sophisticated woman—the epitome of eroticism.

"I was the star who introduced sex to the screen, but it was sex in good taste," Negri told interviewers;[3] she would have been insulted had someone labeled her "decent." She became fitful and snarled when her whims were not pandered to. She wanted fresh orchid petals strewn on her dressing room floor every day and gleaming gold handles on the door to her limo. She wanted the things she owned to conform to the image she held of herself, which was one of a passionate and desirable woman. But she could also be a refined lady, an intriguing contrast to her wildcat behavior.

Pola Negri created a spectacular image for herself—a curvaceous woman who wore fabulous couture and had an exotic voice that added to her mystery. Her Polish accent hinted at Old World castles and culture. Negri's gypsy blood, mixed with the Slavic in her, created a delicious lugubriousness when she sang the nostalgic old gypsy melodies. She sang melancholy songs as if she was happy to sing them and happy songs with a touch of regret. Negri understood that good fortune could end at any moment, that her wonderful world could fall apart before her very eyes.

Although she had a challenging childhood, Pola Negri felt born to entitlement and could be as imperious as any queen. Americans, having no queens of their own, relished her aura of opulence. Negri never spoke of her ancestry, never admitted to being one of the people. She walked around in thousand-dollar furs and storied jewels worth more than a million. Negri dined like a queen, drank the best champagne, and cultivated a love of opera and fine art. She was a sophisticated woman with exquisite taste who also had a rebellious streak.

This streak is what her admirers loved most. This animal nature she possessed was like nothing they had ever seen before, and it was the key to her sex appeal. Mary Pickford and Gloria Swanson were both big-name stars, but they never stepped outside of the good-girl image. Swanson and Pickford only played at being grand. Everybody knew that their image was purely fictitious—that underneath their sophisticated clothes, they were simple women.

Negri made men stumble and women stare. She possessed a unique timelessness and she seemed to have experienced everything the world had to offer. Even when she was acting, Negri could never stop being herself. Her ideas and experiences put the finishing touches on the writer's script, making a director's job easy. According to her work ethic, it was her job as an actress to energize the words on a page. She poured a part of her own life into every part she played, and she always demanded intelligence from her audience.

Film critic Harry Carr may have summed up Negri best in his 1925 *Motion Picture* article "The Mystery of Pola Negri." Carr, who knew Negri well, describes her as "cruel, condescending, overbearing, humble, contrite, generous, sweetly reasonable, gracious with a charm that would disarm an ogre, disagreeable, ungracious, winning, forbidding. In other words, Negri is every kind of woman—according to the mood of the moment." Admiring Negri for daring to "change her emotional clothes in public," he concludes: "Whatever she does, whichever way she takes, hers will never be a tamed heart. Pola will be a beautiful, highly educated, cultured barbarian to the last day of her life."[4]

I

Early Years in Poland

In her final film, *The Moon-Spinners* (1964), Pola Negri utters a line that screenwriter Michael Dybne wrote just for her. Playing a mysterious, world-weary jewel thief, Negri says, "I have survived two wars, four revolutions, and five marriages." Other than the exaggerated number of husbands (she was married twice, once to a count and once to a prince), the line is pretty much true—and makes an excellent introduction to the tumultuous life of Pola Negri.

Pola was born into a changing Europe and a new century. As peasants moved off the farms to the factories, the cities grew gray, the air became thick with smoke, and most people despaired of trying for a better life. People who labored twelve to fourteen hours in the factories rarely dared to raise their heads. They went home to fall into bed, only to do it all over again the next morning. Poland had been under the rule of the Russian czars for decades, and most people seemed to accept this with a fatalistic spirit.

An underground spirit of rebellion was growing among the Poles, however, and Jerzy Chałupec was one of the men who eventually took action against Russian rule. When he was twenty-one, the traveling tinsmith captured the heart of thirty-one-year-old Eleonora Kelczewska, a refined young Polish woman who had never been married. Her sisters, who had taken more traditional husbands, tried their best to end her engagement to the Slovak-gypsy immigrant, but Eleonora would not be dissuaded. When she saw the tall, handsome Slovak, she knew she wanted nothing else but him. Ignoring the age difference, she married the man she loved in 1892. The newlyweds settled in Lipno, a small town between Warsaw and Bydgoszcz, and Jerzy set up a metal workshop that soon began to prosper.

Pola was born on January 3, 1897, as Barbara Apolonia Chałupec—

although in later years she claimed the last day of the century, December 31, 1899, as her birthday. She never doubted that her parents loved her. She was the youngest, and the sole surviving child of three. Her mother doted on her, adorning her hair and clothes with ribbons and preparing special treats just for her. Jerzy often rushed home from work at lunch to whirl her in his arms. "I was my father's pet," Pola remembered. "He never returned home without bringing me something, and he always took my part when I did something naughty. My mother was very stern and strict—like Polish mothers of the old school—while my father was light-hearted and gay. He had flashing black eyes and wonderful teeth. I have never seen someone so handsome."[1]

Skinny and prone to illness, Pola required a lot of nurturing, and her parents feared for her. They were afraid of losing her, like their two older children. Although she didn't appear strong physically, Pola loved to climb trees, and inevitably she fell out of one. Naturally, her father came running to the rescue. She had to be carried to the hospital in Torun, which meant crossing the Russian-German border. The incident almost cost her an eye. She was told to keep her feet on the ground after that, but Pola found that impossible.

Because she had no siblings, Pola tended to be a loner, and as her parents often pointed out, she lived a rich life inside her head. Her father gave her the pet name Zamyslona, or "meditator," referring to her need to sit alone, daydreaming. Barbara Apolonia Chałupec sensed that she was different from the other little girls in her neighborhood, whose ultimate purpose in life was to grow up and get married. It was fine for them, but not for her. She had a burning desire to be noticed.

For a while, things worked out well for the small family. Jerzy Chałupec was a tinsmith, like his father and his grandfather before him. He worked hard in his workshop, and soon he was doing well enough to send for his mother and his brother. They all lived in a five-room wooden house. The home was not a palace, but it felt safe. Eleonora had her dream man, a little doll of a daughter, and a maid to help her out. She was devoutly religious, as was Jerzy's mother, so family activities revolved around the principles of faith and the Catholic Church.

When Pola was almost eight years old, Jerzy started being away from home for hours and hours. He would disappear and then return, only to leave again. Fond of spending late nights in local bars with friends, he began to associate with underground revolutionaries who were organizing against the Russian regime. In 1903 he was arrested and sent to prison. "Despite the fact that my father was a foreigner, he fought for Poland in the revolution of 1905," Negri wrote twenty years later. "Poland in 1905 was not the free country it is today. Our people were ground down by Russian, Austrian, and German oppressors, and nowhere was our lot worse than in the provinces governed by Russian officials."[2]

Jerzy's brother Paweł took their mother back to Slovakia, fearing that the Russians might take repressive measures against them. Eleonora sold the house in Lipno, which was in her name, to help pay for her husband's defense, and moved with her daughter to Warsaw. She had enough money to rent a small attic room on Browarna Street and buy a small grocery store in the Leszno area of Warsaw. No longer a young woman, Eleonora worked hard all day at the store, then went to visit her husband in Warsaw's Pawiak Prison at night.

Eleonora did not turn out to be a very skillful merchant, however. After a few months of letting customers run up large tabs, she reached the end of her savings and the store went bankrupt. She tried to stay positive, praying and hoping for the family to be together again, but often sank into depression. Pola became very close to her mother in their poverty and solitude. Eleonora struggled every day of Pola's childhood to put food on the table. "She came of gentlefolk and had always been provided for," Negri wrote later. "She was unfitted to work."[3]

Pola started attending a general-admission parochial school in Powisle, but her grades were weak. Arrogant and rebellious, she also had trouble fitting in with her peers. The girls at the parochial school made fun of her looks. She wore country braids and old clothes but behaved as if she was better than any of her classmates—a combination the other children didn't understand. Pola was pretty, with an air of edginess and mystique, which made her stand out from the other girls. They excluded her from their circles. Even so, Pola believed she was better off than most. She knew she wasn't born to live in dirty Powisle and breathe the rotten stench of the river, but she didn't want to be a complainer. The other girls had fathers to fend for them, and Pola could no longer hide behind hers. She had to find her own way to stay strong.

The Pola Negri story truly begins in 1911, when the thirteen-year-old girl was admitted to the Warsaw ballet school. There are several different accounts of how she managed to change the course of her young life, but clearly, Pola knew from an early age how to make the most of any opportunity she was given. A. A. Lewis, the writer who worked with Negri on her autobiography, retells her story of being discovered:

> They lived in a slum, the worst section of Warsaw. Her mother took in some roomers; a couple who were in the opera came. Pola was twirling around the living room, the way children will, and this couple said, "She should be a dancer," and they took her to the ballet school which was part of the opera and Pola was enrolled. They gave her a scholarship. Her mother had no money at all. Pola's beauty, charm, and talent were immediately recognized. By the time she was thirteen or fourteen, she was playing featured roles. Pola's mother thought theatrical entertainments were frivolous, though she loved the opera. Because the ballet was connected to the opera, and because Pola finally admitted to her difficulties at parochial school, Pola's mother allowed her to become a dancer. She worked very hard to take her Mama out of the slum.[4]

By day, Pola's life was devoted to the rigors of mastering ballet; by night, she learned history and arithmetic from a neighbor down the hall, who was a dedicated teacher. She kept up with her studies, thankful to put the Catholic school behind her. Although her health was somewhat delicate, she excelled at dance. Girls who sneered at her because of her background had to acknowledge her talent. She had poise, despite being a poor child with a father in jail. In 1911 she made her stage debut as one of the twelve lucky ones chosen for the swan dance in *Swan Lake;* she wore a white-feathered cap and a dress to match.

The stage became Pola's comfort zone, where she felt loved and adored by everybody around her. All she had to do now was show how much she deserved it. Her talent and her high-strung nature gave her an extra advantage. Onstage she courted attention, even when she danced in a group and had no spoken lines.

Neither of Pola's parents made it to her swan debut. Her father was still in confinement—he had lost his appeal and was being transferred to Siberia—and her mother was slowly recovering from the pain of the separation from her husband. Eleonora had spent all of her love and most of her money on him, and now there was no hope of reconnection. Pola was initially told she couldn't see her father until he was released, but her mother made an exception. She brought Pola to Pawiak Prison on her confirmation day so her father could see her in her veil.

In her memoirs, Negri recalls that she cried all the way to Pawiak. The cheap shoes she was wearing had split their seams during her confirmation rites with a loud, undignified rip. She knew those were the only shoes her mother could afford, but that was little consolation. This was the day she officially became a person in her own right, and it had been ruined.

Eleonora scolded Pola for her tears, asking her to brush the incident aside and dry her eyes for her father. Jerzy had not seen his daughter for years, and Eleonora wanted to cheer him up with the sight of a pretty, smiling girl and the happy image of his beautiful family back at home. He needed to believe that the world still had good things in store for him in case he managed to return from the frozen North.

Pola tried to cheer up, but once she saw her father, she broke down again. He was noticeably older, his face gone as gray as the walls around him. "My father's cell was a small, narrow rectangle with one side torn away and barred, so that whatever he did was in full view from the corridor. He slept, woke, ate, paced, relieved himself, and washed, all in public. This must have been the worst thing about prison for him. He was such a private man who kept his thoughts private and adored private places that were all his own," Pola wrote in her memoirs.[5] Her father seemed a stranger, not the man she remembered from Lipno. All he had left was his sense of pride and honor. Pola slipped her fingers between the cell bars, not minding that the steel was grimy and her dress was pristine white. She tried to hug her father, but the guards jerked her away.

After Eleonora's shop went out of business, she found work as a cook for Madame Fajans, a wealthy Jewish widow. The widow's two sons came to visit every Friday night, bringing their families for dinner. To cook for them, Eleonora had to learn the principles of kosher cuisine. She interviewed all the Jews she knew about their eating habits, taking longhand notes that she and Pola studied together. They became experts on the Jewish dietary code. Madame Fajans was so impressed by Eleonora that she never treated her as an employee but as a friend. They often attended Pola's performances together.

When Eleonora and Pola met Casimir de Hulewicz, the vice president of the Imperial Theater and director of state theaters, everything started falling into place. De Hulewicz offered Eleonora his assistance. He became her confidant and supporter, and he treated Pola like his own daughter. The refined, wealthy landowner from Ukraine was prominent in Warsaw society circles, and he also had connections to the Russian elite. His appointment to the Imperial Theater was an honor that gave him even more prestige.

Soon Pola was dancing leading roles. Even though she was still a child, she had a woman's face, with generous lips and expressive hazel eyes that flashed the same way Elizabeth Taylor's do in her films. Pola's figure was beginning to fill out, and the first signs of her tempestuous nature were emerging as well. Music was in her blood. She could bring any character to life.

From the beginning, Pola was enchanted by other performers. She made it a point to see the great actors, opera stars, and pianists perform whenever she could. She wanted to be well rounded. Many dancers cloistered themselves in their ballet world, never developing an appetite for other artistic mediums. Understanding that one art form could enrich another, Pola varied and expanded her studies. She studied a museum exhibition as closely as she would a mannequin in a dress shop window. She learned that the lines of the landscape and the mannequin's pose could both be incorporated into her dance. Structure was at the core of movement, so she spent a long time studying it. If she was to dance as a cloud or a leaf or a snake, Pola had to know how that kind of movement originated. If the dance was to reflect something intangible, like the wind, an echo, or a song, she had to learn the art of translation. She discovered how to turn steps into evocative movement that would be etched into her audience's memory.

"I want to be the world and everything in it!" was how Pola described her visions of her future career.[6] First she had to know everything. Then she would become everything.

She went to hear the famed opera singer Feodor Chaliapin, who once sang before the czar and chose to perform a revolutionary song in defiance of the regime. Arrested and facing exile to Siberia, Chaliapin had pleaded guilty—but only to having too much vodka while toasting the health of the emperor. Naturally, the judge could not convict him for something so noble. Chaliapin later became Pola's lifelong friend. She supported personal liberties; her belief in democracy and freedom was her strongest ideal. Chaliapin was a rebel, just like her father. She was drawn to men of spirit and conviction; she respected and appreciated them. Pola herself was never given to compromise. She lived for the day when no one would tell her what to do.

Pola was so focused on her dreams of a great and successful career that she didn't realize she was ill. Ballet rehearsals started to leave her too weak to perform, and she was diagnosed with the onset of tuberculosis. Upon hearing the news, Casimir de Hulewicz paid for her stay at Zakopane Sanitorium. It was during those three months of rest and relaxation in the mountains that Pola made up her mind to become an actress. With her lungs forever delicate, she knew she would never possess the vitality for a professional dance career. Acting seemed less strenuous physically, but it still tugged at the emotions. Pola knew she had a volatile temperament and thought it would be best used onstage with words—besides, she could make a living at acting.

At the Zakopane library, she came across the poems of the Italian poet Ada Negri. She loved them so much that she recited them to other patients in the evenings. The sorrows and exhilarations of those poems were very similar to her own. Impressed by Ada Negri's poetry, Negri adopted the poet's last name as her stage name. Unlike her Polish surname, Chałupec, the Italian "Negri" set off her nickname "Pola" nicely; the vowels standing out between the consonants provided just the right amount of punch. And so Barbara Apolonia Chałupec began the next phase of her life as Pola Negri.

After returning from Zakopane in 1912, Negri enrolled in the Warsaw Imperial Academy of Dramatic Arts, where she completed the three-year curriculum in one year. She studied hard and was soon cast in plays, earning better and better roles each time. Negri's personality could fill a stage and transmit an electric charge to the audience; her fiery, dramatic eyes conveyed emotion to the back rows of the theater. The techniques Negri learned for the stage were going to prove invaluable later: "I learned how to gauge an audience accurately and elicit greater laughs or tears by certain little tricks of technique—a cocked eyebrow, a break in the voice, a way of walking across the stage."[7]

Casimir de Hulewicz constantly watched the development of his protégé. He knew Negri had great potential, but her career needed proper management. He didn't want her to get locked into one role. He had seen too many actresses of forty play the same parts in the same performances as when they were twenty-five. Negri was a born dramatic type, and she learned her craft very quickly. De Hulewicz told her to bide her time—he would tell her when to make the right moves. He also promised to introduce her to all the right people.

By the time she turned fifteen, the life of the actress Pola Negri was fully launched. For her graduation performance she played Hedvig in Henrik Ibsen's *The Wild Duck*. She debuted in 1912 in Warsaw's Small Theater as Aniela in *Śluby panieńskie* (Maiden vows); she was coached by the renowned Polish actress Honorata Leszczyńska. The Warsaw newspaper *Kurier Warszawski* credited her "boldness and bravery" for such a young debut as an actress. The Polish reviewer added, "We are sure to see her again many times in the future."[8] After the debut, she continued to get offers for other roles. She played Clara in Hermann Sudermann's *Sodom's End*, starred in *Krzywda* (Damage), and was beginning to earn a salary. Her wages now made it possible for her and her mother to move from Bednarskiej 11, where there was only access to a shared outhouse, to Senatorska 6, where they could have their own bedroom and a bathroom inside the apartment.

Negri wrote later about the thrill of receiving her first payment for acting: "It was ninety rubles, amounting to something like forty-five dollars in American money at the rate of exchange before the war. Ninety rubles was a fabulous amount in my eyes. I rushed out to buy an armload of the most expensive flowers for my mother. When I burst into the room and thrust them upon her, she scolded me severely for my extravagance."[9]

Negri later moved on to the Rozmaitosci Theater, where she repeated her role as Hedvig in *The Wild Duck*—a role that resonated with her personally. "Hedvig was a girl I could completely understand," she wrote in her memoirs. "At fourteen, we had both been robbed of what might be called normal childhoods by the poverty of our families. We were both withdrawn, hypersensitive, given to poetic fancy, and possessed of a keenly developed sense of responsibility for our parents."[10] Thrilling as the stage work was, Negri recognized that it could easily lead to a dead end. Some Rozmaitosci actresses in their fifties were still playing ingénues. Yes, they had an audience, but their days were numbered. Negri began looking for other opportunities. After watching a few films from other countries, she had her eye on motion pictures—a new, slowly developing form of entertainment.

Then came 1914. World War I broke out, and the Germans overtook Poland, putting the Russians on the defensive. The battle over Warsaw continued. At one point, Negri and her mother sat in the dark in their apartment for three days, listening to the explosions. "Our apartment building was riddled with bullets," Negri recalled later, "and so many shots were embedded in the walls of my room on the seventh floor that I was unable to enter it—even to get my clothing."[11] The world seemed to be collapsing around them just as Negri was finally making money and they had begun hoping for some stability in their life. Thanks to Negri's hard work, they could afford to eat better, dress better, and find adequate housing. But bombs exploded around them, fires blazed, and lives were torn apart. Negri and her mother finally packed their bags, desperate to escape, but they heard a blast as they were headed out the door. The very bridge they were planning to take to safety was destroyed.

The theaters where Negri worked were all closed. The government requisitioned one to use as a hospital and planned to do the same with the others. Negri feared that the war would destroy the acting career that she had built. Eventually, the theaters reopened and she resumed acting for the stage, but she was becoming even more focused on making a career in silent film. With its roots in the art of pantomime, this medium could make full use of both her acting talent and her lively, expressive face.

Her break came when she was noticed by Alexander Hertz, owner of the Sphinx Film Company—Poland's first major studio. After seeing Negri in Gerhart Hauptmann's play *Hannele,* he put her under contract. One of the pioneers of Polish cinema, Hertz handled the entire production of his movies, from operating his own camera to painting his own scenery. Despite a shoestring budget, he always got things done on time. Negri made films with him by day and performed live in the usual stage plays at night. She understood that Hertz was giving her a unique opportunity, but she still wanted to maintain control over her artistic development. At this juncture she wrote her own screenplay, *Niewolnica zmysłów* (Slave to her senses), in which she played an exotic dancer who achieves a meteoric rise in her career—just as Negri hoped to do. Creating films in the early days of the Polish cinema was a makeshift process. "For actors we had to draft the services of friends who aided us merely for the amusement it provided them," Negri wrote later. "We made the interior scenes in a photographic studio, moving the furniture from my apartment when it was required. The exterior scenes were made in a nearby beer garden, which was loaned to us by the proprietor on condition that his daughter could appear in one of the scenes."[12]

As Negri prepared for the role at home, she played Arabian music and doused herself with exotic perfumes to create the right mood. Eleonora watched her stay up to write feverishly one night and prance around in harem pants the next. Negri didn't mind being two people at once. At home she was the good girl who took care of her mother, and for the camera she was a sexual dynamo. She wanted to be adored, she wanted to excite men, and she flirted with them—wanting them to associate her name with desire.

She did indeed turn heads, especially Ryszard Ordynski's. She had already starred in his Warsaw theater production of *Sumurun* in the role of an exotic dancer. The story called for Negri to be murdered by the Sultan of Baghdad after she insults him by having an affair with his son. When Max Reinhardt, Ordynski's friend and associate, decided to revive *Sumurun* in Berlin, Ordynski recommended Negri. The role changed the course of her life. "Max Reinhardt was the god of the German theater," according to film historian Scott Eyman. "He was the D. W. Griffith of Germany. He was the one everyone looked to—he could do anything, vast spectacles with hundreds of people coming in and off the stage. He had great taste in actors. Almost every actor who went on to fame and fortune came through Reinhardt's training school, from Emil Jannings and Conrad Veidt to Ernst Lubitsch and Pola Negri."[13]

Negri was already a star in Poland, but Germany had a more widely recognized theater district and a large cosmopolitan audience. Before she left Warsaw for Berlin, she did one last Polish movie for Sphinx in 1915, *Czarna książka* (The black pass), also called *The Yellow Ticket*. It tells the story of a young Jewish woman in czarist Russia who, after her father's death, is determined to become a medical doctor. She falsifies her identity in order to gain acceptance into the university, thus hiding her Jewish heritage and avoiding the anti-Semitic oppression rising in Russia. She is forced to find lodging in a brothel, and when she can't pay the rent, she is coerced into "the trade." Shamed, she attempts suicide, but her beloved professor and mentor restores her to health, only to discover that he is her true biological father. Her Jewish heritage was the result of the kindness of her adopted parents taking her in as a baby when she was abandoned by her real mother—the young girlfriend of her professor.

Negri felt she was perfectly suited for the role. It was one of only a handful of times when she played an innocent character who was pure in body and mind. Writing in 2013, Polish film reviewer Michal Oleszczyk commented on Negri's "thoroughly modern screen appeal" ninety-five years after the film was made. "She has Clara Bow's quickness and Louise Brooks' sultriness, as well as a strong, physical presence that's never frail," he wrote. "It's her intelligence, not her body, that's on display in the film. What's more, she's amazingly good at conveying uneasiness with the compromises she needs to make in order to study."[14]

Meanwhile, offscreen she was learning how to handle her affairs in the movie business. In an effort to keep Negri, the Sphinx Company refused to grant her a suspension to appear in *Sumurun*. Negri argued that because she had signed her contract as a minor, the company had no legal hold on her. She felt no animosity toward Hertz, but she knew that Reinhardt's vision was bigger and bolder. He would capitalize on her talents and help advance her career. She was grateful that Sphinx had given her a start, but it was time for bigger and better things.

2

The Move to Berlin

Born Maximilian Goldmann in Baden near Vienna in 1873, Max Reinhardt had a commanding presence. Forthright but gentle, he was a man who knew how to put on a show. As a young actor, he played mainly depressing character roles, to the delight of the critics, but these roles didn't satisfy him. Reinhardt wanted to work on more uplifting, exuberant projects that would also be more lucrative.

Reinhardt was a protégé of Otto Brahm, director of the Deutsches Theater in Berlin. The productions there leaned heavily on naturalism, a school of thought that tended toward "doom and gloom," shunning God and promoting science. In 1901 Reinhardt cofounded an avant-garde literary cabaret called Schall und Rauch (Sound and smoke), an allusion to a line from the famous poet Goethe. To Reinhardt, the theater was "a place for display, spectacle, magic," according to writer Otto Friedrich. "The revolving stage was his specialty, and so were the mysterious lighting effects that nobody else could duplicate. Reinhardt abolished the walls of conventional theater sets; he abolished footlights and curtains; his actors moved out into the audience and made it part of the spectacle."[1]

Schall und Rauch metamorphosed into the Kleines Theater, which became home to contemporary as well as traditional productions. A high point was the lavish production of Shakespeare's *A Midsummer Night's Dream* in 1905. By then, Reinhardt was an established director. "He had become so important that in solid middle-class families everybody skipped the newspaper headlines to read Alfred Kerr's article on the previous night's performance," writes film historian Lotte H. Eisner. "Berliners often went to the Reinhardt theater several times a week, for the program changed daily."[2]

Reinhardt succeeded Otto Brahm as director of the Deutsches Theater, then opened the Kammerspiele Theater next door. The new venue was ideal for more intimate works. To keep his theater ensembles populated, Reinhardt started an acting school where actors—many of whom became leading men and women—were trained in modern acting techniques.

When Reinhardt took Pola Negri under his wing as a theater actress, he offered her help and a great deal of invaluable advice. He made sure she received German lessons, set her up in an apartment with an older woman to look after her, and served as her confidant and friend.

Reinhardt believed in self-discipline behind the scenes. Onstage, however, he allowed his actors a great deal of freedom and independence. He never imposed his concept of a role on actors but encouraged them to look within. He felt that the most satisfying result of his work was not getting what he wanted from rehearsing with actors, but revealing each actor's own personality and allowing actors to express the secret of their being. Reinhardt found it better to guide, rather than govern, his performers. He made very detailed preproduction plans, then let nature take its course, giving actors the freedom to move their characters around, to collaborate—an approach that worked for the whole troupe. His concept of *Gesamtkunstwerk,* or "total work of art," meant that actors should pool their skills. They were free to change how they expressed their roles, inspiring the other actors to reinterpret as well.

Describing Reinhardt's methods as they worked together on their first production, Pola Negri said it was surprising how little talking the director did. "Prof. Reinhardt's method of rehearsing is very simple," she wrote. "Instead of making an elaborate explanation to an actor about the way he wants a role played, he allows the player to do what he wishes until he appeals for advice and direction. In this way the actor thinks he is actually creating the role. The psychological effect is amazing."[3]

Under Reinhardt's tutelage, Pola Negri could develop herself. She was learning when to dramatize and when to hold back. In the theater, each night's performance became a contest to see who really owned the stage. Negri would let other actors think they had it and then would win the audience to her side. Even if the audience disagreed with what her characters did, they still admired her portrayal.

The famous German film actors Paul Wegener, Albert Bassermann, Theodor Loos, Eduard von Winterstein, Conrad Veidt, Werner Krauss, and Emil Jannings all worked in Reinhardt's troupe early in their careers. He helped them mature from good to great actors. Reinhardt didn't just place people onstage; he was a master of lighting who remolded their faces.

Opposing the stark atmosphere the naturalists favored, Reinhardt wanted everything to have warmth, if not magic. He appealed to the audience's imagination.

The generation of directors before Reinhardt had conformed to a distinctive type of stage setting: bare, matter-of-fact figures and forms. Reinhardt saw a more compelling world full of color and allure. He was not sold on German pessimism. His sets created a panorama bursting with life, where light spilled toward the actors from multiple sources: windows, mirrors, stars that twinkled. His productions brought splendor to the eye and enraptured the audience. Reinhardt believed that even negative emotions presented onstage could spark some flicker of pleasure.

Negri made good use of her time in Berlin. She left her mother in the care of a reliable young writer friend and went out in search of new opportunities. Negri appeared in a series of film shorts, some of them comic, which capitalized on her sense of fun and her gift of comedic timing. However, she saw herself more as a femme fatale. As fate would have it, she met a director whose own comedic bent was taking a turn toward tragedy.

Ernst Lubitsch met Pola Negri while he was a character actor with Reinhardt's theatrical group, but he soon got involved with the German film industry. By age twenty-one, Lubitsch had developed his own slapstick persona on-screen: Meyer, a Jewish archetype who became a favorite of the German audience. Lubitsch looked to movies as a way of supplementing his theater paycheck. In 1915 he wrote and directed a one-reeler called *Fräulein Seifenschaum* (Miss Soapsuds).

Lubitsch was part slapstick and part intellectual. Negri knew that people saw him as a prankster and a clown, but she recognized his brilliant mind. There was nothing physically commanding about Lubitsch, Negri recalled in her memoirs, but she admired "the agility with which he expressed his often brilliant thoughts and the witty manner in which he indicated he was two steps ahead of anybody else in any intellectual gambit. A steady stream of eloquence flowed out around the cigar eternally planted between his lips."[4] As the Meyer shorts faded in popularity, Lubitsch leaned more toward directing. He was able to say more behind the camera.

United Film Alliance (UFA) was the largest film company in Germany, and the motion picture industry was making strides there despite the hardships of World War I. After Lubitsch went to work for UFA, Negri also received an offer to work for the studio. She accepted with the stipulation that Lubitsch serve as her director. Even though he was relatively new to the field, Negri trusted him fully.

The war placed German theaters in a critical situation. There were shortages of everything, from raw materials to money for building stage sets. Forced to abandon his grand productions, Max Reinhardt had to experiment with lighting to make up for the mediocre props. Before, the lighting just added to the spectacle; now, it made up the show. Shifting effects created moods, particularly with lights crossing the stage at every angle. A gleam or a glare animated cheap sets. Oscillating shadows made alleys look haunted, cellars foreboding, the evening sky fitful.

Reinhardt was not an expressionist, per se; he just knew how to create contrast onstage. The expressionist cinema that appeared after the war borrowed heavily from his techniques, using lighting to connote the dark forces within. For Reinhardt, the world was not a horrific place, but one full of surprises.

Although Lubitsch had his own brand of talent, his films bear the stamp of Reinhardt's influence. The lighting tricks he employed are reminiscent of Reinhardt's stage shows. Characters surge out of the darkness, or light pierces a blackened sky from a central point above, typically a window or a candelabra. Costumes and furniture glitter with opulence. Lubitsch liked to leave space around the protagonist, grouping the extras so the audience never forgot who was at the center of attention. Negri did some of her best work under Lubitsch, because he let her dominate the screen. The people to the left and right of her often got shut out of the frame as the camera narrowed in on her. No matter how she fared as a character, Negri emerged from every Lubitsch film a winner. The talent of the cameramen she worked with helped as well. "You had great cameramen back then who understood black and white films," film historian Anthony Slide observes in an interview. "They really did everything themselves. They lit the scene. They operated the camera as if they were a one-man photographic department. You also find that many of the stars knew the value of the cameraman, so they would select their own personal cameraman to film them."[5]

Lubitsch possessed an exceptional intuition. He understood people, and he knew what would make an impression on the audience. He could expose people's foibles with what became known as "the Lubitsch touch," using wit and innuendo to convey what was really going on. A fully clothed

Negri could tease a man sexually by letting him manicure her nails. Nothing else was needed—the audience could assume exactly what was taking place. Lubitsch could slyly get a sex scene past the censors because it was so underplayed, but at the same time it was so natural that it didn't seem contrived. In Lubitsch's films, Negri was always a woman who used her beauty and femininity to her advantage and was fully aware of how indispensible she was.

Lubitsch understood Negri's range, whereas many people did not. He also understood the sophistication that she could deliver, and she trusted him completely. The two became artistic partners in this new, uncharted field called motion pictures.

3

With Lubitsch in Germany

The silent era was, of course, the beginning of the invention of a new language—the language of film. Everything had to be made from nothing, and many mistakes were made before standards were established. "The extraordinary thing about those early days of films was that we all invented ourselves as we went along," Negri said afterward. "There were no guidelines."[1]

Just as the director needed new equipment to accommodate his ever-growing vision of light and motion, the actors needed to adjust the skills of their craft to these visions. The use of the close-up, for example, forced performers to develop a very different performance style because of the intimacy of the lens. They had to leave behind the broad, exaggerated gestures that stage actors needed to reach the balcony from a distant stage. With this new approach, the audience felt they were experiencing the performer in a way they had never thought possible. Every gesture, every expression or emotion was made more powerful through the lens. A good director could give the audience the impression that they were standing right next to the actor. Via the camera, one could enter a room and stand beside the actor, walk around and behind him or her, see every side, know every line. Actors and directors alike knew they were facilitating a very different kind of relationship and that they were involved in creating the first true stars. It wasn't that there hadn't been stars before in opera or theater, but this was the birth of a new kind of stardom—one that created a personal and emotional relationship with the viewer.

Pola Negri was passionate about being challenged in her roles. She had boundless enthusiasm and energy for discovering new things about herself through each character she played, and she was eager to bring her excitement to the camera. She was aware of how this energy could be placed very powerfully in the frame and then transmitted directly to each

23

person in the movie theater. Such awareness allowed her to make a successful transition from stage to screen. Quite a few stage actors were left behind because they continued with their grandiose stage style, which looked ridiculous on the screen. Some cinema actors, of course, had no theater background—they just learned film acting from the ground up. Negri's dramatic training and her experience working under Reinhardt created the perfect formula for success.

In 1918 Pola Negri and Lubitsch made *The Eyes of the Mummy Ma*. They were a perfectly balanced team; she was emotional and he was analytical. Throughout the many movies they made together, they were always able to successfully rework the same themes with a refreshing new take: blind passion coupled with raw nerve, unrequited love as a cause of death, pain that was almost too much to bear.

The Eyes of the Mummy Ma tells the story of a romantic triangle in which a man loves a woman, the woman loves another man, and nobody gets what she or he wants. Emil Jannings, who had acted alongside Negri and Lubitsch under Max Reinhardt, played one of the lovers. By all accounts, Jannings tended to be unpleasant behind the scenes. He kept away from other actors, and he spoke in monosyllables. His fellow actors thought he took himself too seriously and was too imperious. However, audiences sat riveted when he played small parts. Jannings later starred with Negri in *Madame Du Barry*—ironically, as a king with a submissive streak.

During the filming of *The Eyes of the Mummy Ma*, Jannings had to stab Negri at the top of a flight of stairs. Instead of staggering backward, she decided to fall down the whole flight, trusting that her dance training would let her control the fall. Lubitsch warned her against taking such risks, but Negri ignored him, certain she could handle it. As the cameras rolled, however, Negri's heel caught in the hem of her dress. She went down in a tumble and lay there, dazed but unharmed, thanks to a knowing friend who had scattered pillows at the foot of the stairs. "Lubitsch was swearing wildly at me, first at me and then at Jannings for not having caught me," Negri wrote later. She also quoted Jannings's response to Lubitsch: "How was I to know what she was going to do? Did I ask you to hire this crazy Pole?"[2]

The scene stayed in the film and left audiences gasping. Although Pola Negri and Jannings worked together after that, they were less than friends offscreen. Professionally, they had a lot in common. Their careers followed similar trajectories: Germany to Hollywood, then back to Germany. There was no love lost between them, but they could portray mutual passion well enough on film.

Carmen, also billed as *Gypsy Blood,* was the next Lubitsch-Negri production. There was already an American version of *Carmen* with Geraldine Farrar, but Lubitsch was not impressed—he was certain he could top it. Negri had her reservations. She believed a silent film could not be made successfully from such an iconic opera, but Lubitsch saw *Carmen* as a classic tale. He convinced her when he told her this would be her chance to play a real beast.

In *Gypsy Blood,* Pola Negri plays the passionate and greedy La Carmencita, who is desired by most men in town. A low-class girl with an itch for grandeur, Carmencita chooses Navarro (played by Harry Liedtke, another Reinhardt veteran) and brings him to ruin with her outrageous demands. A factory employee and a sensuous gypsy dancer, she is also a thief. Any man who gets involved with her finds himself trapped in a web of lies.

Undoubtedly, La Carmencita gets her way more times than she should. She steers Navarro—who, despite his uniform, is more passive than militaristic—away from his fiancée and his military obligations. La Carmencita trifles with him, calling him a canary and watching him squirm as she seduces other men. Even with her hands tied behind her back, the temptress snatches back a rose from Navarro's lapel, only to display it seductively between her teeth.

Trying desperately to win Carmen's attention, Navarro becomes a military deserter, a murderer, and a fugitive camping in the mountains. He soon becomes disheveled and despairing, with a perpetually mournful expression. Lacking the carefree attitude of the Gypsies around him, Navarro cannot shrug off the atrocities he has committed.

La Carmencita, on the other hand, doesn't think twice about what she has done. While Navarro is tormented by his disgraceful deeds, La Carmencita is at her most divine. She becomes the lover of Escamillo, a top bullfighter. No longer the gypsy girl lost in the mountains, she attends the bullfight adorned in lace and jewels like a true lady. She doesn't realize that her past is about to destroy her. While caught up in watching the spectacle of the bull's violent death, La Carmencita feels the surprise of a sword driven through her. Navarro is the man behind the blade. A fellow cutthroat has goaded Navarro, convincing him that he is a cuckold who needs to defend his manhood—it is an affront that La Carmencita has cheated on him with a bullfighter. Navarro extracts his revenge swiftly, before he has a chance to reconsider. La Carmencita, his life's pulse, now lies dead and unavailable to any man, including Navarro.

After the movie was released as *Gypsy Blood* in the United States in 1921, the *New York Times* described Negri's character: "She does not seek to have and to hold; her sport is to capture and destroy, for to destroy the captured is to carry the conquest to its natural conclusion. She hunts and kills in disregard or ignorance of posted fields and closed seasons. She possesses all of the natural artfulness of the female of the species without the protective finesse of the civilized variety."[3]

Ultimately, it is La Carmencita's fate we mourn, not Navarro's, although he commits suicide soon after her death. When she is out of his life and out of the picture, we miss her on-screen. Navarro is such a depleted wreck that he fails to hold our interest. La Carmencita, even as she lies in the gutter, is the one who wins our sympathies, as cruel as she may have been in her torment.

With her dove-white skin, raven hair, and beguiling smile, Negri's La Carmencita was not the stereotypical gypsy. She plays the role with complexity and charm, eloquently expressing her character's moods, impulses, joys, and fears. With her features soft and vulnerable and her eyes charismatically intoxicating, Negri is incandescent as she exhibits her abundant personality on-screen. Each action is a specific communication of a thought or feeling that culminates in La Carmencita the cigarette girl, not Pola Negri the actress. In 1927 she told an American magazine that La Carmencita was her favorite role. "I understood her. I loved her. I was her. It was like playing an organ with innumerable stops. Every emotion could be touched upon."[4]

The *New York Times* wrote in 1921: "Miss Negri's Carmen is no studio puppet: she is no grand operatic queen without a vivifying voice. She is a tempestuous, intemperate gypsy girl, a magnetic, unmoral animal, a free-living, free-loving savage of capricious appetites and a consuming zest for satisfying them. Nothing is precious in her eyes."[5] *Photoplay* was impressed by the film's authenticity as well as Negri's performance: "This Carmen, as played by the intense Negri, is a very real sort of Carmen who refuses to tidy herself up before the camera for the very good reason that Carmen herself was not a tidy person. You feel the background strongly; you feel that it is genuine; that this is the real Seville, and these the real characters around whom the opera was written."[6] Not everyone agreed. A review in the trade journal *Wid's Daily* called Negri's Carmen "about the crudest, most boorish, unfeminine hoyden that has ever been presented" and commented that the film was done with "a heavy Teutonic hand."[7]

The film conquered another reviewer's anti-German sentiments. "We had been feeling strongly on the subject of this importation of German films," Harriet Underhill wrote in the *New York Tribune*, "but *Gypsy Blood* has convinced us. We wouldn't have missed it for the world, and if American producers are wise it will set a new standard for pictures. The story unfolds so naturally on the screen. The play is a slice of life; the camera discovers the characters doing ordinary homely things and records their actions on the film." Praising Negri's "gorgeous performance," Underhill called her "a powerful actress, who is fascinating, beautiful in a way that has character for its foundation, and intelligent."[8]

Carmen premiered in Berlin as Germany was losing World War I. Champagne flowed inside the theater, accompanied by gunfire outside. Negri shimmered in a beautiful, expensive gown from an exclusive dressmaker. The guests at this gala affair were not in the mood for defeatism, even as shots rang out and added to the drama of the performances. The audience stayed in their seats, Negri's ferociously life-loving Carmen providing a welcome escape from the violence that was taking place in the streets. When the party was over, people slipped out of the theater two at a time, hoping to find their way home safely.

Negri herself had to sneak through the streets to the subway alone, keeping her back to the walls. A successful movie star one minute, she became a moving target the next, but the incongruities of life did not faze her. Military skirmishes were nothing new to her—she had survived the Germans in Warsaw. "The Polish revolution of 1905, the great war, then the Kaiser's abdication and the revolution of 1918. . . . My life truly has been a drama of great scenes," she wrote later.[9] She was not distressed by dangers that were not of her own making, although she had to protect herself against them. Like La Carmencita, Negri was not going to give in to her fears.

At the end of World War I, when Poland was given back to its people, Eleonora received word that her husband, Jerzy, had regained his freedom. However, he would not be returning home to her in Warsaw—he had found another woman. Eleonora blamed this on the fact that she was ten years his senior, according to Negri's memoir, but Eleonora waited for Jerzy anyway, in hopes that he would return to her when he became ill or needed her.

But Jerzy never resumed contact with Eleonora, or with Negri. Given his early affection for his daughter, one can imagine that he rejected Negri because she was part of his previous family in his previous life, not because she had done anything wrong. Negri tried to think well of him because, despite everything, her mother refused to speak ill of her husband. His abandonment was understandable when he couldn't break out of prison, but how to explain those later years after he had been released? Negri had to come to terms with the truth—she was part of a past that Jerzy chose not to reclaim.

Rebellion was Jerzy's strongest suit. He loved liberty, and he was willing to fight for it. Refusing to bend to the whims of people he did not respect, he had perceived the occupiers' rule as grossly unfair. Jerzy never considered the negative impact his revolutionary activities might have on his family, however.

Many years later, Negri told the story of her life for the Hearst newspapers in America. She romanticized it, enhancing certain facts and fictionalizing her past. This mitigated the pain that accompanied her memories, while at the same time making her biography more attractive for readers. In the installment where she talks about the separation from her father, she says that after the Cossacks abducted him from the house and burned the place to the ground, she never saw him again. No mention of the heartwrenching trip to the prison or the hands that clutched hers through the bars. No speculation on "the other woman" who became Eleonora's successor. It was easier for Negri to denounce the occupiers than to say her father no longer wished to see her. In her 1970 memoir, though, she reveals the facts about her father's refusal to see Eleonora and Negri after his release from prison.

Negri often kept her emotions in check in real life, but such restraints were cast aside on the film set. She was paid to emote, to turn pain into anger. Whenever an on-screen lover shortchanged her—broke an engagement or sabotaged her plans—Negri was always scripted for a payback. Every leading man became a lover who made her feel like the most important thing in his world; if he could not live up to the task, he lost his title. One might say that Negri ultimately got back at her father by keeping a legion of male admirers reacting to her slightest frown. Each saw himself as the man who could wipe away her sadness and give her all she desired. While women saw her tantrums as a mark of independence, men were enticed by her outbursts.

Negri was most certainly not a poor, downtrodden, suffering little creature. She played roles in which her characters suffered and felt pain, but she always brought out the essence of a woman who made her own decisions. Acting not only accommodated Negri's true emotional nature; it also created a clear path to financial stability.

Lubitsch was a key catalyst in Negri's pursuit of independence. Although they were never lovers, there was an intimacy to their conversations. The essence of the relationship between Lubitsch and Negri was not unlike a marriage, and they had a great deal in common. Both were outgoing, up-tempo people, and they got along very well. Everybody loved Lubitsch. Not everybody loved Negri. She could behave like a diva, even very early in her career when she was still in Germany. Lubitsch's humor and patience equipped him to deal with this. He had a slow fuse and almost never lost his temper; he could soothe and deflect people with his wit. Also, he was one of those directors who genuinely liked actors. Having been one himself, Lubitsch knew firsthand the anxieties, fears, and insecurities of being onstage or in front of the camera.

Negri's seriousness and drama plus Lubitsch's boyish attraction to lowbrow humor made for an electric combination. Lubitsch was a great director but also a very intelligent man. His little jokes and his ability to poke fun at common anxieties made the day bearable. Negri was the perfect match for him—a serious actress, but also a round-faced, plump-lipped Polish girl, so pretty that she invited a pinch on the cheek. When she and Lubitsch got together, they both gushed with enthusiasm and good humor. "He was so funny," Negri recalled later, "that I even laughed when the jokes were on me."[10] Lubitsch exploited the ridiculousness of Everyman. His characters were real people, quick to jump and slow to learn. His movies portrayed a Negri who was cruel, but he gave her every right to be, by showing the vultures flocking everywhere she looked. At UFA, Negri worked with other directors. She remade *Czarna książka* as *Der gelbe Schein* (The yellow ticket) with Paul Stein and filmed *Komtesse Dolly* with George Jacoby, and then she worked with Stein again on *The Last Payment*. However, it was Lubitsch's Negri that audiences clamored for most—a woman with admirable skills as a wrongdoer.

Lubitsch was the perfect director for Pola Negri. He understood that however she characterized herself, she had the intelligence to play serious roles with great pain and suffering, as well as the ability to be light, witty, and sophisticated.

In 1919, Negri and Lubitsch's *Madame Du Barry*, the tale of the French king Louis XV and his tempestuous mistress, broke box-office records everywhere in Europe except France. There, people protested in the streets about the way French nobility was portrayed. They objected to having a German director malign and criticize their aristocracy. The historical angle also caused concern on the other side of the ocean. Financial backers thought that Americans might be put off by a historical title, so the film was released as *Passion* for distribution in the United States. Nevertheless, the role cinched Negri's reputation as a world-class actress. As Jeanne Du Barry, a sweetly smiling shop girl with a mischievous streak, Negri was an enigma that demanded further study. Her Du Barry was never truly fiendish or arrogant—just fond of making the world dance to her tune.

Lubitsch wasn't a French history buff, but he knew it was the details that enriched a movie. A love story played better if it was framed in visual majesty. A king had to be regal, despite being inept as a ruler, but his oversights were less forgivable inside a sumptuously decorated eighteenth-century palace. Lubitsch believed the people at the top of the social ladder squabbled as much as the people at the bottom, so he emphasized petty jealousies in all the threads of the plot. Negri's Madame Du Barry is never power-hungry in the same way nobles are. She simply believes that the best-looking girl should be the belle of the ball.

When Jeanne, the future Madame Du Barry, appears before the king with a petition, the Court kneels down in front of him as he grandly extends his hand to her—and she jumps into his lap and coyly allows the lecherous old king to retrieve the scrolled petition she has placed under her bustier, between her breasts. As he reads it, she moves up against him, batting her eyes suggestively in a deliciously titillating moment. It's sensuous, but in a very comic and lighthearted way, with one riveting element: Negri, a woman in control.

Even as a young performer, Pola Negri was never really a girl. She was always a woman, with a woman's sexuality and a woman's drive and desires. This set her apart from all the other leading women of her time, in Europe or in America. She was the antithesis of Mary Pickford. Pickford was a remarkable actress who played mainly adolescents—

always the girl shy about her sexuality. Even in her early twenties, Negri seemed worldly, mature, and always sure of herself among men. In 1920 the *New York Times* wrote: "She makes Du Barry real, as fascinating as she has to be, with as much of the appearance of dignity as she must have on occasion, and as contemptible and cowardly as she was. She actually wins sympathy for a woman who cannot at any time be admired. This is an accomplishment."[11]

Lubitsch biographer Scott Eyman agrees, commenting on Negri's exuberant high spirits, which are "girlish, almost Mary Pickfordish," in the first part of the film. "If it's possible for an actress to believably play a character who sleeps her way to the top and still remain innocent, Negri manages to pull it off. Later, she marries, gains the name Du Barry, and grows imperious and willful, which Negri communicates through body language. Lubitsch ventures into territory Von Sternberg would later make his own when he shows Jannings kissing her feet and quietly doing her nails. Negri's quiet, cat-that-ate-the-cream satisfaction is perfect; because she is sexy, she doesn't have to play it sexy."[12]

By the time Jeanne arrives at the palace, her flirtations have already caused one death. She stands up Armand, her first lover, by choosing to go to a masked ball with a wealthier prospect. Armand is left waiting by the sidelines as he watches her flirt with other men. One of them is her escort, Don Diego. After Armand challenges the Spaniard and kills him in a duel, he is thrown into prison.

When Jeanne meets Louis XV, we learn that he is as much a child as she is. Jeanne has lived such an impoverished life that her wants are still primitive. She craves creature comforts and indulgences—a lavish table invites her to steal a bite, and a thickly quilted bed delights her. The king's little-boy antics are quite another story. Try as he might, he can never escape the responsibility of running the kingdom, with advisers constantly seeking his ear. Jeanne tugs at his heartstrings by inventing infantile games and having him fit dainty shoes on her feet or clip her fingernails; when he accidentally nips her, she reproaches him for his clumsiness until he is properly contrite. And so the king, the ruler of France, becomes her slave/daddy. But try as he might, Jannings's Louis XV cannot conquer Negri's teasing Jeanne. He can touch her, but only on her terms and conditions. She doesn't need his love and merely plays at getting it—she considers him her protector and nothing else. When Jeanne is held up to public ridicule, the king pulls strings and keeps her in the palace by arranging a fake marriage to the profligate Count Guillaume Du Barry.

As Jeanne rises to the top, she never tries to help the people she left behind. Children are starving and peasants gather at the palace gates, but Jeanne ignores them. She goes back to playing Blind Man's Bluff with the king and his nobles and strolling the palace's manicured gardens, a magical place removed from everyday concerns. Jeanne wants to be a savior for one person only: Armand, the tall, moody student of modest means who is imprisoned as a result of Jeanne's coquettish tricks. Once she has the king's ear, Jeanne wheedles a pardon that spares Armand's life. Jeanne confesses her love to Armand, hoping that he still feels the same about her, but his manhood is insulted to the core once he learns that Jeanne has been appointed his guardian. Although she pursues him shamelessly, he views her with contempt and leaves her to join the mob.

Meanwhile, the king has contracted smallpox, and he wants Jeanne to attend to him. She won't stay at his bedside, and he dies far from her consoling arms, angered that Jeanne has gotten away from him. The people storm the Bastille. Madame Du Barry, deprived of honors and wealth, is thrown into prison. Armand, her former lover, is now a judge on the revolutionary tribunal. He tries to rescue Jeanne from the death sentence, but the revolutionaries repay his tyranny by shooting him. As Armand sinks to the floor, Jeanne rushes to his side, knowing that her own fate is sealed. She clutches at her dead lover, blood on her hands, until she is pulled away to her execution. A stone-faced executioner awaits her at the guillotine and Armand's murderer stands nearby. Still hungry for life, Jeanne starts praying, entreating God with every ounce of her being: "One more moment. Life's so sweet." The ropes around her tighten, nonetheless. In the European version not only does the guillotine come down, but the executioner throws Du Barry's head out into the crowd. This was considered too strong for the American censorship boards, so an alternate ending was created: as her pleas for mercy go unheeded, "The End" flashes on the screen, masking her death.

The *New York Times* complimented Negri's on-screen personality: "Her moving picture is stamped with her individuality, and largely because of her definite pantomimic ability. It is not physical beauty that wins for her. She is lovely in many scenes, it is true, but some of her features are not beautiful, and she makes no apparent effort to pose becomingly without regard to the meaning of her performance. She is expressive. That is her charm."[13] A *New York Daily News* reviewer commented: "As an actress she has vivacity, a radiance, which endows the historic character of Madame Du Barry with life. Her power and versatility as an emotional actress are reached by no American screen star I can call to mind. She is lovely, possessed of a beauty that combines vivacity and intelligence with the charm of perfect control."[14]

Because Jeanne Du Barry was a historical figure, Negri prepared for the role by reading extensively about her and studying her portraits. "I had boundless enthusiasm for the character of Du Barry," she wrote later. "How I knew the soul of that little milliner! Like me, she was the daughter of an ironic fate. Next to Carmen I like the role of Du Barry the best of all I've played."[15]

Lubitsch gave Negri's Du Barry an authentic palace. Frederick the Great's summer palace in Potsdam, called Sanssouci, had a look reminiscent of Versailles. Massive amounts of equipment and a cast of five thousand had to be moved to the location, and housing had to be found for the cast and crew.

Audiences and critics were stunned by Lubitsch's control of scenes and continually compared him to D. W. Griffith. Reviewing the two directors' work today, one may say that Lubitsch is even more capable, efficient, and sophisticated than Griffith. Lubitsch choreographed large groups of people within a confined area—a city square, for instance—with great ease. *Madame Du Barry* and its American version, *Passion*, became Negri's and Lubitsch's calling card for the world market. When the film played in the United States, Americans had not seen such spectacle come out of Europe before. Nor had they ever seen an actress like Negri, who could not only hold her own with her leading men but almost obliterate them. "*Passion* comes like a bolt from the blue," *Motion Picture* announced, "and a few more bolts of a similar nature will cause the American producers to realize that they no longer have a monopoly."[16]

Madame Du Barry's Berlin premiere in 1919 coincided with the opening of the UFA Palace, which, with four thousand seats, was the largest movie house in Europe. A new era had begun for the industry, with *Madame Du Barry* as its forerunner. The reaction was overwhelming; Negri was hoisted up onto shoulders and hailed as a queen. Representatives from all over the world, from each of the giant movie companies, were in attendance.

Among the many celebrities and political dignitaries present was

Charlie Chaplin. Albert Kaufman, the German representative of Famous Players–Lasky (later to become Paramount Pictures), made the introduction. The graying Chaplin was older than Negri had expected, and he looked it. Without the comical mustache, his face was sad. "He had tiny feet, elegantly enclosed in black patent leather and gray suede button shoes," Negri wrote later, "and an enormous head that made him seem top-heavy."[17]

Chaplin was on a mission to strike up friendships with German actors, and he urged Negri to give America a try. The cream of the crop of screen actors gathered in Hollywood, he told her. Meanwhile, agents were competing with each other in their pursuit of Negri, making promises and buying her gifts. Ben Blumenthal, head of Hamilton Pictures, gave her a diamond and pearl bracelet and promised to arrange for Negri's German films to be shown in the United States. He assured her that he would get her a contract in Hollywood, and she was starting to believe it.

With the premiere of *Madame Du Barry* such a great success, theater owners across Europe began to defy the ban on German films that had followed the war. As the movie traveled from country to country, Negri, Lubitsch, and the crew waited to see what would happen. Would the Negri film break the ban, or would the law be enforced if theaters broke it? When the American version was released, Samuel "Roxy" Rothapel tried it out in New York's Capitol Theater, giving it one night to become a hit or end its run. Negri and the crew waited to hear how it fared. *Passion* racked up 21,000 admissions on the first day. People lined up for hours, and thousands were turned away. The box-office grosses for that day alone, a Sunday, totaled twelve thousand dollars, at ten to thirty cents per ticket, and fifty-five thousand dollars for the week. During a two-week engagement, 350,000 people saw the movie. The rave reviews started pouring in.

The picture was first billed as an Italian film, with Negri's name alone on the advertisements. Later, it was called "a European spectacle," again to disguise the fact that it was made in Germany. UFA had a hard time finding an American distributor because of anti-German sentiments. Associated First National Pictures acquired the *Madame Du Barry* rights for forty thousand dollars, while other distributors were too fearful to buy it. The company exercised caution in promoting it, but the reviews were so outstanding that worries were eventually brushed aside. Author A. A. Lewis comments:

Pola Negri and Lubitsch were the ones who broke the embargo on German films, not Fritz Lang, not Murnau, not any of the great Expressionist directors. . . . That film, *Du Barry,* played for months and months and months in theaters in New York, Paris, London, everywhere. We must remember, of course, that it was a silent film so there was no language problem. A German film didn't have subtitles. It had the same titles that any English-speaking film had, and the rest was in pantomime, and Pola was a brilliant silent film actress. Brilliant. And she and Lubitsch were what Von Sternberg and Dietrich became years later.[18]

A cablegram brought Negri and the *Madame Du Barry* crew the big news of the film's success overseas. They had made film history in more ways than one. Negri's name was to be placed on the marquee. Also, the film had been so universally praised that the ban on German films was broken. More films were requested to be shown in the United States, some of them Negri's. Negri had been at the top of the German film industry for nearly five years, and there was still a place for her there, but it was clear that Negri needed to go to America. She had outgrown Europe.

America was the great filmmaking machine that wanted to absorb anyone good, no matter where they came from. The success of the picture in America meant that almost all the entire cast and crew were immediately offered contracts in Hollywood, but Negri did not want to jump into anything too fast. She wanted to be respected as a great artist who could, at the same time, look glamorous and be promoted as a star.

With every new picture, Negri had gained the admiration and captured the imagination of the public. She was glamorous and talented, yet there was no steady partner in her life. That situation changed during a trip from Warsaw to Berlin. During an altercation with customs, Negri was brought before the man in charge, the very handsome Count Eugene Dombski. He was proud to help such an attractive damsel in distress.

Not long afterward, he invited Negri to dinner and stated his intention to marry her. Negri's mother urged her to accept. Both of Dombski's parents were dead, but he had two sisters, Irena and Ludmilla, who were not fond of their soon-to-be sister-in-law. The couple was married, nonetheless, on November 5, 1919, at the Catholic Church Wniebowzziecia Najwietszej Marii Panny in Sosnowcu, Poland.[19] Once the newlyweds made their home in Dombski's large, heirloom-filled home, loneliness and disappointment set in for Negri. Because Dombski's work often kept him away for long periods of time, he left Negri alone with his younger sister, who oversaw the functions of the household. Restless and bored, Negri spent hours looking out the window and longing for the big, exciting world she had been part of just a short time ago.

This was far from the marriage of Negri's romantic dreams. She had a show-business personality that craved being the center of attention and did not suit the role of homemaker and wife, where she felt unappreciated. In her memoirs, she spoke of the feeling of being isolated among her new family; they shared a common bond with their mutual history, friends, and events of which Negri knew nothing. She never felt part of the conversation. "I was married just a year and a half," she wrote later. "My husband wished me to give up my work and take my social position as the countess. I could not do it. Happy as I was during the first few months of marriage, I felt constantly the urge of my ambition. My work was really my first love. It had lifted me from poverty, restored my mother to health and comfort, and given me a position in the world of art that I loved."[20]

Her isolation ended when Ernst Lubitsch arrived from Berlin to visit. He was there to remind her that she still had a contract with UFA, and she had to meet her obligations. Lubitsch helped Negri secure permission from her husband to go back to Berlin and fulfill her contract. She eagerly left her life of desolation and headed for the arms of her true family, where she was happiest and always felt the most at home.

4

Postwar Berlin

At first, Pola Negri did little socializing in Berlin. Friends offered her invitations, but she declined; books were her main entertainment. Her friend Paola Loebel, a Jewish intellectual, and her social circle did their utmost to urge Negri to go out, and they finally succeeded. Loebel and her friends took Negri to play tennis during the day and to local hot spots after dark. The social whirl offered relief from the slow tedium of her marriage to Count Dombski. Negri adored the dances coming over from America and the freedoms they embodied. America was young and in love with itself, and jazz spurred Pola's natural rhythms. Americans danced to show they were aware of what they could do, while Berliners danced because they didn't know what else they could do. America suited Pola's personality.

Germany was struggling with postwar reconstruction, political anxiety, and the need to pay war reparations required by the Treaty of Versailles. Prices were rising and the traditional moral values of the past were declining. People who still had money spent their nights at clubs, singing and dancing. Cabarets thrived. Paris was bringing on the Roaring Twenties, and Berlin became equally decadent. With the crumbling of the aristocracy, film stars became the wealthiest and most admired members of this new, seemingly amoral society.

So much was changing—not only in the news, but also in Negri's life. With her newfound riches, she started to invest in jewels. Currencies, along with governments, were always in a state of flux, but she knew that diamonds and pearls held their intrinsic value. Negri bought part of the Hohenzollern collection. A famed Berlin jeweler, Margraf, proposed that she purchase the valuables because only a big-name movie star could afford such a significant expense.

The Hohenzollern Dynasty had ruled Prussia, parts of Poland, and Romania for over five centuries. After World War I, the heirs of the monarchs were forced to sell the family's most precious ornaments, and Negri was able to buy exquisite diamonds and pearls that had remained in the Hohenzollern family for centuries. She acquired a dazzling bracelet with a 150-carat emerald set in diamonds, a 30-carat diamond ring, magnificent pearls, earrings, clips, and a diamond tiara. "Film stars were rapidly replacing the old aristocracy as fantasy figures," she wrote in her memoirs. "We were the ones making the fabled sums of money and living the glamorous lives, while the great families were being forced to sell their possessions in order to survive."[1]

While in Berlin, Pola received sad news from Poland. Jerzy Chałupec had died on the front lines in 1920, fighting the Russians as a Polish soldier during the war. Negri's mother went into mourning. Later, in her memoirs, Negri said that her mother called Jerzy a hero and forgave him all his faults. Eleonora now locked herself into the role of a martyr, a suffering widow who dressed in black and lit candles, even though so many years had passed since the day Jerzy had abandoned them. Perhaps she was mourning all the wasted years when she could have renounced her marriage, sidestepped her religion, and perhaps found happiness with another man—Casimir de Hulewicz, for instance, whom she never allowed to be more than a friend.

With this chapter of Eleonora's life closed, Negri begged her mother to leave Warsaw and come to Berlin, but her mother refused the invitation, just as Negri now refused any advice on romance that Eleonora had to offer. Her mother did not accept Negri's lifestyle in Berlin, viewing her as a married woman who was acting like a single girl. Eleonora urged Negri to return to Dombski, but by then Negri and Dombski's marriage existed only on paper. Dombski wanted a stay-at-home wife to bear children and attend social events. Incapable of appreciating the artist in his wife, he felt that she should leave her career for him. Of course, the driven Negri wanted nothing to do with such a future of submission and was willing to sacrifice anything for her career. The couple agreed to lead separate lives without getting a divorce. Negri kept living and working in Berlin, and Dombski maintained his residence in the countryside, occasionally going to Warsaw on business.

Negri could not be alone for long, however, and in time she found herself a suitable lover in Berlin—or maybe it was he who found her. Wolfgang George Schleber was the wealthy owner of a large textile enterprise. Negri dubbed him "Petronius" because his aristocratic profile reminded her of the main character of *Quo Vadis?*—a popular novel set in Roman times. Petronius had wanted to meet the famous Polish actress for years. They finally met and were immediately smitten with each other.

Negri was fundamentally a romantic. She loved poetry, champagne, caviar at midnight, and promises made in the moonlight. Petronius was a refined young man, attractive enough to get his way without much effort, but he was also practical. The word was that he had conducted affairs with many beautiful women in Berlin. When he faced Negri for the first time, he called her "the most sheltered woman in Berlin" because of how difficult it had been for him to meet her. Negri was not discouraged by Petronius's reputation as a lady's man. She liked a man who knew more about the art of seduction than she did; that was the kind of teacher she craved.

Pola was physically alone and emotionally adrift until Schleber found and intoxicated her, offering her exactly what she had been missing. He appreciated every moment he could spend with Negri and never pushed her into anything. Petronius introduced Negri to the world of luxury, bookstores, art galleries, and libraries full of secrets and useful information. Each date with him was exhilarating. He understood her needs and cultivated her higher instincts, as well as her sexual desires. Sex was no longer a duty, as in her marriage, but grew as the result of their mutual feelings. He taught Negri to marvel at the male physique, through the great art and sculptures of the masters. She felt fulfilled in this relationship, dazed and enthralled to have someone in her life she actually wanted to spend time with. Negri devoted several pages of her memoir to her affair with Schleber and called their first few months together the most glorious of her life. "He had found in me an unfulfilled, tormented young woman and had shown her how to exalt in the pleasures of giving and receiving love."[2]

Petronius opened new doors for Negri. He taught her how to drive and showed her how to pair good wine with a meal. While their friends limited themselves to jazz, Petronius introduced Negri to Beethoven, Bach, and Mozart. He took her to the theater or a concert every night. At last, Negri felt appreciated. She loved being able to develop her various interests and expand her horizons with her new lover.

But she was also jealous. She was constantly suspicious that her lover was cheating on her. This trait proved to be detrimental to her stardom, and any lover who failed to understand this about her placed himself in peril. When Petronius failed to turn up for a date one night without explanation, Negri became hysterical. She raced her Mercedes through the night to his hotel for a surprise visit, dragging Lena, her old caretaker, along with her. Petronius was not in his room, so Negri bombarded him with phone calls and stuffed notes under his door with a myriad of curses. Her lover had to repent for hours before he was allowed to tell his side of the story. He explained that he was attending a bachelor dinner where Prince Hohenlohe was one of the guests. It was improper to leave before the prince did, and the prince stayed until four in the morning. Negri still would not believe him. Petronius had to phone and wake up a sleeping friend to attest to his whereabouts that night. Negri eventually forgave him, but only after he bought her a puppy and a twenty-carat diamond ring.

For Negri, a jealous rampage was as exciting as love. She now used emotion as a weapon and a tool. She never disguised her feelings, never held back, and every explosion of her emotions was like a safety valve releasing the pent-up pressure inside. As an actress, she knew how to add drama to every nod of the head, every twitch of the eyebrow. Now she used these tricks in her love life.

She was fascinated with living large: posh apartments, limousines, and wealthy and influential men. She always played to an audience, whether she was throwing a fit in front of her offscreen boyfriend or pledging her undying love to her on-screen leading man. Negri played as dramatically for one person as she did as for a full audience, and she knew how to make intimates out of a group. For her, one man's declaration of love, if it came with kisses to spare, could equal the thunder of applause from a room full of adoring fans.

People were fascinated by Negri's personality and the way she looked and moved—she impressed everyone who looked her way. Being a person of grand ideas, Negri wanted a career that was also on a grand scale. She never played the bespectacled nurse or maiden aunt in her films; she was not a girl next door. She stood out as an exotic woman, mysterious and passionate, who seethed with emotion. While other women approached sex gingerly, Negri showed she was up for it, without reservations. Her body tempted every time she walked across a room, and the sway of her neck or the dip of her shoulders advertised her love of rhythm. She danced with anybody who asked, or by herself whenever she felt like it.

By this time, Pola Negri had created a powerful, sophisticated image for herself, on the screen and off, owing in part to ballet school, acting lessons, wigs, greasepaint, wardrobe, music, poetry, and literature. She had a broad vocabulary and could speak five languages. But above all else, the attention and care of the many people she had met throughout her career helped her craft her final image. They all left a mark on Negri, and more than once they protected her from herself.

Petronius regularly sent Negri to a sanatorium to keep her in good health; her sensitive lungs needed to revitalize on pure mountain air to filter out the toxins of the city. He was getting used to having Negri alongside him, but she could be fire and ice and almost had to be reconquered every night. Petronius wanted some assurance from her; he wanted Negri to wear his ring. He insisted that she divorce Dombski.

A civil divorce would not be enough for Negri; she wanted an annulment, which was even more difficult to obtain. However, as if out of spite, Eugene Dombski refused to set Negri free. Petronius was doing everything to make her feel happy. He would drive for hours to spend time with her on movie locations. He accompanied her wherever she asked him to go, regardless of the hardships involved. Negri felt guilty that she could not obtain the divorce. No matter how many times she asked Dombski to end the marriage, his answer remained unchanged.

In 1920 Negri filmed *Sumurun,* later retitled *One Arabian Night,* with Lubitsch. Max Reinhardt donated the sets from his stage show for the production, which made the shoot almost effortless. In addition to directing the movie, Lubitsch reprised his role as Yegger, the lonely hunchback—a clown in the performing troupe in which Negri plays Yannaia, a dancer. Lubitsch's Yegger is an exaggeratedly melancholic soul. Twisted and bent over, he appears to be frowning even when he smiles.

In *Sumurun* Lubitsch gave himself the opportunity to play a dramatic role for the first time. He was well known, at least among German audiences, as a comedian, but it remained to be seen whether audiences would accept him in this new light. The film contains plenty of action and exotic decor worthy of Aladdin. Lavish rugs, tapestries, and lamps dress the indoor scenes, while grand pavilions, a bustling marketplace, and a twinkling palace can be seen in the background. Thugs and spies crouch in corners, dash around alleys, and hide in trunks, trying to get away with what they can, but eyes and ears are everywhere and confrontations are unavoidable. However, this visual feast is secondary to the energizing performances of Negri and Lubitsch.

In the harem scene, Negri's dance is a subtle but powerful beckoning with just the slightest rippling of the fabric of her costume. She instinctively knows that too much motion would make her just another pair of gyrating hips. Her strength and allure come from her stillness as she stands in the center of the room, firmly grounded, her silhouette barely visible through the swaths of fabric hanging off her form. As she allows the men to feast their hungry eyes on her, she is a woman victorious.

This temptress is a variation of the hard-to-get girl from *The Yellow Ticket* and a precursor to her role in the later film *Hotel Imperial*. Yannaia is a fiery little creature, not one to squander love. She doesn't accept what men are willing to give; instead, she fits them into her plan. Sometimes her plan is to wind up with one man, but she will love him as she chooses. She does not want passion to get old, and she refuses to be degraded, whether a virgin or a whore. Yannaia wants to be happy.

The hunchback knows that his beloved little harem dancer is not as promiscuous as she appears. She is a child who has come up from the slums, where she experienced hurt and fear, to become a favorite of the Sultan. None of the men she dances for would want to know the real girl, the girl Yegger knows and loves. Yannaia is the sun and the moon for him, a shining force in a desert land where ordinary people fade away. She, on the other hand, wants nothing to do with him because he is ugly and deformed.

Because he would rather die than accept Yannaia's refusal of his heart, Yegger drinks a poison that promises everlasting sleep, but it fails. Fate is not ready to let him rest yet. While he sleeps off the poison, someone drags his body from one place to another. He wakes up and stumbles upon Yannaia cheating on the Sultan with the Sultan's own handsome son. Mistaking Yegger for a ghost who has returned from the dead, Yannaia screams so loudly that she wakes the Sultan, who slays both her and his son. Yegger returns to his role of clown. At the end of the movie, we see him strumming his mandolin, his painted features distinctive in the moonlight and his face immobile as a statue.

Lubitsch knew what characters Pola could create on-screen. In film as in life, she had men but remained independent. She liked the glamour of being in love, but that was as far as it went. In every relationship she seemed to gobble up her man like a mantis. The men all did everything she asked for, but no man could take Negri away from Negri. In that respect, she was very different from her mother.

As a director, Lubitsch was no pushover. He knew how to have his way, too. Lubitsch made Negri live up to his vision for the duration of each shoot. He would always show the Negri he wanted to show, because she truly listened to him on the set. Also, she thoroughly enjoyed working with him. "Those early years of my association with Mr. Lubitsch were miracle years of delirious work and overwrought nerves," she wrote later. "Together we hunted plots, created characters, built up and tore down."[3]

Lubitsch created characters that were made to be led astray. Life was a game until matters came to a head, and calamity would always strike before you could anticipate it. Lubitsch immunized the audience to pain with satire and then took their breath away with each denouement. Every slight bit of amusement they saw on-screen pointed to some irreversible sadness: untimely death, long-term regret, or never-ending loneliness. Lubitsch's keen grasp of human nature told him that audiences wouldn't feel as distraught about the clown's misfortunes if they were allowed to laugh at his gags, so there were plenty of them.

By the time American audiences saw *Sumurun*, released as *One Arabian Night* in October 1921, they had already seen *Passion* and *Gypsy Blood*. *Photoplay* described Negri as "her usual glowing, gorgeous, theatrical self" and praised Lubitsch for his "extraordinarily splendid performance."[4] *Motion Picture* called Lubitsch's hunchback "one of the most poignant portraits which the screen has shadowed" and Negri's Yannaia "almost as splendid," but rated the film as less worthy than its predecessors. "There are all sorts of complications and most of them prove tedious to the audience."[5] *Motion Picture Classic* singled out Negri's performance: "Here is passion untamed, enmeshed in fine acting. All the fire and abandon that mark her Carmen are to be found here."[6]

Meanwhile, Hollywood offers for Negri and Lubitsch kept coming in. These offers were setting a groundbreaking precedent: Pola Negri and Lubitsch were the first foreign team to be invited to America, although they ended up not leaving for America together. Negri left first and went to Famous Players–Lasky (later Paramount), which billed her as a big international star, and Lubitsch arrived later by invitation of Mary Pickford to direct her film *Rosita*. The Hollywood studios understood that Negri and Lubitsch were a powerful partnership. Although they fought like tigers, they loved each other, respected each other, and truly brought out the best in each other. Lubitsch was the kind of director who recognized Negri's gunpowder personality on the screen. He knew how to surround her with beautiful sets and frame her so she didn't obliterate everything else and overwhelm the movie. He knew just when to cut away from her and tame her explosive personality. Lubitsch was a genius and Negri was his instrument—a partnership that was echoed in the later pairings of Stiller with Garbo and Von Sternberg with Dietrich. The studios also realized Negri's strong audience draw in the United States.

Jesse Lasky at Famous Players had lawyers negotiating Negri's contract and was trying to bring her to Hollywood just as he had promised, but Negri couldn't leave Berlin right away. She owed UFA two more pictures. She also felt obliged to her Petronius, who would feel abandoned if she made the voyage across the ocean without him. Berlin was his home, the place where he lived and worked. His business operations there generated significant income, and he would never consider moving away from Berlin. Meanwhile, Negri was not legally able to marry him, and the larger world was beckoning her. She explained to Petronius that they could have a long-distance relationship; he could visit Hollywood, and she would return to Berlin between pictures. Negri wanted the best of both worlds—companionship and freedom.

As she prepared for her departure to Hollywood, the American press engaged in a flurry of speculation about Negri's personal life as well as her film future. Herbert Howe of *Photoplay* interviewed her in Berlin for an article called "The Real Pola Negri." After running out of superlatives—he called her "the Supreme Coquette," "a Divinity," and "a Goya woman"—he wondered whether American directors would understand her as well as Lubitsch did, "or whether they will expect fire to be always cool and a tiger cat as tame as one of the curly ingenue lambs." He expressed hopes that she would escape the standardization process. "There are plans for putting her in modern American stories, for ladyfying her, tricking her out in pretty clothes, I take it," he wrote. "I hope I'm wrong." She told Howe that marriage was not in her plans. "I have plenty of time. The next five years are for my work. . . . The happiest day of my life is when I see America."[7]

Negri wasn't in America yet, however. There was one more movie to be made: *The Mountain Cat*. Comedy was not usually Negri's style, and the shoot presented challenges both physical and artistic. Petronius braved severe, snowy weather to visit Negri when she was housed in a remote Bavarian ski lodge during the filming, bringing champagne and caviar to make his love happy. Of course, the crew also benefited from the luxurious deliveries, which were trekked in on donkeys. Ernst Lubitsch was taking a chance on this new material for Negri, and he, too, was challenged by the harsh terrain and climate, but in the end the film was a success.

The Mountain Cat is a satire interspersed with slapstick. Negri plays wild Rischka, a bandit living in a vast, frozen wasteland engulfed by snow. The only woman in her father's band of thugs, Rischka has grown up with the boys. She has no manners. The closest thing she gets to a bath is throwing herself down in the snow and rubbing it on her face. She sleeps in a tent on a pile of rags. Like everybody around her, she eats with her hands and blows her nose on her sleeve.

When Rischka falls in love with Lieutenant Alexis (Paul Heidemann), her courting behavior includes pushing her beloved off a mountain and stealing him away from the general's daughter, who is anxious for a proper marriage. She disrupts his engagement party by shooting down a chandelier and tossing her wine glass to the floor so she can drink straight out of the bottle. In the end, however, Rischka returns Alexis to his fiancée and goes back to her former boyfriend, a thief among her people. She realizes her true nature—that she is more at home living with her wild mountain tribe than among the highly refined.

Although this was not Pola Negri's most noted film, it proved she was just as good at comedy as she was at drama. Negri was now ready for her move to America, but she ended up making the trip alone, without Lubitsch. Scott Eyman, author of *Ernst Lubitsch: Laughter in Paradise,* comments:

> Well, they had a breach on *The Mountain Cat.* Lubitsch seems to have gotten a little tired of Negri's demands, Negri's temperament. At this point Lubitsch was ascending in his own right, and, I believe, Lubitsch thought she was giving him insufficient credit for his part in her rise to fame and fortune. Pola was beginning to treat him as subservient, which was well calculated to get his hackles up. He was a delightful and charming man, but he was Ernst Lubitsch, in the process of creating a career second to none. Some people could create, but no one could really do what Lubitsch did and he was aware of his gift. It wasn't that he needed to be a level above Pola Negri, he just didn't want to be put on a level below. So, after *The Mountain Cat,* there was a period where each of them was brought to America. Mary Pickford brings him, and Pola is brought by Paramount.[8]

As the moment of Negri's departure neared, Petronius felt dismissed. He promised he would meet her in Paris and take her to dinner, but he never showed up at the train station. There were no more calls or letters. He had always taken care of her, and now he was gone. It was a painful repeat of her father's behavior, but perhaps she should have expected nothing else. Men turned into phantoms overnight in Negri's universe. They remained in the world but became invisible.

5

Switzerland to Paris to New York

Negri now headed to St. Moritz for the Swiss opening of *Madame Du Barry*. She traveled with Lena, her maid, and Paola Loebel, who gave Negri English lessons and functioned as her secretary. Negri now found that she had to study constantly, whether it was scripts or languages. She had learned German in Berlin, and her relationship with Petronius helped with that. Negri was still lonely for her lover, but there was no remedy like a wide-open future. She was on her way to the country where she knew she would achieve her dreams. Her first stop was St. Moritz, then Paris and New York, and finally Hollywood. She had done nine films in Poland and twenty-four in Germany. It was time to see where else her talent might lead her.

St. Moritz offered clear mountain air for her fragile lungs. Negri nestled herself in her hotel for the first few weeks to compose herself, pray, and meditate. She was still tormented by the thoughts of another failed love affair. She was a movie star—tens of thousands of people adored her. Yet Petronius had bade her a cold farewell.

Negri's name was on everyone's lips all over St. Moritz, and people schemed to meet with her. She found that she could generate publicity by simply hiding, and again she became the talk of the town. The manager of the theater where *Madame Du Barry* was to premiere insisted that she make an appearance at a charity ball scheduled after the movie. Negri agreed to attend the formal dinner only and then return to the hotel.

Loebel set out Negri's evening gown, along with stunning jewelry. Since people wanted to see a star, it should be an unforgettable experience for them. Negri describes in her memoirs how she decided to cancel her appearance at the last minute, declaring that she could not attend the party

47

without Petronius. Loebel lectured her on keeping appointments and maintaining her image. People needed her to show them that life was grand, and she shouldn't let them down. Negri still refused to go, so Loebel and Lena dropped the bombshell: they had received word from Berlin that Petronius was seeing another woman. The news spurred Negri's sense of revenge, and she attended the ball. Her appearance delighted the organizers. Next morning her hotel suite was as thick as a garden with bouquets of flowers, many from admirers who had titles—nobility was paying its tribute to the woman who played Madame Du Barry. Plans were made to throw a party in her honor.

Negri soon tired of Switzerland. Having to be nice all the time became very draining, and she was longing for peace and quiet. She missed having a private life. However, from here on, there was to be no more hibernation time for Negri. She insisted on leaving for Paris early, just in case Petronius would be there. She left St. Moritz discreetly, without making the usual announcement and goodbyes. She needed inner peace, and she was not going to find it in Switzerland.

Paris, the city of love, enticed her with its bustle and eternal mystique. The sidewalks, packed with people she didn't have to talk to, pulsed with life, and that made her happy. She walked around admiring old and new buildings, courtyards, and public squares. Cafés offered cuisine she had never tried, and the great fashion houses sold clothes that satisfied every romantic woman's dreams. Negri went to all the landmarks and found other interesting places on her own. If she was wandering around heartbroken, she was in good company. Parisians understood love and heartbreak—it was their passion. Paris was the place to go for anyone torn up by an affair, and Negri could celebrate her sadness there as in no other European city.

To be in Paris also meant a lot of shopping, so Negri attended fashion shows and spent extravagantly. She drove to Versailles and walked in the footsteps of the real Jeanne Du Barry, who created herself out of sheer willpower and died for her successes. Negri found that all too understandable—her own willpower was a double-edged sword as well. Jeanne Du Barry's success had laid the foundation for her own, and Du Barry's life had become entwined with Negri's future.

Pola began to find her rhythm. She went to the Follies and the Comédie-Française, then out for dinner at the finest restaurants. She kept company with people she knew, but she also made new friends. Ben

Blumenthal of Hamilton Pictures, who had signed Negri to a contract, made sure that the publicity machines were working. Her outings made the papers—everyone knew where she was dining and what she was wearing, and the reporters disclosed the names of all her favorite designers. The evenings when Negri stayed in became a well-kept secret, though; Blumenthal did not want to depict her as an ordinary woman. When he had nothing exciting to report, he fed the press lies and stories about fictitious events. Negri often learned of her own nightlife from the morning papers.

Before the departure for Europe, Blumenthal sold Negri's contract to Famous Players. She did not feel deceived, as it was a common practice. Blumenthal was protecting his interests, but he was also taking care of her finances. He stayed by her side all the way to Hollywood, overseeing all the details to help get her established. Negri felt safe in his company, and Blumenthal treated her like a friend.

In Paris, Tadeusz Styka, the famous Polish painter, asked Negri to sit for a portrait. He was fascinated by her personality. The finished work captured not just her face; it captured her status as an embodiment of freedom, a symbol of an era. In the painter's eye, she was the image of a liberated woman of the twenties. The portrait was exhibited in New York, and later it found a home in the National Museum of Warsaw—donated by Negri herself.

One day Negri received a visit from Casimir de Hulewicz, her angel and ticket out of the slums of the past. After the war, his life circumstances deteriorated dramatically, and he had to leave Warsaw and his position as vice president of the Imperial Theater. Negri found the changes in him staggering. His clothes were now threadbare, and he was sharing a very modest apartment with his grown daughter, Halka. Halka wanted to be a stage star, but she had achieved only the level of a minor actress, playing small parts in the Comédie-Française. She was not in good health—she had developed tuberculosis and could not afford a sanatorium. Naturally, Negri wanted to help. Casimir had funded her own cure years ago, when she was still at school, and he was the closest thing she had to a father. Negri thought it was only fitting that she help her guardian. De Hulewicz refused to take her money, however, even to pay for his daughter's treatment. His pride would not let him accept the generous offer. For a star of Negri's caliber, the sum was not a great expense. She was saddened by the memory of his past elegance and confidence.

Casimir de Hulewicz suggested that he could introduce Negri to Sarah Bernhardt. The rumor was that he had been Bernhardt's lover and that they remained friends after their passion had ended. When the invitation came from Bernhardt, Negri accepted, although she had no idea what to expect. The legendary star still radiated greatness. Despite her advanced age, Bernhardt still sparkled in the society circles of Paris. When they met, Negri found Miss Bernhardt bedridden, yet vibrant. Her face came alive as she talked, and she loved sharing her stories with another actress. She had heard favorable things about Negri and had made films in America herself.

Bernhardt was a living piece of Paramount history, which included Film d'Art, a French film company that brought well-known novels and plays to the screen, interpreted by top stage stars. This brilliant combination attracted literature lovers as well as stargazers. Adolph Zukor bought the American rights to the Film d'Art production of *Queen Elizabeth,* made in 1912 with Sarah Bernhardt. Because the movie was a big earner, Zukor went on to form Famous Players—Paramount's predecessor—with the byline "Famous Players in Famous Plays." To keep his catalog profitable, Zukor favored films made from popular novels: nothing that would challenge the intellect. He signed the stage actor John Barrymore, but many of his players had no theatrical background. Mary Pickford, Famous Players' chief attraction at the time, was not yet a household name. It was Bernhardt who marked the company's inception and remained the symbol of highbrow entertainment.

Sarah Bernhardt was happy to advise her new friend Negri on her career, and Negri was grateful to de Hulewicz for setting up the meeting. He had given her something priceless. Negri left him a substantial check on the sly, making arrangements to prevent his giving it back.

Before Negri left Paris, her divorce papers arrived—Count Dombski wanted to remarry. Because he had converted to Protestantism, the divorce was a civil case; they did not have to seek annulment with the Catholic Church. Negri was now free to remarry, but she was still shaken after the loss of Petronius (Schleber). Eager to bid farewell to her past, she boarded the boat to New York.

Ben Blumenthal and Lena accompanied her to America, and Negri told them that she wanted to spend some time alone on the trip. She worried that her English was not good enough and that she would have trouble adjusting to American ways. On the ship, Ben pushed her to go out and mingle. Any excursion was a chance for big publicity. She certainly didn't lack the wardrobe for an occasion—her trunks bulged with the latest Parisian fashions. Negri tried to persuade Ben that if she kept her head down, the buzz would grow even bigger, and people would see her as elusive—making them even more fascinated with her. "All you have to do is say you want to be alone—and the whole world thinks you are exotic and glamorous. It never occurs to them that you are simply tired."[1] Ben protested a little at first but later admitted she was right.

"The mysterious Negri" was the talk of the voyage. The captain invited her to be his dinner guest, and it would have been bad manners to refuse. So Negri sat at his table in a waterfall of Hohenzollern diamonds, the most honored of his guests. The other passengers stared at Negri in wonder.

The view of New York from the ship made Negri gape herself. The skyscrapers petrified Lena, who thought they would be dangerous to walk near. Onshore, Negri was greeted with full fanfare. The Polish welcoming committee set up a band to serenade her with the Polish national anthem. The Poles who had found their footing in America considered her a member of their community. Negri cried as she sang along with the anthem, recalling memories of home. It was 1922, and the world had been waiting for her. A 1922 *New York Times* headline read "Polish Film Star to Appear in Series of Paramount Pictures," and the article explained: "Pola Negri, the Polish motion picture star who has appeared in *Passion, Gypsy Blood, One Arabian Night,* and other German-made photoplays shown in this country, is coming to the United States to work in a series of Paramount pictures, it was announced by Jesse L. Lasky, First Vice President of the Famous Players–Lasky Corporation, who returned from Europe last Tuesday. Miss Negri's work here is made possible through an arrangement between the Famous Players–Lasky Corporation and the Hamilton Theatrical Corporation, with which she is under contract."[2] According to A. A. Lewis, who worked with Negri on *Memoirs of a Star,* her reception was over the top:

> Pola told me that her arrival in New York City was a great triumph for her. But later, I met Alva Gimbel, whose husband, Bernard, owned the Gimbel Brothers Stores, and she told me that she and Bernard were on the same ship and that anything Pola told me about her entrance into New York had to be an understatement, because she had never seen anything like it. The fireboats came

out with great sprays and bursts of water, the air creating rainbows all over the harbor. People came out in little boats with signs: WEL-COME POLA NEGRI! There was a parade from the pier to her hotel. When she went to the opera, the Metropolitan Opera, to see a performance, she came into the box and the whole audience stood up and cheered. It was that kind of a sensation. She was Pola, the first foreign star to come to America and the first foreign star to become a great star in America.[3]

6

Coming to Hollywood

Pola Negri stepped off the *Majestic* at Ellis Island wearing a small black hat and a white satin dress trimmed with fur, according to news reports, and was instantly barraged by reporters and photographers. The already established actress Mabel Normand was also on the voyage from Europe, returning from a vacation, yet the press almost ignored her arrival as they swarmed around the exotic beauty from Poland. Reporters bombarded her with questions, and nobody waited his turn. Negri was used to more structured interviews, and all the pushing and shoving made her panic. "In my confusion I momentarily forgot every word of English I knew. I could do no more than bow and smile as the cameras clicked away," she recalled. "The next day I read the papers and found it made no difference whether I spoke or not. They had not only come prepared with questions but with my answers too."[1] In Europe, Negri's reputation was established, so she had the confidence to face reporters there. In America, she almost had to start from the beginning again, but she was prepared to show her willingness to cooperate and to make herself a welcome guest.

When the customs officials asked Ben Blumenthal if he had anything to declare, he shot back, "Pola Negri!" That cleverly timed retort became the best quote of the day. Negri was ushered to a waiting limousine and was off to meet her producers, Jesse Lasky and Adolph Zukor. George Schönbrunn, a close friend of Negri's in her later years, commented, "Adolph Zukor and Jesse Lasky, the heads of Paramount, signed her to her contract because she was such a big star in Europe, and she had the personality and looks to be a Hollywood star."[2]

The Paramount enterprise was founded in 1912, and soon afterward it was making its name in the movie industry as its star Mary Pickford made hers. In the beginning, Paramount was mainly a distribution company. When Famous Players and the Jesse L. Lasky Production Company were created, Zukor supplied them with movies. He came into power as all three companies merged during 1916. When Negri was put under contract in 1922, the organization's name was still Famous Players–Lasky.

Negri was the first European star to be courted with an American film deal and taken ashore to receive red-carpet treatment. She knew she was appreciated here and was aware of the great honor she had received. After all the buildup to her arrival, now she needed to meet the high expectations. She had been promoted as a "tiger woman" and a "blazing temptress." If she minded her manners, it could be bad for business and a lot of people might be disappointed.

"Picture for yourself a delicately chiseled beauty, so blue-white in her pallor that she looks as though she had been cut from Carrara marble," urged Helen Klumph in *Picture-Play* magazine. "She dresses all in black or all in white. The gown that she wore as the ship steamed in sight of the Goddess of Liberty was of white charmeuse. The next day at a luncheon at Sherry's given in her honor by Adolph Zukor she wore black satin, heavily encrusted with Spanish lace and embellished by a diamond and platinum plaque as big as a discus."[3]

There were photo shoots and parties, luncheons, dinners, and galas. Negri had numerous rounds of press interviews, and she met the leading gossip mavens. Upon meeting Louella Parsons, she received a tidbit of information. Parsons reported that when she had asked Charlie Chaplin what he considered the most beautiful thing in Europe, he replied, "Pola Negri!"

Adolph Zukor and his wife befriended Negri and helped her take her first steps forward in America. In turn, Negri called her benefactor "Papa Zukor." The Zukors had faith that Negri would become a great movie star in her new country. Beneath her Parisian clothes and European sophistication, Negri was a sensitive and impressionable young woman who was grateful to anyone who took pains for her. The Zukors saw that she was eager to learn. Everything was new and fascinating to her. Negri was thunderstruck by the Ziegfeld Follies. "I was amazed by these gorgeous showgirls who were only required to walk regally across the stage," she wrote later.[4]

Negri knew those women sold some of the same things she did— youth, vitality, and sex appeal—but Negri aspired to stardom. Negri never learned to disappear: not in the schoolyard, or in the ballet line, or in the Rozmaitosci Theater. How did one little starry-eyed Polish girl become a captivating femme fatale while others, who were just as pretty, did not? Some women seek the power of melting into a group, but that was not for Negri. She also knew that she needed to be vigilant—she couldn't let herself be used and tossed aside. The entertainment business ate lovely young women for lunch. In her memoirs, Negri recalled the legs of veteran dancers she had seen in backstage dressing rooms—legs that were a lattice of varicose veins. Where would they be in five to ten years when their legs wouldn't kick anymore and their midriffs broadened? The cruel reality for the professional dancer is that there are always younger, slimmer girls waiting in the wings. Smart chorus girls saved their money while it was coming in. Negri felt that a fat bank account was the best security for a woman.

When Negri left New York for Hollywood, the Zukors each gave her a gift. Mrs. Zukor gave her a silver wishbone, and Mr. Zukor handed her a copy of *Bella Donna*—the Robert Hichens novel that became Negri's first Hollywood picture. The book was being adapted for the screen while she rode the westbound train. As she read, Negri became apprehensive when she realized that she would be playing a shallow, immoral woman. She could not find anything subtle about the character, anything to make the audience side with her. Also, Negri wondered if she and George Fitzmaurice, her new director, would get along. She wished she could work with Lubitsch. Film historian Anthony Slide agrees:

> It's a pity that when she came to America Zukor didn't sign Lubitsch up as well. For example, MGM had the common sense to sign Garbo and her mentor/director, Stiller. Why didn't Paramount have the common sense to sign both Lubitsch and Negri as a team? Lubitsch was assigned to direct Mary Pickford in *Rosita,* and the film was a fiasco because Mary Pickford was not suited to play a street singer. If Lubitsch and Negri worked together at the beginnings of their Hollywood careers, I think it might have been very different. Lubitsch went on to be a great director of sound, but I think he could have made Pola Negri into more of a great American actress."[5]

The train trip gave Negri a view of America that she could only get firsthand. She admired the wide-open spaces and the stretches of desert but suffered in the hot, dry air. Negri thought she would die of the heat, but she made it to Pasadena, where she was welcomed by a crowd and honored with a grand reception.

Hollywood was nothing like New York. At that time, it was a small film-production town where the people, not the buildings, were the center of events. A. C. Lyles, a former Paramount producer, comments on the early days of the studio:

> Jesse Lasky was a genius, as was Adolph Zukor, with talent. He was the man in charge. The second in command was Lasky. Then there was a man named Samuel Goldfish who later changed his name to Samuel Goldwyn. And the director general was Cecil B. DeMille. Jesse Lasky and Zukor wanted to get all the stars they could here—Mary Pickford, Rudy Valentino, and other people. And Jesse Lasky saw a picture with Pola Negri and just thought she could be a very big star here. And the fact that her English was not the best didn't matter. They were silent pictures.[6]

The Hollywood that Negri encountered was often rocked by scandals, with those involved desperately trying to clean up their act before their reputation was shattered by a series of front-page headlines. The prevailing view was that decent, law-abiding citizens did not want to watch unrestrained debauchery on-screen. The Puritan ethic dictated that movies must not promote immorality and that stars should live up to the standards of acceptable behavior.

However, movie stars proved to be hard to control. This was the Roaring Twenties. Scandalous parties were thrown at night. Young celebrities with an endless supply of money had no restraints. The most notorious case was that of comedian Fatty Arbuckle, who was tried for manslaughter for the death of the lovely Virginia Rappe. She died after having sex with him while a larger celebration raged downstairs. Although he was acquitted, Arbuckle's career never recovered. He died broke, abandoned by everyone who knew him. Another scandal involved director William Desmond Taylor, who was discovered in his study, dead of gunshot wounds. Investigations revealed that both Mabel Normand and Mary Miles Minter were among his lovers. Minter, a professional virgin on-screen, never regained her image. Taylor was found to have frequented "queer meeting places" where a patisserie of drugs was wheeled around on tea carts. Normand was uncovered as a cocaine queen, spending almost two thousand dollars per month on her habit. When *Good Housekeeping* magazine declared her too "adulterated" for the American audience, she lost her popularity. Olive Thomas, the actress married to Mary Pickford's brother Jack, committed suicide—reportedly after failing to score a large quantity of heroin, a drug Jack had grown dependent on.

In March 1922, the studio heads appointed Will H. Hays as their arbiter of good taste. The infamous Hays Office inserted behavioral clauses in movie contracts, and the studios could legally drop stars who did not conform to the codes of conduct. Hays, a trusted member of President Warren G. Harding's cabinet, was a shrewd political operator. As chairman of the Republican National Committee, Hays had tilted the nomination to Harding—reportedly, for a bribe—although this didn't come to light until 1928. Hays himself didn't know much about movies, but he had friends in all the right places.

By setting up the Hays Office, the Hollywood producers hoped to avoid government censorship. The studio moguls hoped that Hays would create a smokescreen so they could continue doing what they had always done, while acting as if they were not. In the 1920s, the Hays Office had just enough clout to hurt the progress of an actress like Pola Negri, who was regarded as having too much sex appeal.

The Hays office's first dictate limited the sexual content that could be shown on-screen. There was to be no more carnality, or even an indication of lust. Negri's on-screen behavior implied sensuality, which put it in the category of sexual content. Many of the gestures and expressions that had made her famous were prohibited by the code. She was already high-strung when she arrived; her European "spontaneity" was considered a liability. Instead of being allowed to play women with healthy sexual appetites, she was given scripts in which impure motives led to scandal and disgrace. As a result, she couldn't play a woman who initiated sex for the sake of sex, but she could maintain a veiled sexuality that didn't arouse too much passion or cross the line.

When Hollywood beckoned Negri with the prospect of money, fame, and a stupendous career, she was at the pinnacle of the German film industry. Now she was among Americans who were still reveling in the Allied victory in World War I. There was such a thing as a happy ending, and Americans were sure to have more of them. Germans, on the other hand, had reasons to be sullen in the postwar era. With the whole infrastructure of their once-mighty country destroyed, there was no money for repairs or to feed people. The currency had been so devalued that it took a wheelbarrow of Deutschmarks to buy one loaf of bread. Filmmakers like Fritz Lang found a way to make the misery of the nation work for them. They addressed the themes that were on the minds of the German people: the question of who would take over the world, the effect of industrial mechanization on society, and the wrongly persecuted individual who is forced to take a stand. To the postwar German mind, life was a tragedy.

Pola Negri was said to have gone to America to be able to expand her creative horizons. Just as likely, though, she just wanted to breathe freely, to feel young while she was still truly young, and to stop feeling stifled by Germany's political environment. Germany was going to pay for its mistakes. Negri was one of the few who lived there who was not up to her neck in debt. As a movie star, she had earned a decent income in Berlin and could even afford to give to charity.

Europe, having been "civilized" for hundreds of years, bore the scars of multiple wars over boundaries and territories. America spanned a continent, from ocean to ocean. Its size could swallow most European nations. There was room to realize each person's dreams, with a wide margin for mistakes. As a foreigner struggling with the language and local customs, Negri had plenty of mistakes to make. What she didn't realize was that her creative and personal freedom would be more restricted than she had hoped. Emily Leider, the author of *Dark Lover,* a biography of Rudolph Valentino, provides background on the studio system:

The studios made the films and the studios owned the stars. Stars had contracts with the studios and, really, it was a form of high-paid slavery. They owned you and you couldn't work for another studio unless they released you—as Valentino cruelly found out when he went on strike against Famous Players–Lasky and was not able to work for anybody else while he had a contract with them. So they gave you work. They guaranteed you money and, if you were a star, it was good money. But you didn't have artistic freedom. You didn't have the ability to go where your impulses directed. The executives also intruded upon your personal life. They felt they had the right to tell you what you could and couldn't do, and there are many instances where this led to tragic situations. So, it's debatable whether the studio system was a force for the good or the bad.[7]

Coming to Hollywood

All things considered, however, Negri was lucky to have landed at Paramount, which was the most European of the Hollywood studios. It brought over more European directors and stars than any other, even in the postsilent era. Someone once described the lunchroom at Paramount as "the Tower of Babel" because everyone there spoke a different language. The many Europeans working at Paramount were known for their sophistication, wit, and European style. Clearly, Negri did well by picking this studio as a place to call home.

Negri had a lot of growing up to do, but so did Hollywood. The little production town that promised to make her a star was only just learning how to walk itself. It had started out as a ranch owned by a Mr. and Mrs. Wilcox, who had come west from Kansas. Mr. Wilcox was a real estate man who bought the land as a place to retire. Five years after he settled there in 1886, Wilcox decided to subdivide his land, coming out of retirement to oversee the sales of home plots himself. The ranch became the small community of Hollywood—rural, modest, and pretty as a picture.

Hollywood soon became too good to remain a secret. In 1907, Colonel William N. Selig found it an ideal place for shooting movies. At the time, the rest of the film industry was expanding in New York, but the unpredictable winter weather made it difficult to maintain outdoor shooting schedules year-round. Lost time meant added costs. Southern California had greater appeal because the climate conditions were much more favorable. It also offered wide-open spaces instead of streets clogged with pedestrians. More room and better weather meant fewer headaches and faster shoots. When the Motion Picture Patents Company wanted to gain an advantage over its competitors, it set up shop in southern California. Other independent-minded film companies, looking to buck the trend and film outside of New York, soon found themselves making the trip to Hollywood.

In 1910 there were still no indications of the dynamic future development of the town. It was still a backwater, but that was about to change. Cecil B. DeMille took the place by storm in 1913 after discovering it by accident. He had not even planned to use his cameras there. Disappointed by Flagstaff, Arizona, he stayed on his train to the end of the line and got off at Hollywood. Recognizing the potential of the site, DeMille filmed *The Squaw Man,* a feature-length hit with gorgeous scenery, in this newfound locale. The film became a traveling advertisement for Hollywood, and DeMille claimed the title of the town's official father.

Although the Motion Picture Patents Company had disbanded by

59

1917, Hollywood soon became the second home of most motion picture studios; they kept their business offices in New York but moved production to the West Coast. Hollywood soon became a brand name—the place where movies were made. Some studios actually had sound stages in Culver City or the San Fernando Valley, but Hollywood became the synonym for a southern California location. Pola Negri arrived thinking that Hollywood was a place of artistry as well as craftsmanship. In reality, the town was younger than she was, with the heads of studios still learning the business and trying out one strategy after another.

In Germany, art and film were unified. Fritz Lang, F. W. Murnau, Paul Wegener, and G. W. Pabst inspired each other as directors who delved into the subconscious mind. They left the audience fearing the evil thoughts that were embedded in the psyche. Hollywood tended to be far less soul-searching. It liked its leading men boisterous and it often reduced its women to mere clotheshorses who modeled the latest hairstyles and makeup.

The Hays Office, which mandated script changes, decreed that while housewives and mother characters should be amply rewarded at the end of a movie, lusty ladies must always be penalized properly. This was referred to as the "bad girls formula." By the end of the movie, they were doomed to be abandoned by their leading men, often to die a violent death and make room for a more demure replacement.

Negri did not fit easily into the Hays definition of the standard American way of life. Her characters were comfortable with their sexuality, although they never crossed the line. They were often enigmatic. Her characters slept with men but didn't ask for money. They were dressed in furs and jewels but didn't have husbands. "The Negri women were sexy in every contemporary sense of the word," wrote film historian James Card. "They were neither frail nor caricatures of either evil or purity."[8] American audiences sometimes had trouble understanding these characters' attitudes. Were they a good example of a selfish bad girl getting rewarded, or a good girl led astray into thinking only of herself? The women Negri played seemed to like men but also seemed to be free of them. The powers that be decided that women of the 1920s disapproved of movies that glamorized selfishness. Consequently, the studio dressed Negri up and turned her temperature down, thinking that was what the American audience should see.

The audiences of the time, however, didn't want reality. The silent-era actors and actresses who became stars were abstractions of reality, and audiences wanted that. Their performances were supported by glorious, scenic backdrops and accompanied by luscious background music that amplified the characters' emotions. The movie palaces where the films played were exotic—Moorish, Spanish, Oriental—like Grauman's Chinese Theatre on Hollywood Boulevard. These environments were unlike any others and created a mystical aura. Faces like Rudolph Valentino, Douglas Fairbanks, or Pola Negri would never show up at anyone's church or county fair—such stars were the opposite of the guy or girl next door. These were extraordinary beauties and personalities of both sexes. They were larger than life, both in terms of what the audience was seeing and where the experience was taking place. They possessed people's imaginations in a way that was unique to that film era.

Negri slipped easily into the vibration of the Hollywood star system, which was a glamour machine—she lost no time in orchestrating this in her favor. It was business. As she had done in Europe, she continued to purposefully create the concept of Pola Negri, which was not the same thing as the actress. She knew how to add an extra dimension, so that everyone would notice her—write about her, talk about her, photograph her. This would, in turn, make her more indispensable to the studio and ensure her continuous employment.

Negri rented a large, Tudor-style mansion and started exhibiting her flair for the exotic and eccentric. She was often seen riding around Los Angeles, dressed all in white, in her chauffeur-driven limo. Negri recalled: "I bought a limousine of pure white, trimmed with ivory, and upholstered in white velvet. My chauffeur wore all-white uniforms on sunny days and all black when it rained. I used a white fur lap rug and was usually seen with two white Russian wolfhounds."[9]

Negri was photographed strolling down the streets of Beverly Hills, wrapped in ermine or mink, trailing her pet tiger on a leash beside her. "The tiger's teeth were safely filed," she told an interviewer in the 1940s, "but he might have turned on me at any moment."[10] On the studio lot, she demanded that her surroundings be furnished with taste and attention to detail. Her dressing room was furnished in a Chinese style, and she demanded that fresh orchid petals be scattered on the floor each day. Negri had a gift for knowing how to take glamour to new heights, providing her fans with new fashion trends. "Each important star was expected to set a new vogue in style," Negri remembered. "I brought Russian boots and high turbans with me. I wound jewels on the turbans. There were jewels in my boots, which were made of many colors of leather. These I wore on the streets, and they were widely copied."[11]

All of these antics guaranteed publicity. Jeanine Basinger, film historian and author of *Silent Stars*, reflects:

Pola was a product, not a victim of her own publicity. When you look at a woman who begins in an obscure place in Poland, comes out of it and works with the very biggest names in theater and film in Europe, comes to the U.S., makes a career, portrays different roles on-screen—you have to say: This is a woman who knew what she was doing. She might have been enjoying it, it might have been fun, but I can't believe for a minute she thought walking a tiger on a leash was a sensible plan. I am sure that walking a tiger on a leash wasn't what she wanted to do in her spare time. But walking a tiger on a leash and getting your picture taken helped your job. I always felt when I looked into her career that she was a woman that embraced the idea and understanding that this filmmaking thing, this glamour machine, was growing as a business. If she mastered its practices as well as its artistic practices, she would be on top of the situation.[12]

7

Paramount Pictures, 1922

The film industry was breaking new ground and setting new standards daily. The silent era gave birth to the feature film, the narrative film, and the studio system. It also generated stardom, fandom, fan magazines, and the press that drove it all. The use of long shots and close-ups continued to evolve in Europe as well as the United States, but, thanks to D. W. Griffith, America was beginning to lead the way artistically and technically. With its studio lots and sound stages, Hollywood could save money by producing feature films very quickly.

Controlled lighting was the critical component of this new way of filming. Previously, most shooting had to be done outdoors to get the maximum use of light. If the crew couldn't finish their shots before they lost sunlight, a whole day of shooting could be ruined. Studio shooting relied on the very harsh klieg lights for artificial but controlled lighting. Many crew members suffered permanent eye damage from the dust these lights emitted when they burned out. As a result, there were many lawsuits.

Moviemaking had other hazards as well. The extras and unknowns often suffered under extreme working conditions: heat, exhaustion, hours in heavy makeup and standing on their feet. Even the big stars were bothered by the hot lights searing their skin and irritating their eyes, but they were making too much money to complain—and they knew that every gaffer or script girl dreamed of being in their shoes. Having trained as a dancer and a stage actress, Negri could endure hours of sweat. Part of acting was to smile through each grueling day.

Pola Negri's first two movies in the United States were *Bella Donna* and *The Cheat,* both completed in 1923 and directed by George Fitzmaurice, a man known for his excellent taste. Fitzmaurice is not well known today, but he was regarded as a top-quality, elegant director—a man who knew how to handle sophisticated, melodramatic material that had a European sensibility. It's evident in these two films that Paramount had decided to invest heavily in Pola Negri as a star, for they are lavishly produced and extravagant. These movies are geared toward women. One theater ad for *Bella Donna* read: "The most fascinating love actress on the screen! Pola Negri—beautiful—passionate—dangerous—fifty Paris gowns!"[1] In addition to looking glamorous, in this movie Negri faces some astonishing obstacles that are physically challenging and visually thrilling. She rows across a lake, treks through a desert, and stumbles across tigers, but she never appears frantic, angry, or foolish. No matter what nonsense is going on around her, she is in control and manages each situation with credibility. Perhaps Paramount was just trying to create some kind of cinematic madness around its star to complement her offscreen antics. "Pola Negri's first American picture is, except for the continuously electric Pola, just another vampire-film, deodorized as much as possible to please the censor," a *Time* reviewer commented. "There's a sheik and an English nobleman and a little box of poison and a desert with a prowling lion—and none of it matters very much. Except when Pola appears."[2]

The *New York Times* praised her performance: "Her face is beautiful one second, filled with hate the next; her eyes glow with deep affection and suddenly sparkle with fiery anger. She is good, and then wicked; loving and then the ruthless vampire. Her acting is made all the more compelling by her lithe and sinuous movements, which set off to the fullest extent the beauty of her expensive gowns. There may have been other vampires of the screen, but none possessed the talent of Pola Negri."[3]

The *Film Daily,* a trade paper, noted that crowds were thronging theaters long before show time, and they seemed particularly interested in Negri's appearance: "She has been photographed to look like a million dollars, and the lighting given her makes her appear as someone new and delightful in contrast to the sharp lighting and poor makeup used in her foreign productions."[4] *Photoplay,* however, considered the film artificial. "Negri's first American-made picture does not fit her as well as those tailored in Berlin. Pola is more beautiful but less moving: a passion flower fashioned into a poinsettia."[5]

Negri had initially feared that the costume changes would subtract from the movie's authenticity. She plays a woman whose first husband is taken away for attempting to drown his rival. Later, Ruby (Negri), herself involved in a love triangle, tries to poison her second husband and finds herself doomed for her transgressions. Negri didn't think that a woman with so many problems would be changing outfits every other minute, but her appeals were laughed off and the studio's decision held. She had wanted more artistry, but those too-frequent costumes changes that Negri originally objected to made her into a fashion icon. Gowns were what people paid to see, to escape their own reality of a limited wardrobe.

Negri enjoyed acting with Conrad Nagel and Adolphe Menjou, two actors she admired. In an interview about her favorite leading men, Negri described Nagel as "the idealist, the dreamer . . . with a vibrant force to his personality which precluded all suggestion of passivity." Menjou was the ultimate sophisticate, a connoisseur of the ladies. "He makes women see themselves through his own eyes," Negri explained. "He wisely knows that women grow extremely bored with being taken seriously all the time, and he makes them enchanting doll companions."[6]

To keep herself looking like one of those doll companions, Negri painted her toenails red. She was thought to be the first woman since Cleopatra to do so. When Menjou looked at her feet, he was sure they were bleeding. Other women followed suit, and brilliant-colored toenails became the rage. Girls who had them liked to walk around in open-toed shoes to show them off.

Her second film, *The Cheat,* gave Negri very little dramatic elbow room. Once again she was cast as a clotheshorse in a role based upon her looks. Only one scene gave any clue to what was really going on inside her. Otherwise, the plot was similar to that of *Bella Donna:* a society woman betrays her husband as she falls for some smooth-talking scoundrel, and she is consequently abandoned to fend for herself in a series of life-threatening situations. The audience watches her drag herself through the dirt, never doubting that she deserves punishment. She has allowed herself to be led astray, and justice must be served.

"No attempts have been made to make of Pola 'a nice girl,'" the *Los Angeles Times* reported. "There has been no warping of the part on the mistaken idea that a star must always play a 'sympathetic character.' The part is written, and played, as that of a female cheat—a woman who does not play square with either the man she loves or the man who loves her until the final test comes and her loyalty and courage rise superior to the habits of temporizing and deception."[7]

The Hollywood standard created a new image for Negri. The characters she played in Europe, like Carmen and Madame Du Barry, were working-class girls. Paramount lighting made her less earthy and more glamorous. As the war ended, Hollywood photographers started using orthochromatic film stock and sharp lenses, and they gauzed their lenses for both medium and close shots to disguise facial flaws. No actress was so pretty that she didn't need a birthmark or a laugh line removed, and cameramen went overboard to create the illusion of perfection. The *Los Angeles Times* said of Negri in *The Cheat:* "Her beauty is made strikingly evident by Arthur Miller's photography—made evident without being lighted to the point where it appears flat."[8]

Miller, the cinematographer for both *Bella Donna* and *The Cheat,* said he did what was demanded, but many performers became indistinguishable on-screen. Negri was luminous in her Paramount films, but she lost some of her personality. Soft lighting made her more of a studio product and less of her own person. Negri's strength was always in dictating her own terms. In Lubitsch's films, she was authentic. She showed that the characters she played weren't afraid of being mussed up. The exquisitely groomed women she portrayed for Paramount were reluctant to chip a fingernail. Negri often disliked the pictures she made for Hollywood, but they were doing well at the box office. She was now Famous Players' largest financial asset, and she had to continue to live up to that role. Famous Players–Lasky (which later became Paramount) took care of the new Negri, and Negri had signed a very favorable contract, agreeing to do whatever it took to fit the American star system. They created a new image for her: a bob haircut, heavier makeup, and expensive gowns. Adolph Zukor, who used to own a fur company, knew that the general appearance of the stars was very important.

The critics invariably raved about Negri's performances, regardless of the movie's success. A *New York Times* reviewer admits his disdain for the U.S. release of *The Last Payment* while admiring Negri's performance: "*The Last Payment* is a poor picture in many ways. It is jumpy, it is badly photographed, it is only moderately well directed in its best scenes, its settings are tawdry, its story is theatrical. And so it is not satisfying as a whole. But Pola Negri acts in it. She acts. She doesn't pose a part, she doesn't parade through certain so-called 'action.' She acts, not so vitally as in *Passion* or *Gypsy Blood* or *One Arabian Night,* or even *Vendetta,* but still with sufficient vitality to make her character tellingly real."[9] The critical raves about Negri's acting continued throughout the 1920s and 1930s as she turned in winning performances again and again. At times, she tortured her colleagues with her spontaneous diva fits and bad temper, but she just expected them to accept her passionate and artistic temperament. After all, dramatic fits were what gained her constant coverage in national fan magazines. It was all part of playing the role of a star. According to film archivist and historian Anthony Slide: "The so-called star of Hollywood today bears little resemblance to the real stars that existed in the 1920s and 1930s. Back then, to be a star meant that you had your name above the title. That made you a star and this was very important. It was the fans who determined who were the stars. The studios kept track of the amount of fan mail an individual star received. The theater owners reported back to the studio who was the most popular actor or actress. And so the stars were created—Garbo, Chaplin, Pickford, Negri—and became legends."[10]

Negri wasn't always happy with the movies she was in, but each of them brought her money and fame. She focused on what she could do the best and love the most—and she loved acting in movies. Negri knew how to tell the story with her movements, her expressions, and her splendid eyes. Once in a while, a subtitle appeared, but mostly the camera told the story through her eyes. Perhaps because of that, the camera fell in love with her. And what the camera fell in love with, the audience fell in love with—making Negri a big star. Former Paramount producer A. C. Lyles remembers in an interview: "Pola Negri became one of Paramount's premier stars—stayed a premier star for a long time. I regretted her absence from the screen because I think she could have contributed much more the next twenty-five years than she did, just coming out occasionally to do pictures. She had thousands and thousands of fans. I used to think as a youngster I was the only one in love with her, until I found that every guy was in love with her."[11] No other star was interested in men as much as Pola Negri was. She liked to leave men crying. The girl with eyes full of passion and desire was a born hypnotist who drove lovers to distraction. Her characters chose strong partners but always proved stronger. In an age when a woman needed someone to take care of her, Negri—through her screen portrayals—practically shouted, "I can take care of myself!"

Clara Bow was another larger-than-life film personality who was famous for her vivacious temperament and sex appeal. She was referred to as the "It" Girl—a code word for sex appeal coined by writer Elinor Glyn— and it showed on the screen. Other standouts from that time were the dashing Douglas Fairbanks; Rudolph Valentino, the dream lover whisking the audience away to his netherworld; and Harold Lloyd, who would take on any challenge and jump over any obstacle for the woman he loved. It was a wonderful time for stars who could make the screen come alive. Silent movies illuminated and magnified human nature. The stars weren't perfect, but their imperfections made them who they were.

8

Engagement to Chaplin

Charlie Chaplin was set on romancing Pola Negri from the day he met her. In his book *My Trip Abroad,* written in 1921, he elaborated on her extraordinary beauty: "Pola Negri is really beautiful. She is Polish and true to the type: beautiful jet-black hair, white, even teeth, and wonderful coloring. It is such a pity such coloring does not register on the screen. She is the center of attraction here, what a voice she has! Her mouth speaks so prettily the German language. Her voice has a soft, mellow quality with charming inflections. When offered a drink, she clinks my glass and offers her only English words, 'Jazzboy Charlie.'"[1] Chaplin had already fluttered around Negri at the *Madame Du Barry* premiere in Berlin in 1919. Later, he would not leave her alone after bumping into her in Hollywood. Actually, it was the car she rode in that bumped into his—a minor traffic accident brought the two great personalities together. Their acquaintance soon blossomed into a highly publicized romance that was beneficial for both their careers.

They were two different people from the start. Negri had composure, at least when she was not throwing a fit, but Chaplin had a constant nervous energy that fueled his acting, social life, and success as a businessman and innovator. Negri and Chaplin both excelled, however, at self-creating their images and their careers until they each became legends.

Chaplin soon embarked on a campaign to win Negri's love. He flooded Negri's home with floral arrangements and phoned her incessantly. Although he was known as a miser, he sent her a diamond and onyx bracelet. Soon after they met, Chaplin sent a ten-piece orchestra to Negri's house in the middle of the night to serenade her beneath her bedroom windows while he was home in bed. The gesture convinced Negri that Chaplin was not only creative, but also a romantic.

Then Chaplin told Negri something that touched her heart: he and his former wife, Mildred Harris, had had a son who died when he was only a few days old. Chaplin still grieved this loss deeply. To recover from his own difficult childhood, Chaplin felt sure that having a family was the answer—he wanted and needed children more than anything. Negri didn't want to rush into marriage, but the great Chaplin had located her soft spot. She yearned to have children, too.

Chaplin may not have told Negri that his baby son was born horribly deformed and that his wife had almost died giving birth. Mildred Harris was sixteen to Chaplin's twenty-nine years when she married him—little more than a child herself. Chaplin's passion for young girls was giving him a reputation, and it entangled him further in the years ahead.

Mildred Harris had been a popular actress since age eleven, but Louis B. Mayer wanted her to use her husband's name at all times after she married. Mayer was certain that he could sell her better as Mrs. Charlie Chaplin. Chaplin fumed at Mildred for signing a contract without his knowledge or consent and resented Mayer for using Chaplin's popularity to promote Mildred's films. As Chaplin's marriage dissolved, he and Mildred started hurling accusations at each other. Mildred claimed that Chaplin was unfaithful and treated her badly. He countered that it was she who had been unfaithful—with Alla Nazimova, one of Metro's top actresses. The couple's divorce was final in 1920.

For Chaplin, Negri was a breath of fresh air: unexpected, enticing, and much older than the women he had loved in the past. In fact, Negri needed no supporting at all. She was quite comfortable wearing the pants in the relationship, and this intrigued Chaplin. She was an independent, intelligent woman who matched his own success as an actor and businessperson. She was also ready for love. Negri longed for a romance with all the trimmings, and Chaplin fascinated her—even though he was not the tall, broad-shouldered type she usually responded to. When they met for the first time in Berlin, she admired his hands, "which were never without a cigarette," she remembered in her autobiography. "He used them so expressively that there was little need for a translator." She also loved the way he moved. "He has the grace, precision and timing of somebody trained for the ballet. If he had not become the greatest clown of his day, he could certainly have become one of its foremost dancers."[2]

Negri was beginning to find Hollywood disheartening. Her earlier popularity in Europe was of no importance here, it seemed. At the Famous Players studio, she was given a bungalow that had been built especially for Mary Pickford, which meant that Negri was now their biggest star. Several other stars tried to claim the bungalow after Pickford left Famous Players to found United Artists with Griffith, Fairbanks, and Chaplin. When it went to Negri in the end, there was outcry in the press—she was called "the Foreign Legion." The same critics had a field day when she ordered new furniture. Negri considered the existing furniture uncomfortable, so she asked for a regular couch to rest or nap on. The press reported that what had been good enough for Pickford was apparently not good enough for Negri. Some also criticized Negri for not being present in the public eye enough, interpreting her absence from social engagements as disinterest and disdain. The reality was that Negri's dedication to her film schedule meant early nights and long hours of study.

Chaplin was often Pola's oasis and pillar of support as she worked long hours at the studio and faced the glare of the publicity spotlight. He knew how unkind the press could be, how it could play upon every trifle and turn misunderstandings into a brawl. He advised Negri to develop a thick shell and focus on their budding relationship instead. Chaplin realized that Negri needed quiet time to keep in character, so he often drove her to the beach where they would stare at the water for hours, enjoying each other's company and feeling comfortable together in silence—which was a relief from their arguments. Their political views were drastically different. He leaned left and she leaned right. It didn't help that Chaplin was not very tolerant. He lectured Negri as if his worldview was superior, oblivious to the fact that she had experienced war and poverty firsthand. Convinced that he was always right, Chaplin had little interest in listening. When Negri declined to accept his views as her own, he became contentious and the arguing went on. "I soon reached the place," said Negri, "where Charlie occupied every spare minute of my time—and more. Charlie did not care what orders the studio issued—he would not take me to parties and if I tried to go alone he would come to my house and quarrel, get into such emotional discussions, that even though I went alone I always arrived too late and in no state of composure."[3]

Given the circumstances of Chaplin's childhood, his controlling tendencies are not surprising. His father, who had shown no interest in him or his older brother, died of alcoholism when Chaplin was twelve; his mother was a sickly woman who suffered a breakdown after her husband's death and ended up in a mental hospital. Chaplin had to fend for himself from a very early age. He lived in an orphanage when he was not living in the street—a common plight of children in turn-of-the-century England.

Both of Chaplin's parents were music hall performers, and he made his first stage appearance at the age of five. He always waited for his mother backstage and knew all her lyrics by heart. When she lost her voice and had to interrupt her performance, a theater manager told the boy to go out and continue the show, and little Chaplin stepped in successfully. His mother always dreamed of a spectacular career for herself, but Chaplin achieved one instead. He was touring with a clog-dancing troupe, the Eight Lancashire Lads, by the time he was eight, and show-business jobs came his way from then on. He had a knack for getting people to empathize with him.

Chaplin was a small man with a body that was perfectly suited for acrobatics. He was also admired for his juggling skills. His body language contributed greatly to the persona of the Little Tramp—an amusing little man who never set out to be funny and who kept aspiring to grandeur even though his standard of living fell far short of middle class. Chaplin first came to America touring with Fred Karno's troupe as the Little Tramp, later becoming a world-recognized figure.

Once contracted to Mack Sennett's studio, Chaplin stayed in the United States. In 1913 *Making a Living* featured him as a supporting player, but by his second film, he was already playing the Little Tramp. For *Kid Auto Races at Venice,* Chaplin created his wardrobe from several items given to him by friends. Fatty Arbuckle contributed the pants, so large that a piece of rope had to secure them to his waist. The shoes were courtesy of Ford Sterling, big enough that Chaplin wore them on opposite feet. His jacket and derby were too small, and only the mustache was sized to Chaplin's lip from one of Mack Swain's private stock. Chaplin always walked with an air of dignity even when he twitched or tripped on his uncomfortable clothing.

As the Little Tramp evolved, Chaplin learned to include various dilapidated objects around him as his signature props. A battered stove or a broken chair perfectly illustrated his shabby circumstances and was routinely abused. Chaplin's Tramp took pity on things when no one else took pity on him, which made the audience sympathize even more. He played a man who may have been poor but whose heart never hardened.

In time, Chaplin left Sennett for a better offer at the Essanay Studio, where he fleshed out his character. *The Tramp* sealed his popularity in 1915. Each of his Little Tramp movies told the story of his life from a different angle. *The Immigrant,* for example, was a true story of a stranger in a strange land. Chaplin's films always found ways to derive humor from sadness.

While Pola was in Germany filming historical dramas, Chaplin was working on his first feature. Released in 1921, *The Kid* was produced on six reels at First National and took a year and a half to complete. Industry tycoons objected to its length, but *The Kid* became a hit, taking its place right behind Griffith's *Birth of a Nation* as a blockbuster.

Chaplin joined Mary Pickford, Douglas Fairbanks, and D. W. Griffith to form United Artists in 1919. As Negri and Chaplin were getting to know each other, his main project was writing the script for *A Woman of Paris*. The movie featured Edna Purviance, his longtime leading lady. Whatever his relationship with Edna may have been, it didn't stop Chaplin from pursuing Negri.

A Woman of Paris was based on the life of Peggy Hopkins Joyce, a Ziegfeld showgirl with whom Chaplin had a brief but passionate affair. The clever and ruthless Peggy had five husbands behind her and was living it up on the $3 million of alimony. She told Chaplin details of all the times she had married for money. *A Woman of Paris* tells the story of a girl torn between a wealthy man and a struggling young artist. Chaplin described the film as the first silent picture to articulate irony and psychology. His tempestuous relationship with Negri was also said to have influenced the leading lady's characterization.

Arguing with Chaplin was an outlet for Negri. At Famous Players–Lasky, she had to do as she was told. Chaplin was a vibrant and communicative man who allowed her to blow off steam. Mary Pickford believed the couple could be a match. "You are the only woman who ever understood Charlie. That's why I believe you can make him happy," she told Negri privately.

Chaplin and Negri often dined at Pickfair, the elegant estate of Mary Pickford and Douglas Fairbanks. Pickford and Fairbanks were the reigning Hollywood couple—pillars of their community and the personification of the American Dream of a perfect marriage, even though they had each divorced someone else in order to be together. For the better part of their marriage, Fairbanks and Pickford had eyes only for each other. Their screen images were perfect. He was the robust action hero, laughing in the face of danger, while Pickford was a spunky little girl who looked like a minor until she was over thirty.

Pickford started in pictures before movies listed the stars' names.

Studios thought anonymity would prevent their featured players from asking for more money. An actress with an unknown name couldn't demand a higher salary because she could be replaced by anyone else. But audiences became attached to their favorite screen stars and wanted to see them more often. Pickford was one of them—a feisty little girl who never wanted to fight but knew that she had to. Everyone admired her stubbornness and the way she could tough out any situation. Soon they were asking to see movies with "the girl with the curls."

Pickford had been thrown headfirst into the business at the tender age of four. Gladys Smith—her birth name—had a family to support. Her father had died in a construction accident, and the family needed all the help they could get. Starting in a small theater company as "Baby Gladys," by age nine Gladys had hit Broadway. David Belasco gave her the stage name Mary Pickford when she appeared in his production *The Warrens of Virginia.*

When Pickford found that stage work wasn't steady enough, she started looking into the movies. D. W. Griffith offered her five dollars a day, but Pickford balked at the going rate; she had worked too hard. Griffith agreed to raise her daily fee to ten dollars because she was a teenager. He was starting to shoot a lot of close-ups, and young faces looked best under the scrutiny of the camera. He also hired Mabel Normand, Mae Marsh, Blanche Sweet, and Dorothy and Lillian Gish to add their youthful faces to his productions. Griffith used editing for psychological intensity. With the camera now able to show the smallest details of an actor's face, emotions became more visible. Once close-ups were introduced, performers no longer had to flail their arms or tear their hair to show emotions on-screen. Pickford turned out to be an excellent comic actress.

In addition to proving her mettle in every film, Pickford became a shrewd businesswoman. Well aware that her public adored her, she made sure that her salary reflected the box office. During the ten years she worked at Biograph for Griffith, her wealth grew substantially. In her two years at Famous Players–Lasky, she persuaded Adolph Zukor to pay her five hundred dollars per week—up from the forty dollars he was paying her originally. Pictures like *Tess of Storm Country* and *Rebecca of Sunnybrook Farm* made her "America's Sweetheart." Everybody loved a rags-to-riches story, and it was always up to Pickford to see that all ended well.

At the time Negri became friendly with Pickford, Pickford was a virtual moneymaking machine. Negri and Pickford shared the personal attribute of being close to their mothers and taking care of them. Professionally, they also shared an admiration for Ernst Lubitsch. Pickford had become such an admirer of his films that she had him brought to Hollywood.

Negri, Pickford, and Chaplin had all been entertainers since they were children. They knew what it was like to grow up in the eye of the public—and understood that an audience could leave you flat the moment you stopped being cute. For a long time, Pickford managed to stop aging on camera. She played a twelve-year-old girl in *Pollyanna* when she was twenty-seven. Chaplin retained much of the child in his Little Tramp—a vagabond never sure of his direction but constantly in search of adventure. Negri had more womanly attributes, but her characters were self-indulgent, seizing their moments and childishly thinking that no one would object. Like Pickford, Negri was a member of the weaker sex who proved to be tougher than the boys. The two were never as strong as men physically, but they were empowered by their intuition.

Douglas Fairbanks, who didn't take up acting until he dropped out of Harvard, was a little boy's version of a gallant man. Fairbanks was large and muscular, with broad, cleanly delineated features. Audiences found him likable even when he played a rogue, and younger boys could relate to his portrayal of manhood. The Fairbanks hero was too busy climbing ropes and swinging from the draperies to give in to romance. He could kiss a woman if it needed to be done, and was always up to the task, but for the most part he was preoccupied with fending off enemies and other swashbuckling adventures. Ladies were to be rescued, then set safely aside.

Chaplin had hopes that he and Negri might become the next Fairbanks and Pickford, with a home and a ready circle of friends. Chaplin even bought land near Pickfair and made plans to build a house there. Fairbanks and Pickford were so in tune with each other that they held hands as they counted their movie grosses. One always knew exactly where the other one was. Chaplin didn't want to let Negri out of his sight. She wasn't the kind of girl he typically dated, either. Aside from Peggy Joyce, Chaplin usually went for women he could dominate easily.

Negri and Chaplin became lovers much later than everyone assumed, partly because Chaplin created that impression. On Negri's twenty-sixth birthday (reported by the papers as her twenty-third birthday), which she celebrated on New Year's Eve, Chaplin was late for the party at Negri's house. He had the butler announce that he would be waiting for her upstairs, where he gave her a five-carat, blue-white diamond—which he hadn't had time to have set into a ring—and proposed. Admiring his determination, Negri accepted. After some wine and a violin serenade, their affair was in full swing. Negri found they went together better than she had hoped. She kept trying for the kind of union Fairbanks and Pickford had, one of quiet devotion, but she and Chaplin were too volatile. Negri had maternal longings, but ultimately Chaplin needed more than she could give. She was every inch his equal, but a partnership wasn't what he was after. He wanted a woman who would make him her world. And Chaplin had tantrums of his own. His immaturity was endearing to her, but only for a while.

The "Queen of Tragedy" and "King of Comedy" got daily write-ups in the press, with their battles recounted by special bulletins. Reporters followed Negri and Chaplin around to get the best stories. They were looking forward to an elopement, which might offer opportunities for smuggled wedding pictures. When Chaplin and Negri went on holiday to Pebble Beach, cameras clicked everywhere. Chaplin told reporters that he hoped Negri would marry him, and the vacation became a picnic for photographers. Negri didn't want to say anything official, but she couldn't deny Chaplin's statements, either. Studios thought actresses had more appeal as available women, so Famous Players had taken out a million-dollar insurance policy against her becoming a bride. As a result, Negri couldn't set an actual wedding date until her contract expired, but she didn't mind the wait. Chaplin liked public displays of emotion and enjoyed calling her "sweetheart" in front of other people.

As the papers vied to carry the juiciest news about the couple, the *San Francisco Examiner* claimed that Negri and Chaplin would spend their honeymoon on a trans-Pacific liner as the guests of Fairbanks and Pickford. It also speculated on a wedding date and future plans: "Hollywood's leading prognosticators are also predicting that Charlie and Pola will be married within sixty days; that she will be Mrs. Chaplin when his new mansion in the hills of Beverley is opened for a house warming, and hint that Chaplin will finance her in extravagant photoplays when her present contract with Famous Players–Lasky has expired." Chaplin describes his fiancée later in the article: "Really, she is wonderful! Exquisite! Marvelous! And what an artist she is! In Berlin when first we met, I was thrilled by her amazing personality, by her beauty, by, well, just by the wonderful woman that she is. There has been an attachment between us that is hard to define—an intangible something that drew us together. I have never been more completely happy than at present."[4] Meanwhile, Negri kept trying to fit into the Paramount mold and find a compromise between the studio's demands and what she wanted for herself. She managed to generate so much publicity with the Chaplin affair that the studio was delighted. There was so much space devoted to Negri in the fan magazines that she couldn't really object to Paramount's perpetual portrayal of her in films as a kind of exotic, tempestuous, and difficult personality, instead of as a great actress in great films.

Chaplin was hoping to turn Negri into his own ready, willing companion, and Hollywood wanted Negri to be the proud bearer of the "vamp" label. Theda Bara, Tinseltown's original man-eater, had reigned from 1914 to 1916, when her exaggerated gestures and predictable plots became stale. People wanted stories they could think through, dramas that would engage them. Sex was no longer hidden and was somewhat less mysterious. The soldiers returning from World War I wanted to watch a movie goddess of flesh and blood, with a touch of realism, someone they could see themselves with in real life. Anthony Slide observed, "Pola is unique—a tempestuous exotic compared to Gloria Swanson and Mae Murray. Both Swanson and Murray tended to have bee-stung lips, exaggerated false eyelashes. Negri didn't really do that. She managed to look exotic and natural at the same time."[5] Despite being reined in by both censorship laws and her studio, Negri used her talent to drive her screen lovers to distraction with her hypnotic eyes and gestures.

Having finished *Bella Donna*, Negri was being groomed for *The Cheat*. Chaplin didn't like her being called for movie conferences, because he wanted her at his beck and call. Negri thought that Chaplin, a fellow actor, would understand her professional obligations, but that didn't happen. Once her contract at Famous Players ended, Chaplin wanted her to come work for him. As a partner at United Artists, he could control her career. Negri did not warm to the idea. Chaplin was too mercurial to make sound choices on her behalf. She needed shrewd, objective business management—something Chaplin could not provide.

Despite all the work he put into it, Chaplin did not have a success with *Woman of Paris*, although he claimed that "discriminating audiences" favored the movie. Chaplin seemed to lack the knack for adult themes, while Negri was hoping to play more serious roles. She wanted to do something to change her image. She knew better than to try to direct herself, though. Actresses who formed their own production companies were not, for the most part, their own best friends.

Negri needed clear, expert guidance and career advice. In the meantime, she was trying to bring George Fitzmaurice around. He was to direct her again in *The Cheat,* and Negri wanted to make the most of her performance. Ouida Bergère, Fitzmaurice's wife, was adapting the script, as she had for *Bella Donna.* Negri liked Ouida but could not agree to the first draft of the script. They wanted her to jump from an airplane to the water, from the water to a motorcycle, and from the motorcycle onto a moving train. Only after the acrobatics were deleted did Negri agree to take the part. Next, they argued about the leading man. Negri pushed for Wallace Reid. The front office voiced its opposition, but they arranged an interview. She then realized that the Wallace she knew was gone, and in his place stood a shriveled dope addict. Drugs had turned the strong, healthy all-American male into a gaunt, jumpy old man.

Wallace had been injured a few years back in a train wreck on the way to location, and the studio doctor gave him morphine so he could finish the picture. Reid's dosage was dangerously high; he became addicted, and he drank to mask his addiction. He continued to make films until he collapsed on the set during production and the truth became known. Already in poor health, Reid contracted the flu, went into a coma, and died at age thirty-one. His widow publicized his story, hoping to spare others a similar fate.

Eventually, the constant fighting with Chaplin sapped Negri's energy and cooled her romantic feelings toward him, especially when a reporter quoted Chaplin as saying he was "too poor to get married." Chaplin had never spoken of money problems to Negri, and she felt betrayed by getting such information from a third party. She decided to use this same third party to call off the engagement. When Chaplin read of his broken engagement, he went to Negri on his knees. He tried to explain that the "too poor to get married" comment was meant as a joke; he never thought they would print it. Plus, it was taken out of context. He had been explaining that he needed his picture to turn a profit. Chaplin assured Negri that he never intended to insult or hurt her.

A columnist who had camped out at Negri's house wrote a minute-by-minute description of Chaplin's apology. Other journalists arrived to report on the unfolding story. They were anxious to witness a reconciliation, and none of them would leave. People Negri barely knew phoned to plead on Chaplin's behalf. She finally caved in. It was not about her and Chaplin anymore—apparently, she had to make the whole world happy.

Alma Whitaker of the *Los Angeles Times* took Negri's side in a lengthy essay headlined "Heart and Mind in Grim Battle: A Penetrating Analysis of Romance between Pola Negri and Charlie Chaplin." After outlining what she viewed as Chaplin's cerebral, manipulative neediness and Negri's ongoing battle between her "desperate emotions" and her common sense, Whitaker concluded that this marriage would be a mistake—especially for Negri: "She needs an adorer, a worshipper at her shrine . . . a man obsessed with a great sympathy for her and her art, a man who loves and never questions. But she won't get that kind with Charlie. Charlie can give only intellectual sympathy . . . and admire only critically."[6]

Their tumultuous love affair and on-and-off-again engagement became a gossip columnist's dream. The press followed their every move, and the fans lapped it up. "Pola Negri Is Happy as 'Love Spat' Ends. Chaplin Invites Her to Feast at His Home and She Accepts," declared a *New York Herald* headline. The article explained:

> Pola Negri, "Polish tragedienne," and Charles Chaplin, comedian, were still "made-up" tonight—so much so, in fact, that Charlie invited her to a "love feast" at his home, and she accepted the invitation.
>
> That was the first net result of what Miss Negri termed their "little love spat" of last night. Her emotional reaction to Chaplin's alleged statement that he was "too poor" to marry her right now, resulted in a six-hour break in their engagement and the motion picture world waited, almost breathless, until they had effected reconciliation.[7]

As Negri was learning, gossip greased the wheels of the movie industry. The daily tattler's reports became increasingly popular in the 1920s when Louella Parsons got a column in the Hearst newspaper the *New York American*. She was originally hired to give Marion Davies's career a boost. After Davies, who was the mistress of the newspaper magnate William Randolph Hearst, offered to supply Parsons with insider information, Parsons and Davies formed an alliance. Full of exciting revelations, Parsons's column caught fire. Readers couldn't get enough of other people's triumphs and misfortunes, especially if the other people were celebrities. If times were hard for a celebrity, the man and woman on the street didn't have to feel so bad about their own problems. The papers made the film gods and goddesses seem almost like neighbors to be spied upon.

Parsons knew that it was her job to provide accounts of events that would keep the readers satisfied. Since she couldn't say anything off-color about Marion Davies or Hearst, Parsons salted her column with the mishaps of other famous people as they lived their colorful social lives. Celebrities could be haughty and obnoxious, which was bound to cause sparks. The trick was to be there when they did. A columnist had to go to the big-name events or have a network of spies all over town. Parsons also reported happy events: engagements, weddings, and births. Any good news was just a prelude to the far more popular reports of bad news: lawsuits, marital woes, spousal abuse, and children abandoned to their nannies.

Two other gossip columnists, Hedda Hopper and Sheila Graham, gave Parsons a run for her money. Parsons, who started as an author and screenwriter, was the only experienced journalist of the group, but Hopper, a former actress, knew a thing or two about causing a stir. The same was true of Graham, who had also been in front of the camera as a model. A gossip maven did not need polished literary skills. The three top columnists vied to be the first to break a story and get an exclusive.

Actresses eagerly offered the gossip columnists personal revelations: whom they were secretly dating or which actor had rancid breath. Sometimes the actress wanted to get her side of a story told before the rumors started. Scandals could make or break careers. Hedda Hopper liked to humiliate her enemies in print, and her column bordered on sadistic. Graham was not as vindictive, but her column had fewer readers. Hopper and Parsons could be vicious about beating each other out of a story. Anyone who dared to give information to both of them would become their mutual public enemy. Negri was on the friendliest terms with Parsons, whom she trusted to check her facts.

Before long, rumors started circulating about Negri and the French actor Charles de Roche, who played her leading man in *The Cheat*. De Roche was particularly kind to Negri during the filming. An American role was undoubtedly a move up for him and could make him a more popular actor. The papers hinted that he and Negri might be having an affair, and the speculation caused quite a stir. Chaplin should have known better than to believe the press, but his insecurities took over. Without warning, he went to Negri's house and confronted her about the reports that she had a new lover. She defended herself, pointing out how hard she had been working. Chaplin was certain she was tired for other reasons. He accused her of doing things she had never thought of doing, and Negri threw him out. There would be no more second chances. A. A. Lewis, the writer who worked with Negri on her memoirs, commented in an interview:

> You read Charlie Chaplin's autobiography and he barely mentions Pola. He was engaged to Pola. He was crushed. I had the clippings from all the papers from all over the world, which said "Queen of Tragedy Jilts King of Comedy." That was a headline in the *Los Angeles Times*. He had camped at her doorstep, longing for her to forgive him. All of that, he didn't put in. He didn't come out well so he ignored it. They were all like that. Mae Murray invented her autobiography as she went along. They all did. That was the stuff. Hollywood was inventing itself and all of the people who lived there were inventing themselves. Press departments were helping. So you never got reality. Nobody wanted the real story. Not as it really was. Alas, Pola went along with it too long in her life. There should've come a point where she came back to the very real, very nice woman she was and played off that and her career might've lasted a bit longer, but she was stuck with the glamour image. They all were.[8]

In truth, Chaplin mourned the passing of the affair and tried many times to gain Negri's forgiveness. He persuaded mutual friends to invite her to a dinner party so he could meet her, but Negri smelled the bait and canceled at the last minute. The press reported that it was the end. She later mused, "Love is disgusting when you no longer possess yourself."[9] In an interview with the *New York Herald,* she announced that the engagement was definitely off. "Chaplin is a charming fellow but I now realize that I could never marry him," she said. "He has no qualities for matrimony because he experiments in love. I am glad it is over because it would have interfered with my work."[10]

In her autobiography, Negri wrote that all the accounts of her affair with Chaplin were portrayed differently than they actually occurred. She also stated that Chaplin was like many comedians: he had no sense of humor in his private life. She believed that to have a really great love affair, one needed a sense of humor. This carried over into her work on-screen, as well. In each of her roles, her passion always has a slight undertone of humor—humor that enhances and modernizes her intense performances.

Perhaps Chaplin wanted to be the only fiery character in their offscreen romance. Their intensity as artists and as individuals drew Negri and Chaplin together but ultimately may have been what tore them apart. In a *Movie Weekly* interview in 1923, when Grace Kingsley asked about the Chaplin breakup, Negri said, "An artist should be very, very sure before marrying that the comrade of a lifetime will be able to help and not hinder and distract. When two artists marry, they should mutually inspire each other."[11]

By 1925, Negri had evolved in her views and told the *New York Times* that people in her profession should not marry each other: "By my experience with Mr. Chaplin I came to the conclusion that there is always a certain jealousy—ego—between two professional people which makes happiness impossible. If I do marry it will not be anyone connected with the profession. I want rest with a husband. One temperament in the family is enough!"[12]

In the years following his breakup with Negri, Chaplin had a total of ten children with two different wives. He married sixteen-year-old Lita Grey in 1924, had a relationship with actress Paulette Goddard in the 1930s, and married eighteen-year-old Oona O'Neill in 1943 when he was fifty-four years old. His final marriage was a long, mostly happy one that provided the stability he had always wanted. Negri was dismayed to learn that he still bore her a grudge many years later. He told stories to the press that showed her in a bad light. She tried to be magnanimous in forgiving him, saying "Clowns live in a world of fantasy,"[13] but her tone indicated that she would have been happier if he had found some good things to remember.

9

Gloria Swanson

When Pola Negri arrived at Paramount in 1922, Gloria Swanson was the biggest female star on the lot. Reporters were smacking their lips at the possibility of a rivalry between the two famous women. When the press didn't get what they hoped for, they fabricated plots and dialogue. The public loved to read about the alleged rivalry between Swanson and Negri.

Both stars were under contract at Paramount at the same time, so it was not surprising that each considered herself the number one star. That alone was a good setup for a feud. According to what was written about them, they hated each other. In one alleged spat, according to *Photoplay*, Negri, who hated cats, demanded that the Paramount lot be cleared of over a hundred cats that had taken up residence there. Once Swanson got wind of this, she started feeding the cats to spite her rival. The *Photoplay* article went on to speculate about the politics behind this type of feud, "Negri was a new personality. She had been brought to this country on a calliope of international publicity. Until her arrival, Gloria had been Queen. Negri threatened her reign. Pola was dynamic; Gloria was dynamic. Pola was sensational; Gloria was sensational. Pola was dramatic; Gloria was dramatic. They played the same types of roles. Gloria must fight not only for her place in the arc-light of world fame but she must fight for it in studio prestige."[1] The article also points out that the star who reigned as queen of the Paramount lot would get first choice of stories, directors, casts, cameramen, electricians—all of which would matter more to a star's success than actual acting talent.

Early in Negri's Hollywood career, she and Charlie Chaplin attended an Actor's Fund benefit dressed as Shakespearean characters. Negri looked magnificent as Cleopatra, but she spent the evening in distress because of the purported feud between her and Swanson. Catfights were always a draw. Watching two stars known for their mutual dislike meet unexpectedly in public gave a circus atmosphere to otherwise stuffy public events. A charity benefit was boring after the costumes paraded by, so the press corps was summoned to drum up some drama.

Reports had been circulating that because Pola Negri was to show up at that gala, Gloria Swanson would not be attending. Vying for the same parts at the same studio, the women were considered rivals, but they were going to find themselves in the same room sooner or later. Negri had utmost respect for Swanson. She was already finding that Hollywood was playing a game, and she was sometimes assigned to play the pawn and other times the queen. Charlie Chaplin's published comments about how pretty Negri was and how no one could match her wit and personality only spurred more comparison and rivalry in the press.

The "quarrel" between Negri and Swanson took up a lot of newsprint, but it was a publicity gimmick, not a feud. Theater owners wanted movies to get a boost from the press, which in turn needed to sensationalize the film industry to get people out to the movies. Stories about Negri and Swanson's alleged fights popped up constantly in the press, but neither of them gave credence to the rumors. They were not friends, but neither were they enemies. They were always polite to each other, and neither of them wrote critically about the other in their respective autobiographies. Negri mentioned Swanson more often than Swanson did Negri, but there was mutual respect and understanding in what they did write about each other.

According to Swanson, they started out as friends and invited each other to dinner, which was customary at the time. It was only after the hoopla began about their being enemies and rivals that they avoided talking to each other. *Photoplay* columnist Cal York quoted Swanson in 1925 as saying that *Passion,* the film that brought Negri and Lubitsch to fame, contained some of the best acting she had seen. She then added, "You know, I haven't any grudge against Pola Negri. I don't know why the legend persists—perhaps because it makes interesting reading. But it really isn't true."[2]

Negri said much the same thing. "There were such fantastic stories about my superstitions in the old days," she told an interviewer in 1932. "The famous story about the cats was as well known in Paris, London, Warsaw, and Berlin as in Hollywood. Gloria Swanson and I were supposed to be rivals on the old Paramount lot. According to the press, we were having a bitter feud. Actually I was very fond of Gloria. . . . The publicity made us more exciting to the public. More to be talked about."[3]

When Swanson was credited with saying hateful things about Negri, Negri felt certain that Swanson simply had bad advisers, who purposely misguided her. Even so, it could be hurtful. Chaplin was there to console her—when they were still together—telling her that it would be worse to be ignored. In his autobiography, he called the gossip "a mélange of cooked-up jealousies and quarrels" fabricated by Paramount. "The twisted feline angle was manna to the publicity department."[4]

Swanson had been developed as a star by Cecil B. DeMille, aided by her own driving ambition. Although Swanson and Negri had similar images—vampy, insatiable beauties—they each had their own take on it. They did not vie for parts the way some people assumed. Both Negri and Swanson followed in the footsteps of Theda Bara, the beautiful but heartless temptress—the screen's original sex siren—who made her debut in 1914. Theda was actually Theodosia Goodman, a nice Jewish girl from Chillicothe, Ohio, not a villainous harlot of French-Arab extraction, but people believed the ruse because she made such a good case for it, working the Princess of Sin angle to sell herself.

The concept of the "vamp," meaning a female vampire, gained popularity when Americans discovered Bram Stoker's 1897 novel *Dracula* and were fascinated by the story. Many similar tales were written about the mysterious, bloodthirsty creatures that led innocent people to destruction. In books and in movies, comely female vampires insidiously entrapped their victims, only to later drain them of their blood. Suddenly vampire stories were in fashion—the more dramatic, the better. Porter Emerson Browne wrote a play called *A Fool There Was,* followed by a novel of the same name. In 1914 Theda Bara became evil incarnate when she starred in a film adaptation of the work for William Fox. Moviegoers were fascinated by the idea of characters who couldn't resist a woman even though she would eventually destroy them. For some men, that seemed like an attractive enough way to end a life.

Theda Bara successfully played a beautiful but destructive woman who put every man she came across in mortal danger. The theme of her movies never changed: a demonic temptress leading her victims to destruction. Publicity shots were staged to make her seem preternaturally alluring. In time, Bara's self-created persona slowly began to be perceived as overdone and her merciless expression lost its charm. Audiences became intrigued with actresses who were more of this world.

Gloria Swanson and Pola Negri played true exotics at a time when most women in film were shown standing around in feathers and furs. They portrayed women who were daring—active women who made their own decisions—and exhibited those traits in their offscreen lives as they managed their own careers. "The crucial thing about them was their refusal to be ordinary—to be dutiful girls who behaved properly," says silent-film historian Jeanine Basinger. "They had nerve—real nerve—at a time when very few women in film could make that claim."[5] In an industry that was notorious for destroying women, physically and emotionally, they survived because they were shrewd enough to see that film was a business. Swanson had several male mentors, but Negri had only Lubitsch, who helped create who she was and directed her well. But in the end, each actress had to make her own decisions and be her own guide.

As the "feud" between Negri and Swanson began to feed on itself, the two actresses came to accept that, as far as the press was concerned, they *were* enemies. It was a fiction treated as a fact. At one studio banquet, each megastar sat in her dressing room waiting for the other to make her entrance. Finally Negri entered first, presumably not wanting to waste any more of her evening. She wore a green brocaded gown, a Parisian import, which no one had seen the likes of before. Swanson timed her own entrance for maximum attention. She entered in an identical green gown. The designer had not told either actress that they had bought the very same dress. It must have been tremendously entertaining to watch as Swanson and Negri spent the night keeping a safe distance from each other.

To avoid further friction, Swanson usually filmed at the Astoria branch of the studio in Queens, New York. Negri was left to reign over the West Coast. If the studio made a concession to either actress, the other demanded similar treatment. When Paramount purchased the rights to *Madame Sans-Gêne,* at Negri's request, but awarded the movie to Swanson, Negri was very disappointed—and remembered to mention it when she was battling to do *Forbidden Paradise* with Lubitsch. In an interview, former Paramount producer A. C. Lyles tells about some diva-like behavior between the two stars:

> One of the stories Gloria was telling Mr. Zukor, Mr. DeMille, and me was when she arrived in her chauffeur-driven car and would get out, Gloria would have two beautiful young ladies with a big basket of rose petals which they threw in front of her when she walked so she would enter the studio walking on rose petals. I was

Publicity photo of Pola Negri for *Three Sinners,* directed by Rowland V. Lee, Paramount Pictures, United States, 1928. This photo, which the author observed hanging in the Joe Allen Restaurant in Manhattan, New York, inspired him to learn more about the actress.

Pola Negri's birth certificate, prepared by the City Hall of Lipno, Poland, in 1978.

POLSKA RZECZPOSPOLITA LUDOWA

Województwo __włocławskie__
URZĄD STANU CYWILNEGO w __Lipnie__

Odpis skrócony aktu urodzenia

1. Nazwisko __Chałupec__ ————————————————
2. Imię (imiona) __Apolonia__ ————————————
3. Data urodzenia __3 stycznia tysiąc osiemset ————__ __dziewięćdziesiątego siódmego r. / 3.01.1897/__
4. Miejsce urodzenia __Lipno__ ————————————
5. Nazwisko i imię __Chałupec Jerzy__ —————————
   (ojca)
   ——————————— zawód __blacharz__ ———————
6. Nazwisko rodowe (ojca) ————————————————
7. Imię i nazwisko rodowe __Eleonora Kelczewska__ ————
   (matki)
   ——————————— zawód —————— ————————

Poświadcza się zgodność powyższego odpisu
z treścią aktu urodzenia Nr __11/I/1897__

__Lipno__ dnia 18 kwietnia 1978 r.

Miejsce
na opłatę
skarbową

KIEROWNIK
Urzędu Stanu Cywilnego

ALINA NEJMAN

Pu-M-8 — Zam. Nr 1568/DW/On
1684 — LZG Z-d 4 — 29.3.77 — 663.000 — piśm. 3 kl. A1/39

The Imperial Academy in Warsaw, 1910. Courtesy of David Gasten.

Pola Negri at the time of her theatrical debut in Warsaw, 1913. Courtesy of David Gasten.

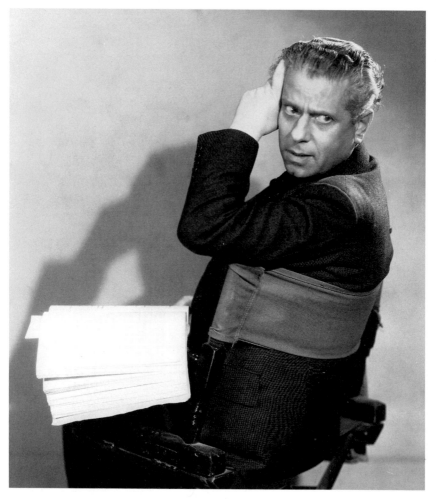

Max Reinhardt, the producer-director who discovered Pola Negri. Courtesy of Photofest, New York.

Pola Negri publicity picture, Warsaw, 1916.

Pola Negri in *The Yellow Ticket*, directed by Victor Janson and Eugen Illés, Berlin, 1918.

Pola Negri, Harry Liedtke, and Victor Janson in *Carmen*, directed by Ernst Lubitsch, UFA, Berlin, 1918. Courtesy of David Gasten.

Pola Negri with Emil Jannings in *Madame Du Barry*, directed by Ernst Lubitsch, UFA, Berlin, 1919.

Pola Negri in *Sumurun*, directed by Ernst Lubitsch, 1920. Courtesy of David Gasten.

Pola Negri with Wolfgang George
Schleber in Alpy, Switzerland, 1920.
Courtesy of George Schönbrunn.

Pola Negri publicity picture, Berlin, 1920.

Johannes Riemann and Helga Molander with Pola Negri in *Sappho*, directed by
Dimitri Buchowetzki, Berlin, 1921.

Cover of *Movie Weekly,* November 5, 1921.

Pola Negri and her portrait by Tadeusz Styka, Paris, 1922.

Pola Negri with producer
Jesse Lasky at the Famous
Players–Lasky Studio,
Hollywood, 1922. Courtesy
of David Gasten.

Paramount publicity photo of Pola Negri, Hollywood, 1922. Photo by Eugene Richee. Courtesy of Photofest, New York.

Pola Negri and Adolphe Menjou, in her first American picture, *Bella Donna*, directed by George Fitzmaurice, Paramount, United States, 1923. Courtesy of Photofest, New York.

Pola Negri in *Bella Donna*, directed by George Fitzmaurice, Paramount, United States, 1923.

Pola Negri and Jack Holt in *The Cheat*, directed by George Fitzmaurice, Paramount, United States, 1923. Courtesy of Photofest, New York.

Pola Negri with Charlie Chaplin at Pebble Beach, California, 1923.

Pola Negri and Ernst Lubitsch working on the story for *Forbidden Paradise*, 1924, at Negri's home in Beverly Hills.

On the production set of *Forbidden Paradise,* with actors Rod La Rocque, Pola Negri, Haus Dreier, and Adolphe Menjou and director Ernst Lubitsch, Paramount, United States, 1924.

Pola Negri with Rod La Rocque, from the movie *Forbidden Paradise,* directed by
Ernst Lubitsch, Paramount, United States, 1924.

Director Ernst Lubitsch with a portrait of his star Pola Negri from *Forbidden Paradise,* Paramount, United States, 1924.

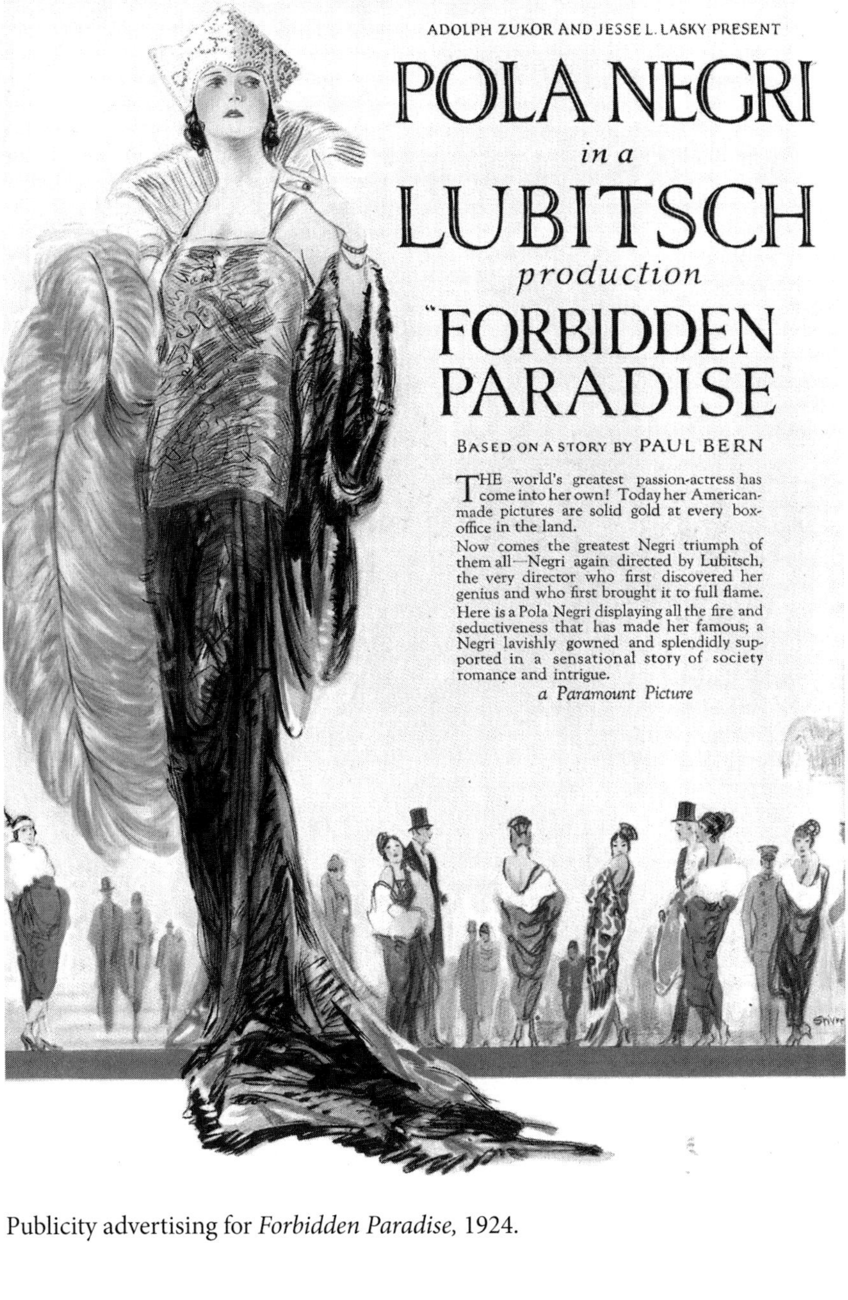

Publicity advertising for *Forbidden Paradise,* 1924.

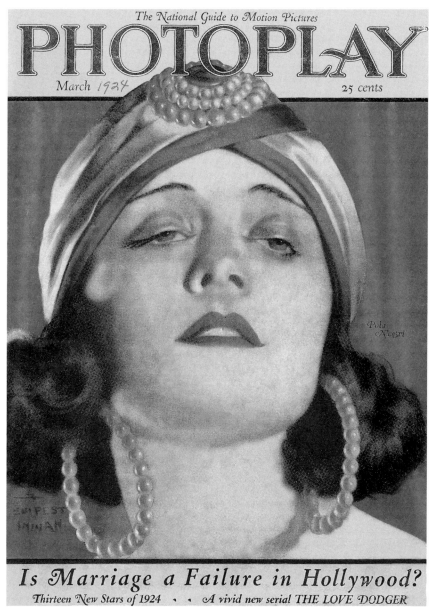

Cover of *Photoplay* magazine, March 1924.

Pola Negri, her mother, Eleonora Chałupec, and Mieczyslaw Brodzinski at the San Francisco train station, 1924. Courtesy of David Gasten.

Feodor Chaliapin, a world-famous basso, was greeted warmly at the Paramount Hollywood studio by his friend Pola Negri in 1924. *Left to right:* Ernest Vajda, Dimitri Buchowetzki, Noah Beery, Negri, Chaliapin, and Mikall Vavitch.

Pola Negri with her mother, Eleonora Chałupec, in Hollywood, 1925.

Pola Negri, star of Paramount, Hollywood, 1925. Photo by Eugene Richee. Courtesy of Photofest, New York.

Cover of *Motion Picture* magazine, August 1926.

Poster for *Barbed Wire,* 1927.

Pola Negri's Beverly Hills home, 1926. Courtesy of George Schönbrunn.

Rudolph Valentino and Pola Negri at the ball given by the Sixty Club, Los Angeles, March 1926. Courtesy of Brother Alexis Gonzales.

Rudolph Valentino with Pola Negri at the wedding of Mae Murray to Prince David Mdivani, Hollywood, 1926.

Pola Negri at the funeral of Rudolph Valentino, New York, 1926.

Director Mauritz Stiller, Pola Negri, and producer Erich Pommer in *Hotel Imperial*, Paramount, United States, 1927.

Pola Negri in *Hotel Imperial,* directed by Mauritz Stiller, Paramount, United States, 1927.

Pola Negri and Prince Serge Mdivani at the time of their wedding, Séraincourt, outside of Paris, 1927. Courtesy of Brother Alexis Gonzales.

The married couple, Princess Pola Negri and Prince Serge Mdivani, outside their château in Séraincourt, 1927. Courtesy of George Schönbrunn.

in awe. It wasn't out at a premiere or something. It was just coming to work. And then she said, "You know what Pola Negri did when she saw me with the two ladies? She got *four* young girls to be there so when she got out of her car, there were four young girls throwing rose petals."[6]

Like Negri, Swanson wanted to stake out her own territory and disliked having other people tell her what she ought to do. When Mack Sennett claimed he would make her a second Mabel Normand, she decided she didn't want to be second to anybody and left him for Cecil DeMille. Swanson underplayed her roles before the camera; she knew less was more on the silent screen. She dramatized her private life whenever she could, however, to guarantee herself coverage in the gossip magazines. When she married Henri, Marquis de la Falaise de la Coudraye, in 1925, some people claimed that she married a marquis so reporters would have something to write about. Confident in her abilities, she went on to produce her own projects with Joseph P. Kennedy (thought to be her lover) under the umbrella of United Artists, but things did not go as planned and the business ended in a complete fiasco. Swanson invested over two hundred thousand dollars of her own money in *Queen Kelly*, but the movie never opened in the United States. Having fired Erich von Stroheim, the film's original director, who had invested six hundred thousand dollars in the project, Swanson had to pay him back—something she didn't finish doing until 1950. She recaptured her fans with *Sadie Thompson* and showed she could sing in *The Trespasser*, her first talkie. By the 1930s, Swanson was focusing on theater, but she took time out to make *Father Takes a Wife* in 1941, which wasn't enough to revive her film career. Not until nine years later did she do something memorable on-screen, playing the unforgettable Norma Desmond in *Sunset Boulevard*—with von Stroheim playing her butler and DeMille as himself. Negri refused the role, in all likelihood because she considered the early version of the script she saw as a mockery of herself.

In the end, Negri and Swanson are both remembered as great stars who hit the front pages with a splash and stayed there. "Front page personalities are born, not made," Swanson said later. "When certain personalities walk across the street they make news; others can commit murder without making the headlines. Barbara La Marr was front page. So was Pola. I guess I am too."[7]

10

Paramount Pictures, 1923–1924

With her first two American films and a broken Hollywood engagement behind her, Pola Negri rededicated herself to her career and told the studio she wanted to act in a different type of role. In a 1923 *Movie Weekly* article, "What America Has Done for Pola Negri," she was blunt about her opinion of *Bella Donna:* "I didn't like *Bella Donna* myself. My imagination of the role was so different! But I allowed myself to be persuaded. They said to me, 'Ah, but American audiences are different! You will not succeed unless you adapt yourself to our ways.' But you see! The picture is making money I believe, however." Grace Kingsley, who conducted the interview in Negri's "cozy boudoir" on the Paramount lot, describes Negri's appearance that day: "Miss Negri wore a gorgeous, silver-cloth negligee and she settled herself gracefully in a big chair. I shouldn't really say settled herself, but rather poised herself. She is always electric, volatile—you never know quite what she may do."[1]

With her innate love of luxury, Negri found many things to enjoy about her movie star life. She loved wearing ermine, mink, sable, silk, satin, and chiffon. Along with the fresh rose or orchid petals strewn on her dressing room floor every day, an ice bucket with the finest champagne was always at hand—for her, Prohibition didn't exist. To help herself unwind, Negri got in the habit of dancing by herself between takes. She was particularly fond of doing the Charleston to rid herself of excess energy.

A three-piece orchestra on the set helped stars to get in the mood for pantomiming their emotions. Negri would Charleston in her dressing room, then continue out the door as she prepared for the camera. People marveled at her energy. She kept busy, but deep inside Negri feared that her screen roles were becoming repetitious. She didn't want to keep playing a determined rich woman who lived in a mansion with no visible source of income, seducing men for some ulterior motive. But eight thousand dollars a week and the double strand of perfectly matched pearls from Zukor fueled Negri's stamina. Having seen the roles she was being given, Ernst Lubitsch agreed. "They make a mistake in trying to make Negri play characters who are all white," he said. "Pola does better when they are a little spotted."[2]

Negri got her wish and landed her next film thanks to her future lover Rudolph Valentino. A film called *The Spanish Cavalier* had been on hold for Valentino, but it fell right into Negri's lap when Valentino abruptly broke his Paramount contract and went on a dance tour with his wife, Natacha Rambova. The studio had the script rewritten for a female lead and renamed it *The Spanish Dancer,* and it became Negri's third Hollywood picture. Negri had great hopes that Lubitsch would be her director and that they could take on Hollywood together. To her disappointment, *The Spanish Dancer* went to Herbert Brenon instead. Lubitsch was busy directing Mary Pickford in *Rosita,* a film with a similar plot, at United Artists.

As Negri prepared to play a dancer on the screen, the great Valentino left town to make a living as a dancer anywhere but Hollywood. In 1923 Valentino was already exerting an influence over Negri's life without even being present. He had been having a run of bad luck, some of which he brought upon himself by making poor decisions in his private life. He had married his second wife before the divorce with his first wife was final, which resulted in a bigamy charge and a night in a Los Angeles jail.

Valentino's decision to walk out on his Paramount contract and go on the Mineralava Dance Tour was another strike against authority. The Mineralava Company produced beauty clay that women used as a cleansing mask. The company was a competitor of Richard Hudnut, the wealthy stepfather of Valentino's wife Rambova. Born Winifred Shaughnessy in Salt Lake City, and later named Winifred Hudnut, Natacha Rambova had grown up with all the advantages, courtesy of her stepfather, but she did not harbor much loyalty toward him. She worked as a Hollywood set and costume designer and tried to make a name for herself as an actress and dancer.

Rambova was creating movie sets for Metro star Alla Nazimova when Valentino took an interest in the designer. Valentino was becoming wildly popular at the time, thanks to *The Four Horsemen of the Apocalypse.* Based on just one scene in that film, the previously obscure actor became an overnight sensation. "The Buenos Aires tango scene . . . turned Valentino into a box-office lion," says Valentino biographer Emily Leider.[3] To Rambova, though, he was just a handsome Italian with a foreign accent—raw material for her creative ambitions. She tried to make Valentino battle writers and directors for script, costume, and actor changes, but he was not good at negotiating or putting his foot down. Valentino was at his best, as a man and an actor, just standing there, chest pushed out and hands on his hips, ready to conquer the first woman who came along.

Rambova so antagonized Valentino's bosses that they decided to get rid of her. Paramount refused to give Valentino script approval on their current project, *The Spanish Cavalier,* knowing that the requests were hers and not Valentino's. Rambova and Valentino drove off to tango for Mineralava, breaking the contract with Paramount at a high point in Valentino's career—and leaving Negri to benefit from their decision by filming *The Spanish Dancer.*

The Spanish dancer, Maritana, is a gypsy who can foresee the future. She is also the lead in her performing troupe and is renowned across Spain for her dancing. When a wealthy nobleman, played by Antonio Moreno, asks Maritana to tell his fortune, she resists. The cards show he will be haunted by poverty, but Maritana also sees something else—a danger hanging over him. As the dancer looks the nobleman in the eye, they feel a mutual attraction, theirs to pursue if they should ever meet again. Later in the film, Maritana is asked to perform for the queen, but palace insiders involved in political intrigue plot to use the dancer against the queen and take power. Luckily, Moreno's nobleman saves the day. He foils the plan of the conspirators and saves the kingdom.

The Spanish Dancer would be a boring film without Negri's face stamped all over it. It is the tilt of her chin and the flash of her eyes that make the audience care. Queens may fall out of favor, kings can be deposed, but the gypsy girl lives outside the law. She will do only what suits her in a world of shifting alliances. As the beautiful Maritana, Negri grabs all the attention. In her swirled skirts and bangles, she is an ode to temptation. Her dancing blots out everyone else.

The studio invested heavily in *The Spanish Dancer,* putting up $250,000 just to furnish the sets. The costumes were lavish and the scenery eye-popping. Negri found Herbert Brenon's direction competent but uninspired. She tried to do her scenes as Lubitsch would have directed her, but

Brenon wanted ironclad control. He and Negri butted heads on the set, airing creative differences with each take. Negri's clashes with Brenon made for a creatively explosive working relationship, and in the end they were considered a victorious pairing.

Lubitsch had a much more trying time with *Rosita,* since English was not his first language and Mary Pickford was not a credible gypsy. "I always thought the results were pretty terrible," Pickford said later. "I didn't like myself as Rosita. I think it was my fault, not Lubitsch's."[4] The film became a disappointment to the investors. However, Lubitsch was granted a three-year contract with the newly established Warner Bros., and went on to become one of the greatest directors of all time.

Negri and Pickford maintained their friendship, knowing their films would be compared. Although Pickford did not make a good Latin tease, having always done sweetheart roles, she thought it was worth taking a chance. Nonetheless, both women refused to compete. The slightest rift between them would have been a windfall for the press.

Sometimes making movies was a dangerous business. *The Spanish Dancer* left Negri with a scar on her face. Brenon was showing Antonio Moreno how to hurl a boot at Negri, but the director's aim was so accurate that the spur of the boot cut into Negri's eye a fraction of an inch from her eyeball. She ended up with twelve stitches, and the mark never faded completely. Years later Moreno ran his hand across it when he saw her. "I gave you that," he said regretfully, as if the incident had been his fault. Negri was touched by his gesture.

Negri was now hailed as the "Goya woman." With her raven hair, milky-white complexion, and eyes of fire, Negri's Spanish dancer did indeed resemble the famous painter's women subjects. Nonetheless, Hollywood still wanted her to embody traditional values. Even when she got to play a part like the gypsy dancer, the Hollywood code required her to play women who had lost their way and needed somebody to set them straight so they could become decently moral again. Negri's characters had to give the men who adored them back to their abandoned wives or allow themselves to die as a warning to other wrongdoers. As Lubitsch's *Carmen,* she did not have to make such sacrifices.

In *The Spanish Dancer,* Negri's character Maritana goes out of her way to redeem her bad deeds and prove herself to be honest. She takes pains to return money that her friends have stolen, rescues the queen's son from certain death, and saves her own passionate kisses for the only man she will have now: the self-sacrificing nobleman. She tries to show others that she is sweet and honest, as if saying, "I'm not really a gypsy, not as you know them to be."

Reviewers agreed that Negri was headed in the right direction. "After being wasted in *Bella Donna* and *The Cheat*, Pola Negri comes back to her own in this picture. She is again La Negri of *Passion*," said *Photoplay*. "She portrays almost every emotion conceivable, and does each and every one admirably."[5] The *Film Daily* said the film would please those who favor "colorful, romantic pictures," but the reviewer asked, "Why not use the old combination? The star appears to better advantage here than she did in either *Bella Donna* or *The Cheat*, but Pola is still not doing the big things that she did under Lubitsch's direction."[6]

Three of her 1924 films followed the same mold. In *Shadows of Paris*, *Men*, and *Lily of the Dust*, she plays a manipulative woman who undergoes a complete metamorphosis after falling for a good, decent man with impeccable values. Marriage to him would be her biggest reward, if it were not for her past. All three movies tell a moralizing tale: These women cannot be accepted the way they are. The harlot must be converted.

Negri never minded her characters deviating from the norm in Lubitsch's films. They could cheat people all their life and play each day away. In *The Mountain Cat*, instead of adjusting her behavior to suit an elegant home, Rischka skates across its polished floors like a child, not caring if the sophisticates consider her ill-bred. If her face seems more flawed in the German films, due to harsher lighting, her laugh lines only indicate a zest for life. In Negri's Paramount films, her beauty is superficial and her expressions seem muted, yet she is still worth watching. In *Shadows of Paris*, based on the French play *Mon Homme*, she shines in two contrasting roles. The film gives Negri a great opportunity to display her histrionic talent, and she excels in portraying both a brazen girl in a den of Apaches— turn-of-the-century Parisian thugs known for brutal muggings and attacks—and the elegant mistress of an Avenue Marigny mansion.

Negri plays Claire, also known as the Blackbird. In Negri's first scene, which introduces her as the Blackbird and a member of the underworld, she wears an ungainly checked skirt, a tight bodice, and a very ugly feathered hat, with her hair plastered to her cheeks. When she learns that her Apache sweetheart Fernand (Charles de Roche) is believed to have been killed in battle, this queen of the crooks decides to masquerade as a war widow and a Polish countess. With her new identity as Claire, she meets the influential Raoul de Gramont (Huntley Gordon), the prefect of police, who eventually marries her. As the Countess, she wears the latest Parisian creations, with costly gems at her throat and on her ears, fingers, and wrists.

After the Blackbird establishes herself in high society, she can't resist the temptation to return to the Apache dive occasionally and spend an evening with her old companions. Clad in her short, shapeless skirt, she leaves her elegant home by the back door and sneaks off to make merry with her real friends, unaware that she is being watched by Georges de Croy (Adolphe Menjou), her husband's secretary.

Claire has never forgotten Fernand, the Apache who became a brave soldier and was thought to have died on the battlefield. When she discovers that Fernand is alive, she tells him where she is living and how he can get into the stately house. Fernand believes her to be a servant. Claire receives her former companion of the underworld after she has adorned herself with most of her expensive jewels. He is intoxicated by her beauty, which is enhanced by her wonderful gown and glittering jewels. But the thief in him wins out and he steals bracelets and rings from her. For the first time Claire sees Fernand not as the man she loves, but as the thief he is. In 1924 the *New York Times* praised the action of the film: "As the best picture made in America with Miss Negri, *Shadows of Paris* will interest everybody who sees it, and those who are a little fastidious about Parisian atmosphere will find that the action makes up for what is lacking in some costumes and scenery. Mr. Brenon has done a good piece of work, but it would have been much better if he, like Ernst Lubitsch, had given a little time to what he evidentially considers trivial scenes."[7]

In *Men* and *Lily of the Dust*, Negri was pleased to be directed by Dimitri Buchowetzki, a Russian who had directed her German film *Sappho* (released in the United States as *Mad Love*). *Men* was Buchowetzki's first American picture, for which he also wrote the script. Aside from Lubitsch, Buchowetzki was the director who was able to bring out the best in Negri. Columnist Harry Carr described in a 1925 *Motion Picture* article how Buchowetzki helped Negri achieve her fiery best by having lengthy conversations before a big scene:

> They just talked and talked, and he watched her like a cat. Finally, her eyes would light up in a way that showed her interest had been won. In other words, Pola's genius was throwing out sparks. If

possible, he sent her out in front of the camera that instant, for that instant was the divine moment.

Handled that way, there is no finer actress than Pola Negri—living or dead. But it is a strenuous job for a director. Very few who have tried it ever care for the job a second time. Handling dynamite is something that few men care to undertake as a steady job.[8]

The plots of *Men* and *Lily of the Dust* follow the typically trivial, shallow stories of the time—a woman finds herself with a man she does not love to improve her social standing, then hates what she has become—but Negri's performances in both films show the audience that she is indeed a true actress.

Filled with deft touches and original ideas, *Men* is a perfect early example of a symbiotic relationship between the director and his actors. The characters in this film display great spontaneity in their roles. The lighting is dreamlike and the large crowd scenes are as effective as anything yet executed on the screen. Buchowetzki displays impressive dexterity with minimalistic and metaphoric devices, such as filming the skyline of Paris to introduce the location of the story. He uses close-ups of ankles and feet trudging along wet pavement to portray the sense of a bustling, weather-beaten city.

Under the direction of Buchowetzki, Negri exudes enthusiasm in a role that she clearly enjoys. The film gives her the opportunity to exploit all of her impressive acting range as Cleo, a poor waitress in Marseilles who rises from rags to riches. In the opening sequences, Cleo stands out against a backdrop of gloom, grime, and the most destitute residents of Paris. She takes a healthy swig from a bottle of milk while waiting for her tray to be filled with orders. This setting is in stark contrast to the elaborate and elegant world Cleo eventually finds herself in when she is seduced by the Baron (Edgar Norton). In these scenes, lavish costuming enhances Negri's physical beauty. Whether she is in a drawing room or a rundown tavern, Negri's Cleo thoroughly enjoys being surrounded by admirers vying for her attention.

The *New York Times* gave the film, and especially Negri, a warm reception: "No carnival or masquerade scene has been pictured as beautifully as the one inserted in this film. . . . *Men* has so many fine and delicate nuances that it will be appreciated by everybody as one of the best entertainments the screen has offered. Pola Negri at her best."[9] *Photoplay* again compared Negri's performance to her role as Du Barry. "The story is a little trashy and its treatment a little threadbare," the reviewer commented, "but the fiery, heavy-lidded Pola of *Passion* is back."[10] *Time* called *Men* "all woman, for it is all Pola Negri. . . . She plays with all the matchless glow of her temperament the role of a young woman who hates all men for what a few of them have done to her, until the right young man awakens her love."[11]

Pola Negri's second American picture with Buchowetzki, *Lily of the Dust,* was based on Hermann Sundermann's novel *The Song of Songs.* Again, the critics accused it of having an improbable plot, but it was still considered a directorial and acting gem. Negri's performance is once again inspired by Buchowetzki's direction, which is full of suspense and "fine touches of subtle suggestion."[12]

The tale takes place in a small German garrison town before 1914. The alluring Lily is employed as the librarian of the garrison's book collection. There has been a steady increase in books being checked out by the soldiers since the attractive Lily began working at the library. The dashing young Lieutenant Prell (Ben Lyon) eventually catches Lily's attention. One morning, she hides behind a door, expecting to surprise Prell. When the door opens, she is face to face with the intimidating Colonel Mertzbach (Noah Beery), who has come to investigate the sudden taste for literature among his men. He is captivated by Lily's dark, playful eyes and soon asks for her hand in marriage. Persuaded by his wealth and status, she accepts and leaves her memories of Prell behind as she and Mertzbach set off for their honeymoon in Berlin.

The couple seems to be content, and Lily enjoys being showered with gifts from her Colonel. But Prell soon arrives on the scene to take back what was stolen from him. He takes Lily in his arms, kissing her long and passionately. When the jealous Colonel discovers them, a duel results and Prell is wounded. The *New York Times* praised the performances of the soldiers, especially Lyon and Beery, but was most generous to the film's star, Negri: "She is quick to betray her emotions such as anxiety, affection, nervousness, interest, pleasure, and despair. Her eyes are soft and as usual, wonderfully expressive. She gives one the idea that the whole trouble is her eyes, or at least, her eyes and her facial beauty. She does not flirt. Men flirt with her and then, in entertaining them, she finds trouble. . . . Pola Negri will win many admirers by her sincere performance as Lily in this cleverly directed photoplay, which is for the most part, a stirring entertainment."[13]

Although Negri's films had thin plot lines, she was not making bad films. She knew she could do better, though. She missed the magic she had created with Lubitsch—a director who knew how to work with a European star. To Negri's delight, they were to be reunited later that same year.

11

Forbidden Paradise

Ernst Lubitsch enjoyed living in Hollywood, but he had yet to find his directorial stride. Since Mary Pickford imported him from Europe to make the disappointing *Rosita,* he had worked for Paramount, United Artists, and Warner Bros. without really finding a niche. None of his films had been particularly profitable—which was what the studios cared most about—and his latest film for Warner Bros., *The Marriage Circle,* hadn't gotten much of a reception. Negri and Lubitsch now lived next door to each other in Beverly Hills, and they became part of each other's everyday lives. Seeing his Hollywood prospects grow dimmer made Lubitsch depressed. Negri had always known him to be cheerful, and she wanted him out of the doldrums.

Meanwhile, Negri was building an arsenal of goodwill, although she still had detractors. She became a role model to girls and young women, who considered her a trendsetter. When she painted her toenails, they painted theirs. When Negri put on a turban in lieu of doing her hair, turbans sprang up everywhere. Russian boots and Grecian sandals were seen on more feet because of Negri. However, she could not enjoy her success while Lubitsch was down. One day she started reading Melchior Lengyel's book *The Czarina,* a tale of Catherine the Great's life, and thought of Lubitsch. "Before I was half through, I knew that I had found what I was looking for and bounded across the lawn to his house, waving the book in my hand like a victorious banner," she said in her memoirs.[1] This was a story she could sell to her studio bosses, she knew, and she would make them take Lubitsch too. She was convinced that *The Czarina* had her name, and Lubitsch's, on it. It was to take them to the top.

In 1924, based on the success of her previous movies, Negri was able to present the owners of Paramount with her own material. She showed them *The Czarina* and suggested Lubitsch as a director. The Paramount bosses acknowledged that Negri and Lubitsch made a good team. Warner Bros. agreed to allow him do a picture with another studio. Given the chance to work with Lubitsch, Negri became a sweetheart again. *The Czarina* became *Forbidden Paradise,* an acclaimed American masterpiece featuring Negri as Queen Catherine, Empress of Russia. Negri plays a queen who is used to having her own way until she falls for an officer who is already attached to one of her ladies-in-waiting. The officer's part went to Rod La Rocque.

Working with Lubitsch on the movie, Negri felt so carefree that she took La Rocque on as a lover. Hollywood was starting to feel like home, and she was laughing and loving again. La Rocque was both ardent and amusing without trying too hard.

Catherine the Great's wardrobe kept the costume department working overtime. In one scene, Negri runs through connecting corridors to descend a winding stairway—a duplicate of one in St. Petersburg's Winter Palace. It was a tricky scene to shoot, and Negri was concerned she would trip on her gown. Lubitsch asked her if she was the same girl who had thrown herself off the staircase in *The Eyes of the Mummy Ma.* Negri countered that she was three years older and ten times wiser. So Lubitsch put on Negri's dress and demonstrated how the run should be performed, keeping his ever-present cigar in his mouth, and never once tripping. Negri was in stitches. She could laugh herself silly with Lubitsch and still turn out sophisticated work. "To Pola, going back to Lubitsch's direction was like taking off a tight pair of shoes," Harry Carr said in 1925. "He didn't want her to be beautiful or sympathetic."[2]

Negri found a comrade in Rod La Rocque. She did not love him so much as she liked to be with him. She had stopped putting pressure on herself to find that one great love. La Rocque paid attention to her without smothering her. Of French descent, he was an American boy from Chicago who could transform his look to fit European roles. He could be steamingly romantic one minute and light and breezy the next. One day when Negri was trying to think of a birthday present for him, she rummaged through her jewelry box and found the loose diamond that Chaplin had given her. Long hours on the set left her with little time to shop, so she had the diamond set in a ring for La Rocque, placing the stone in a masculine design. Chaplin found out about the present and reportedly told La Rocque he would wrench it off his finger.

"As long as she lives, Pola will never have another part which so perfectly fits her character and temperament as this petulant, arrogant, passionate, Slavic queen, who had humor and shrewdness as well as power and strength," Harry Carr wrote in the *Los Angeles Times* on November 12, 1924. "From every standpoint . . . this is one of the great pictures of motion-picture history."[3]

Jeanine Basinger describes the importance of this film:

> *Forbidden Paradise* marks probably one of the greatest films Pola made. She gets to play Catherine, the Empress of Russia, with Lubitsch in control, understanding the range she has. Catherine is so awesome. On the one hand, she is imperial and authoritative and aristocratic. On the other, she is flirtatious and slightly comic—very appealing and cute. She is charming and luscious and wonderful. So, here you get this creation that is Lubitschian in range and Negrian in range. The two mesh perfectly in making this woman come to life as an enchanting but dangerous creature. Or a dangerous and enchanting creature, depending on the direction you want to come in."[4]

The magical juxtaposition of serious and comedy that Lubitsch brings to all his films surfaces in a scene where the camera enters a cavernous, lavishly decorated hall. Everyone in attendance is sobbing and the scene appears to be one of enormous tragedy—until the tragedy is revealed as the Empress's (Negri) cutting her hair. Everyone is weeping over the fallen locks. It is the classic Lubitsch scenario, where the viewer expects one thing and gets the opposite. The film initially presents itself as a serious drama, believable and tragic, then unravels into delicious moments of comedic play—which suited Negri perfectly. In this role she returns to her roots, inhabiting a world of drama and tragedy that was, at the same time, light and sophisticated. The film allowed her to be the fabled Pola Negri who had been born on film in Europe.

"May Pola always have [Lubitsch] as a director and may he always have Pola to direct. The combination develops the best dramatic talent in both," said *Photoplay.* "Pola's Catherine is what one might call a good bad woman. But her wickedness is done gorgeously and regally."[5] The *San Francisco Examiner* praised Negri's interpretation of the beautiful queen who is "one moment a romantic girl, falling in love with all who momentarily strike her fancy and then, on the other hand, a woman keen and skillful in the handling of the reins of the government."⁶ "What a combination!" said trade paper *Film Daily.* The reviewer told exhibitors, "You can make all the promises in the world for this and it will live up. . . . Pola comes into her own again and does her best work since *Passion.*"⁷

Finally, America saw the Negri that it had been longing to see: a bold freethinker with a strong heart, an open mind, and stylized European manners. Her Catherine the Great regally presides over affairs of state while surrendering to her own human desires. She registers a queenly sense of command, although she stops at nothing when pursuing a lover. Coolly detached one minute, she is wanton and willing the next. She subjugates her lover until he learns that one man will never be enough for her. The Queen can afford to be promiscuous, and any of Catherine's loyal soldiers would gladly serve as her conquest. Lubitsch emphasizes this fact in the movie by having Catherine pin a medal on her latest acquisition as the camera moves down the line to show rows of handsome young men wearing identical medals: the Queen's mark of commendation. It was subtle enough to get past the censors, but the audience got the message.

There was so much preparation involved in her roles, and the movies followed each other so quickly, that Negri was constantly working and studying. Always short on time, she stopped attending social affairs. Lubitsch told her that people had started calling her aloof and speaking negatively about her. To stay in the game, she should keep her backers happy—shake hands, give hugs and kisses. Hollywood was composed of a few chummy cliques, and other actresses were angling to take her place.

Lubitsch showed Negri a clipping that called her "The Star Who Is Too Superior to Come Out into the World" and stated that Negri obviously wanted to live in an ivory tower. Lubitsch warned her that unless she altered that opinion, her days on top were numbered. Knowing that Lubitsch never gave meaningless advice, Negri began a tireless campaign. She let magazines display photo spreads of her home. She went to the name parties, and she gave interviews and commentaries. People wanted to see a star on whom they could pin their fantasies, and Negri tried not to disappoint. The press noticed.

"The unfavorable publicity which was the direct result of her arrogance toward the press and her intolerance of direction was severely damaging her prestige," Eunice Marshall wrote in a *Screenland* article called "The New Pola." "She was a stranger in a strange land and she met only coldness and hostility on every side. True, she had done little to win affection, but still the lack of friendliness hurt. So, being a woman of intelligence, she about-faced."[8]

Negri and Lubitsch remained great friends, but after the success of *Forbidden Paradise*, they each went their own way. They still had miles to go in their own careers with much more success to come, but they had created an exceptional body of work together, and every film they made together stood on its own.

12

Becoming a Star

With the demand for movies growing greater and greater during the Roaring Twenties, Famous Players–Lasky, now known as Paramount, built a bigger, better-equipped studio, with offices fit for its growing success. Pola Negri, as one of its top actresses, was given lots of incentive to stay. After Gloria Swanson left the studio to make her own films, Negri's salary was increased to $7,500 a week for the first year of her contract, $8,500 for the second, and $10,000 a week for the third. Negri's new contract also guaranteed her a European vacation. Before she left, Paramount threw a lavish champagne-and-caviar party for her at New York's Ritz Hotel.

By now, movies had become ingrained in the American psyche. Style and success came to those who were throwing cash around, thinking big, and acting bold. Actors had to get themselves noticed if they wanted to be talked about. American audiences were attending more movies than ever, and the studios had quadrupled their output.

Memories of wartime shortages were still fresh, so people did their best to compensate for them with jazz, gin, and all-night parties. Negri was not a flapper, but she was progressive—someone whose strong sense of herself helped lead the march toward change and new development. There was a new, postwar world in the making, and she wanted to sample every bit of it. The year 1924 found her at the glittering premiere of Marion Davies's *Yolanda,* a much-touted movie. The film was a romanticized look at history with breathtaking scenery and lavish costumes and was emblematic of those Davies made under the supervision of her lover, the powerful tycoon William Randolph Hearst. Davies entered the California Theater flanked by Charlie Chaplin, Negri, and sisters Norma and Constance Talmadge. The women wore low-cut gowns that bared their backs and shoulders, and all four were dripping with jewels. The crowd lining the entranceway cheered. Seeing live movie stars was as exciting as seeing their movies. One after another, the limousines pulled up. Onlookers screamed, caught up in the glamour.

The people who made the stars famous were also in attendance. The industry bigwigs, their spokesmen, and the press reporters were all there. Elinor Glyn, the British-born writer and social climber, also put in an appearance. Glyn had coined the term "It Girl," with "It" meaning sex appeal. A prime example of the It Girl was Clara Bow. The opposite of a vamp, she did not intend to undermine men; she conquered them just to have a good time. You would never see Bow, or a character she played, attending an evening lecture or reading a book—bowling alleys and pool halls were more Bow's style. Negri scoffed at the concept of the It Girl. In her opinion, women were meant to be mystical creatures, never disclosing what they were thinking.

Negri would not place Marion Davies in the same category as Clara Bow. Davies was a born comedienne with a quick wit, but Hearst insisted on casting Davies in heavy-handed dramas, because he didn't want to see her poke fun at herself. He found slapstick particularly demeaning and would not hear of her taking a pie in the face. Hearst had to admit that Davies had an infectious sense of fun and could charm the audience with her humor, so he had some jokes added to *Yolanda*. He liked to see Davies in ribbons and curls, especially since she was competing with Pickford.

In 1924 the place to be seen was at parties held at San Simeon, the castle-like home that Hearst shared with Marion Davies. Hearst was a powerful man, and everybody wanted to be invited to San Simeon. Guests at San Simeon were guaranteed a mention in the newspapers, because Hearst's gossip columnist, Louella Parsons, was usually there. Everybody loved to be entertained at a party with Davies, who made sure that all of her guests had fun. If Hearst was around, however, frolicking in the pool with a cocktail in hand was replaced by a more sedate sit-down dinner.

Negri found Davies admirable for her honesty, living as Hearst's mistress and letting the chips fall where they may. She respected Davies's life choices. Nobody threw parties like Davies and Hearst, and Negri became one of their inner circle. Hearst tried to give Davies nothing but good press. He had ventured into moviemaking before he met Davies, but his interest in film peaked as she entered his life. With her talent, however, Davies would undoubtedly have kept her foot in show business even without W. R.'s financial backing.

Davies was born Marion Cecelia Douras, a mostly Irish girl, the youngest of four daughters in a Brooklyn family. "Showgirls always come from Brooklyn," she said after becoming a Ziegfeld Girl. Her older sisters also had some success in show business, and they changed their last name to "Davies" after seeing it on a billboard advertising a real estate firm in Queens. One of Davies's sisters, Reine, married theatrical producer George W. Lederer, who boosted the Davies girls' careers. Naturally vivacious and personable, Marion Davies was considered the most beautiful of the four sisters.

She was not Hearst's first showgirl. In fact, he had married one, Millicent Wilson, also a dancer, who became the mother of his five sons. Millicent did not so much disown her past as turn her back on it. She devoted herself to high-society life, joining clubs and supporting charitable causes. (Davies's interest in charity was later thought to result from wanting to follow in Millicent's footsteps.) Millicent was eighteen years younger than Hearst, and Davies was fifteen years younger than Millicent.

Davies met Hearst when Millicent was expecting a child. He did not consider it cheating on his wife when she was in no condition to have sex. Hearst had enough money to be able to avoid the consequences of his infidelity. He decided to maintain a double life, running off to meet Davies and then coming back to be with his family. Davies tried not to be jealous of the time he spent with the family, but she couldn't help but feel bad when he left her. Originally, Hearst had political ambitions, and a divorce would not have served him well. Once it was clear that he had little chance of being voted into office, he changed his mind and requested a divorce from his wife. Concerned for the future of her children, Millicent refused to sign the papers. There were also rumors that she did not want to hurt her social standing.

Finally, everyone came to an understanding. Hearst kept up the semblance of being a family man, although he did not hide having a mistress on the side. Millicent remained in New York and Davies lived with Hearst in Santa Monica and San Simeon.

Despite the thirty-three-year difference in their ages, Davies really cared for Hearst. She had other lovers here and there, usually married men—she was especially fond of her leading men—but this affair was different. Davies loved Hearst as her provider and protector, but most of all she appreciated him for the person he was. He, in turn, was warmed by her presence. People jokingly remarked that Hearst was built "like the back of an elephant," as he was a large, lumbering man. When Davies entered his life, Hearst's appearance seemed to change and soften. Davies had a large family: sisters, brothers-in-law, her mother, and assorted nieces and nephews. Hearst was generous to them, buying them houses and making sure that Davies's father, a lawyer, landed a high-salaried position.

As a result, Davies's entire family was doing exceptionally well, and she also enjoyed her life to the full. She smoked, drank, and loved to entertain. Her friends never minded her slight nervous stammer. She was always as eager to tell a bawdy joke as she was to hear one. She also became a perfect mimic, able to do impressions of Mary Pickford, Gloria Swanson, and Pola Negri.

Charlie Chaplin was someone Davies would put everything aside for. They always had a great time together, doing pantomimes for each other, engrossed in their own private party. Chaplin later assured the public, and Negri, that their relationship was strictly platonic, but everybody around them assumed they were having an affair. Hearst suspected it himself and hired detectives to keep him informed. Davies was forever under his watchful eye, whether he was at home or on the opposite coast.

In addition to Negri, Davies had a lot of show-biz girlfriends, such as actress Constance Talmadge and writer Anita Loos, but she always sought out male company. Chaplin dined and danced with Davies at the Montemarte, Hollywood's first swanky nightclub, never taking his eyes off her. The gossip columnists perceived this as passion. Chaplin was under pressure to marry another girl, Lita Grey, who was regarded as a young Hollywood sex symbol. He had been grooming Lita for the movies since she was seven years old. Because of him she was getting small parts to play, and at sixteen she was signed for the role of a dance-hall girl in *The Gold Rush*. One day she felt nauseated while filming. She was pregnant with Chaplin's child. Under the circumstances, Lita's mother demanded a wedding. Then a second event put Chaplin's life into even more chaos.

Thomas Ince, a well-known movie producer, was supposedly shot on Hearst's yacht, *Oneida*. Officially, it was announced that he died of acute indigestion, but many saw that as a cover-up, since the death sounded suspiciously sudden. The party on Hearst's yacht was to celebrate Ince's forty-third birthday. The guests who came on board included Ince and his mistress, actress Margaret Livingston (not his wife, Nell), as well as Elinor Glyn, Louella Parsons, and Chaplin.

It is believed that Chaplin was asked along only so that Hearst could watch his behavior with Davies. Parsons and Chaplin later denied being on the yacht. Clearly, Ince's death was a direct result of something that happened there. Whether he died at home two days later or instantly from a gunshot wound is still disputable. There were whisperings that everybody who was present on the yacht that day had been sworn to secrecy.

Ince's body was cremated two days later. Chaplin's secretary, Kono, allegedly saw a bullet hole in Ince's head as he was carried off the yacht. Hearst was known to be a crack shot and kept a diamond-studded revolver on board. According to one version of the events, Hearst saw Davies and Ince talking in the dim light of the lower galley and assumed the worst. Ince resembled Chaplin, with his large head of wavy hair styled in a similar fashion. Perhaps the alleged bullet was meant for someone else.

Rumors abounded, but the investigation of Ince's death was closed to his widow's satisfaction. Hearst did not attend the funeral, although he quietly provided Ince's widow with a trust fund.

Soon after the incident, Chaplin made up his mind to marry Lita Grey. They divorced after their two children were born, and Lita got a $625,000 settlement when she threatened to name five prominent actresses with whom Chaplin had had relations during the course of their marriage. Marion Davies and Pola Negri were to be among those, but Negri had not gone back to Chaplin. She now referred to their relationship as "mad love" and wondered what had gotten into her at the time.

Davies was a good friend to Negri, who was a fellow smoker and drinker. Having grown up in a large family, Davies took people for what they were and had no need to put on any airs. She would lounge around San Simeon in slacks amid its antique chairs and grandiose statues and still act the lady of the house. For Hearst, Negri was the spirit of the company, and Davies loved Negri for her intelligence and her slightly theatrical manner.

Negri and Davies remained friends because they were not forced to compete. Davies was a madcap blond, Negri a bewitching brunette. Pretty little Davies was never really a threat to beautiful, grand Negri. Besides, Davies could handle female jealousy if it came her way. She had three sisters and had gone through all the hair-pulling stages of learning how to get along. If Negri was huffy, Davies put her arm around her and calmed her down with a joke. Even though they had both been close with Charlie Chaplin, their interest in men differed.

Negri developed a friendship with another actress who had connections to Chaplin. Mabel Normand had been a fellow passenger on the boat that brought Negri to America, and they became friendly over the years. Normand was comfortably attractive rather than pretty. She was a comedienne, not a sex symbol—a funny girl who could fall on her rear and get up like a lady. She traded pies-in-the-face with Chaplin and Fatty Arbuckle but didn't let that take anything from her in people's eyes. She worked with Chaplin in the early days of his career with Mack Sennett Studios, where she encouraged him as he refined the character of the Little Tramp.

By the time Negri and Normand got well acquainted, Normand's career was pretty much over. She was getting bad publicity and having work problems because of her cocaine use, which came to light in connection with the murder of Paramount director William Desmond Taylor. Normand found herself in a very difficult situation. She was considered a suspect, although she could not be charged with Taylor's death. In 1924 another scandal arose when Normand's chauffeur shot Denver oilman Courtland S. Dines with a gun that belonged to the actress. Dines survived, but Normand's reputation was tarnished further, and audiences didn't consider her a barrel of fun anymore. Normand was grateful to receive compassion from Negri. Most of her friends didn't want their names associated with someone involved in two murders; they were afraid it would shed a bad light on them.

Negri always had very strong opinions about her leading men. In a 1925 interview with Helen Carlisle for *Movie Weekly*, she spoke frankly about each of them. She described Ben Lyon of *Lily of the Dust* as "a forerunner of the first generation to come after the World War, a generation which, we hope, will be unscarred by harsh experience, permitted to keep its illusions until maturity is reached." She considered him a gallant man and saw him as someone whose appeal would be "felt strongly by women older than himself, for he brings back to them their own youth and their first love. He is, indeed, every woman's first sweetheart, impetuous, eager, flaring into jealousy with a rush of hot words, stormy, sulky, boyishly engaging—an unusual and quite intriguing screen personality."[1]

Negri viewed Conrad Nagel of *Bella Donna* quite differently. "Nagel also conveys the impression of youth to the screen, but it is youth in which the spiritual dominates the physical. Constitutional inhibitions guard him from the reckless, prodigal gestures of a less repressed nature. His appeal to women lies in the fact that he represents those qualities she most desires in a husband: constancy, devotion, with just that right suggestion of dignity which gives him rank among men."[2]

According to Negri, Jack Holt of *The Cheat* was "a high type of clean-cut American manhood. Like Conrad Nagel, he is schooled in repression, but his appeal is distinctly physical rather than spiritual. He is the masterful, commanding type, reserved, almost coldly assured. The clinging-vine type of woman is especially attracted to him, for his manner is protective, essentially masculine."[3]

She placed Robert Frazer, who played opposite her in *Men,* among the screen's great lovers: "His outstanding quality is his deep sincerity, and it is this which is building up an army of Frazer fans all over the country. Nothing awakens response more rapidly in the feminine heart than an assurance of sympathy and quiet understanding, and these qualities, coupled with the dignity and repose which distinguish the Frazer personality, have a direct appeal to women everywhere."[4]

She characterized Antonio Moreno of *The Spanish Dancer* as "a flame, dying quickly." He was also suggestive of "the glamour of romance, the flower-hung dusk of Old Spain, the twanging of a guitar beneath a latticed window, a copper-colored moon swinging low in the tropic sky, a song tossed like perfume upon the languorous breeze."[5]

She knew Rod La Rocque of *Forbidden Paradise* for being cultured, for having "a keen appreciation of music and literature. He is markedly idealistic," she added, "yet it cannot be said of Rod that he seeks the shadow rather than the substance." He was "of fine physique, athletically inclined, vigorously masculine. His is a complex personality, in which the mental, physical and spiritual qualities are blended to a high degree." He was the only one of her on-screen lovers that aroused her maternal instinct.[6]

Edmund Lowe of *East of Suez* was one of "the handsomest" men she had ever known. "He is the ideal Grecian type," she proclaimed. "I like just to sit on the set and look at him, so classic are his features."[7]

In a *Photoplay* interview from the same era, Negri spoke of her changing views about happy endings in the movies. When she first arrived in America, she held the European point of view that the happy ending was not true to life and therefore constituted a jarring note in any form of drama that held itself as art. After a few months in America, she began to understand why melancholy drama could not thrive in this new frontier of commercial moviemaking—it was a matter of national temperament. This preference for the happy ending was a reflection of the breathless speed, the bustle, and the joyful scramble after the dollar that any American could participate in. This was in stark contrast with the meditative, profound tone of European movie endings, which were considered too gloomy but were probably more true to life. Negri reflects on the two art forms: "It was when I returned to Europe on my last trip that I came suddenly to the realization of my changed attitude toward the expression of theatrical emotion. I went to see many plays, and some of them were tragedies—artistically and intellectually excellent. But their emphasis upon human misery, their appeal to the spectator's self-pity, their cynical insistence that life was a hoax, fidelity impossible, love a sham, and justice a delusion, undeniably had a depressing emotional influence upon me."[8] Although Negri tended to be wordy, interviewers never cut her off. She revealed a sound mind when her intellectual side was allowed to shine through. If fans read what Negri said or just looked at her photos, she gave the impression of being larger than life, with an image to match.

In public, Negri was imperious, careful to uphold her public image. An incident at the Claridge in Paris illustrates this beautifully. Checking in, Negri rejected a deluxe suite, claiming that she needed an entire wing of the hotel. She was surrounded by mountains of suitcases and had a whole retinue of people at her beck and call: a maid, a secretary, bellboys, publicity agents, friends, and other travel companions. The actress Nora Bayes was honeymooning in the wing Negri had requested, and she did not want to move. Negri had made Bayes's acquaintance years before and thought a lot of her. She was sure Bayes would give up her rooms once she heard who wanted them.

"Tell her to jump in the Versailles fountains," Bayes answered when she heard of Negri's request. Bayes considered herself a star in her own right, a vaudevillian who had made inroads in musical comedy. She requested that Negri join her and her husband at the Follies-Bergère. First they met in Negri's rooms for cocktails. Bayes wore ermine and pearls. According to Howard Greer's written account, which Negri quoted in her memoirs, Negri decided to arrive late, refusing to appear before the other guests. Greer, a costume designer who had designed many of Negri's film outfits, described Negri's entrance:

And in swept the radiant Pola. It was worth waiting for. She could be the most ravishing and fascinating person in the world when she thought her audience was worthy. Her dress, that night, was a sheath of crystal embroidery and around her shoulders she carried a voluminous chinchilla cape. An emerald of one hundred and twenty carats was set in the diamond bracelet on her right wrist. On one finger, she wore her glittering ninety-four-carat diamond. Around her throat was the diamond chain with a yellow diamond pendant the size of a golf ball, which had once belonged to the Hapsburgs.[9]

Bayes and Negri sized each other up, then made their way to the theater. Every eye was upon them. When the curtain came down, people forgot to applaud—they were too busy admiring the two stars.

While in France, Negri spent time with Casimir de Hulewicz, as well as her mother. She had set Eleonora up in an apartment on the Riviera, where the climate was much more agreeable than Poland with its frigid winters. Eleonora had left her Warsaw properties to the relatives who remained there. She had lived through many years of poverty, often getting by on the kindness of the Sisters of Mercy, but thanks to her daughter's success she was her own woman now. A. A. Lewis remembers that "Pola was devoted to her mother. She was also a devoted Catholic. She was devoted to both her church and her mother—and her mother was a very religious woman. Pola was a very moral woman. She was not the vamp legend would have you believe."[10]

Negri learned from her mother that her first husband, Eugene Dombski, had been remarried to a Danish countess. Having been away from home for quite a while, Negri had a new perspective on the old days. Things that had seemed so important in her early years seemed quite insignificant now. Her failed marriage paled in comparison with what she had to go through daily in Hollywood.

Negri's mother felt that property was the safest investment; one should always own the roof overhead. So Negri bought a home in France—an eighteenth-century château named Rueil-Séraincourt. It was just outside Paris and a world apart from Hollywood. The château was in need of restoration, painting, and other work. She gave the task of overseeing the remodeling to her old mentor Casimir de Hulewicz. Negri had money, and she wanted to spend it. She was always glad to help those who had helped her.

Negri was still a draw in Europe. When she went to Berlin, crowds threw flowers and cheered. Admirers gathered in front of the hotel, awaiting her arrival. By now, Negri had made films in numerous countries and had proved that she was indeed a great star. She knew how to keep people interested in every aspect of her life so her audience would keep following her to movies and reading her interviews. Even with her stomach churning, feet sore, and head throbbing, she knew she had to answer the same old questions and smile until her face was numb. Negri never tired of the prima donna act.

Throughout her life, Negri quietly donated time and money to a number of charities—for tubercular children, for instance, in remembrance of her own painful experiences. But that didn't make as good copy as a hellbound love affair. Negri's film-star longevity owed to the fact that her life was never banal or boring, even for a moment. She was a star: a man-eater, not a nurturer. She won the admiration of crowds by putting her charms on display, and she knew very well how much wealth she could amass by doing this. It was not only about her beauty. She had to create the aura of a temptress, a legend to match her image, no matter which hotel she patronized or who she bedded. She wanted to stay within the realm of her fans' fantasies. Her reality was composed of banquets, limos, flashbulbs, and everything else that the gossip columnists or other celebrities reported it was.

The whirlwind year 1925 found Negri engaged in several more movie projects. In *East of Suez*, directed by Raoul Walsh, she played a Eurasian half-caste who is taken prisoner by a barbarous mandarin. It was during the making of this film that she first met Rudolph Valentino. Walsh casually introduced him to Negri when they both happened to be at the director's house. Valentino was inspecting a horse that Walsh had for sale. The introduction of the two future lovers certainly did not take a romantic turn that day. At the time, Valentino was still married to Natacha Rambova, and he was preoccupied with other events in his life. None other than Marion Davies made a more meaningful introduction later.

Playing Mariposa, a Latin dancer who wins the heart of all of New York, in *The Charmer* was a source of great satisfaction for Negri, although once again reviewers found her performance far superior to the vehicle. "Pola gamely tackles a poor story and plays it as gallantly as though it were a masterpiece," said *Photoplay*. "Her gay spirits soar far above the hokum comedy and her sincerity overbalances the triteness of phony dramatic situation."[11] The *New Yorker* agreed: "Pola Negri's vibrant quality is lost again in another picture."[12]

In *Flower of the Night* she plays a dancer named Carlota, the descendant of a high-ranking Spaniard, who works as a dance-hall girl. Paul Bern directed the film from a story written for Negri by Joseph Hergesheimer. The *New York Times* review praised her performance: "Not once during the registering of the varied moods of Carlota, daughter of a sad, disillusioned Spaniard, does she strike a jarring note; she is just as one expects her to be. She is subtle, smiling, quiet, and disdainful when occasion demands, and in other situations she portrays vividly distraction and also depicts the strong willpower of the character in checking hysteria. There are close-ups of Carlota which do not stop the story but give a clear conception of her feelings in moments of anguish and in periods of excitement and fear."[13] The *Film Daily* told exhibitors that the film was slight in plot but that Negri played "a dashing Spanish vamp likely to hold them with her performance."[14] *Time* said, "She plays Pola Negri as well as ever, and that in itself is probably a sufficient accomplishment."[15]

The theme of a woman getting the better of a man is a common element of many Pola Negri films—unless, of course, she has to sacrifice herself for the greater good. She told interviewers, "I have been called a man-hater. That is very far from the truth. I have never been able to depend on them. The woman who is able to depend on them is most successful with them."[16]

In *A Woman of the World*—based on the novel *The Tattooed Countess* by Carl Van Vechten—Negri comes out on top again, literally whipping her man into submission after having gained his love and admiration for breaking every social taboo. Most of the movie is filled with humor and comic insights. It pits a big-city girl against small-town America, simple folk against a lady of broad perspective, libertine against fervent conservative.

Malcolm St. Clair, the director, was a great fan of Lubitsch and had a flair for comedy, having worked his way up from newspaper cartoonist to playing a Keystone Kop in Mack Sennett comedies to directing for Sennett. He allowed Negri to play a big-city bad girl with tongue in cheek. She isn't really out to lead all men astray, but rather to make them question their own core beliefs.

A Woman of the World begins with an enormously glamorous Negri, playing Countess Elnora Natatorini, enjoying the balmy breezes of the Riviera. She exudes glamour and mystery with her long cigarette holder, luxurious chinchilla wraps, and a butterfly-and-skull tattoo on her arm. The European men fall at her feet. But Countess Elnora has her heart set on gaining the love of one man. When she discovers that he loves another woman, she decides to forsake France and the Mediterranean and plunge into the depths of the American Midwest, to the small town of Maple Valley, Iowa. Her cousin Sam Poore (Chester Conklin, another former Keystone Kop) and his plump wife greet her at the train station. Although they know nothing of the finer things in life, they are greatly impressed by having a countess visit the community.

The contrast between this sophisticated European creature and the silos and cornfields of Iowa is quite comic and charming, and Negri is wonderfully amusing. The Countess, with her confidence and individuality, manages to baffle, alarm, awe, and delight the sheltered residents of Maple Valley through various scenes and events, including a county fair where a sign announces that anybody can "talk to a real countess" for twenty-five cents.

Maple Valley is run by Richard Granger (Holmes Herbert), a narrow-minded district attorney who crusades against drinking, dancing, women smoking, and frivolity in general. Upon meeting the Countess, however, he falls under her spell. The clerk he sends to deliver flowers to the alluring Countess falls in love with her himself, which angers Granger. In a bizarre plot twist, the district attorney finally is horsewhipped by the bobbed Countess into the man he must become to marry her.

Against this absurd backdrop, some serious events unfold and problems arise, but Negri displays the worldliness of the true sophisticate who can be at home in a small town or the mansions of Monte Carlo. She brings the gift of acceptance and generosity to the narrow-minded people of Maple Valley, who then discover their own acceptance and generosity toward her. Their mutual plea to accept each other on their own terms is a very forward-thinking theme. The Countess can treat the townspeople with kindness because she understands her own world and knows who she is. Because she doesn't need society to tell her who she is or what she should be, she can confidently remain herself, no matter who considers her strange or naughty. The New York Times again praised Negri's performance: "Miss Negri is just as stunning and as conscientious as in any of her other pictures."[17] Photoplay celebrated the return of the passionate Pola: "Awake! Negri fans, from your long siesta. The fascinating, continental Pola is with us once again. A dangerous, cynical, tempestuous Italian countess she is, wearing a tattoo—insignia of an amorous adventure."[18] "I am a woman of the world, not the world's woman," is the Countess's motto throughout this picture. She knows enough about human nature to accept the local customs, but she doesn't have to eat hot dogs or take a pie in the face to be part of the community. And she doesn't mind letting everyone see that she is a girl who's been around.

The movie was both praised and criticized; some people considered it delightful, whereas others found it outrageous. Negri never lost her composure, however. She was used to startling people both before and beyond the camera.

13

Finding Valentino

As Pola grew more certain of her audience, a new man appeared on the horizon. Fate seemed to play a hand in that romantic development. Valentino biographer Emily Leider explains: "Valentino apparently saw *Madame Du Barry* before Pola Negri came to this country and supposedly he wrote her a fan letter right after he saw it at a private screening. He described himself as a worm worshipping at the foot of a great star. Valentino had a tendency to describe himself in abject terms, so I'm not surprised that he would take that approach to Pola Negri, and I think she loved it. And he ended up working for the same studio as Pola Negri, which was Famous Players–Lasky, later Paramount."[1] Negri didn't know it yet, but a number of things were happening in Rudolph Valentino's life that kept leading him to her door. It seemed that every turn he made brought him closer to Negri.

His Mineralava dance tour was an instant success, and people were fighting to get seats for it. Natacha Rambova, his second wife, didn't know how to tango until Valentino taught her the moves, building on her years of ballet training and classical dance practice. She and Valentino duplicated the tango he had done in *The Four Horsemen* and supplemented it with exotic eastern numbers. Their costumes, designed by Rambova, were stunning. Rambova wore black, backless dresses with a flower in her hair. Valentino was attentive and adoring as they danced; he was deeply in love with her, or with his idea of her, while she remained cool and remote.

Whether or not Rambova loved him, she at least loved to dance. Valentino styled his moves to hers on the stage, so their hearts and bodies seemed joined as one. Audiences were wild to see the star of *The Sheik* in a live performance. Watching the tango was akin to watching a love game between two people, with the woman goading the man on, then holding him back until she was ready to fall into his arms. The audience shared in Valentino's triumph as he danced with her across the floor.

Once they learned about the success of the tour, Famous Players asked Valentino to return. If they expected him to return gratefully, they were disappointed. Valentino was making more money on the dance tour than the studio paid him, so he requested a healthy sum to return to movies. He went back on Paramount's payroll for seventy-five hundred dollars a week and the promise that he could help select the scripts. Naturally, that was Rambova's doing. If the studio moguls thought they owned Valentino, she was going to make them change their minds.

Meanwhile, Negri was keeping herself in the social swim. Since she was not always up to going out but did not want to appear antisocial, she did a lot of entertaining at home. She had spacious quarters where houseguests could stay overnight. One of her frequent visitors was Feodor Chaliapin, the Russian opera singer, who passed through Los Angeles on concert tours. As a child in Warsaw, Negri had heard him sing, so she was thrilled to have him perform in her living room. Feodor would play her piano while her friends gathered around. Negri loved having her home reflect the Old World culture. She had the deepest respect for people like Chaliapin.

While Negri was creating her own happy home, Valentino was becoming a beleaguered husband, and he could not understand how it had come about. He used to think he was successful in every area of his life, but Rambova rejected everything he held sacred. She did not want to love, honor, and obey him, or have children. He, on the other hand, had spent years on tours, making compromises, thinking it was all for her. Now he wanted and needed a family to come home to. He expected Rambova to be grateful that his longings were so simple.

Valentino was born in Italy under the name of Rodolfo Alfonso Raffaele Pierre Filibert Gugliemi di Valentina d'Antonguolla—Rodolfo Gugliemi for short. His father, a veterinarian who specialized in farm animals, earned enough to keep his household among the middle class. There was order and discipline in the house. Valentino's mother had married in her early thirties and was thoroughly devoted to her husband. She was of French extraction, possibly a descendant of aristocrats. She was pretty, with fair skin and pitch-black hair—hair that brushed little Rodolfo's face as she leaned over to kiss him goodnight or regale him with stories. Her two other children, Alberto and Maria, did not have such privileges. His mother's vivid imagination was reserved for Rodolfo as he constantly begged her to tell him yet another story. In fairytales good always wins, and evil gets punished, so his mother's stories developed a sense of justice and decency in little Rodolfo, whose high sensitivity made him the black sheep of the family. He was his mother's best-loved child, because he required constant care and attention.

Rodolfo's father punished him frequently. The boy had a short attention span, found it impossible to sit still, and did poorly in the classroom. He was given to climbing trees and fond of scaling cliffs and straddling fences. His mother worried about him, and his father kept him within strict limits. Valentino's father died when the boy was twelve, after contracting malaria while formulating a vaccine for horses. His last words to his sons were: "Mother and country."

Valentino had his heart set on becoming a cavalry officer, but to achieve that, one had to be a brilliant student from a wealthy family. Valentino was just average. He tried to get into the naval school, but he couldn't pass the physical—his chest was two centimeters too small. Noticing that he had a way with animals, his mother sent him to an agricultural school. Valentino learned how to landscape, build stone walls, and plant flowerbeds, but also to train horses, break bulls, and tend cattle. He proved himself athletic and able, which kept the work coming in.

Valentino could never steer clear of romantic distractions, and he was always in love with some girl. He was usually attracted to fair-skinned girls with long, dark hair. He had a Romeo-type personality. He could sing and play the mandolin and wasn't really interested in an ordinary job. Slicked-back hair, a Fiat, and a tuxedo became his calling cards. He spent a lot of time at dance clubs, where he polished his skills. He could step out with the best of them, and he practiced good etiquette. Women found him a willing escort. Valentino shunned the middle-class respectability his family had worked so hard to achieve—he had a hedonistic bent and the heart of a gigolo. The "black sheep" label seemed fitting for the graceful, handsome young man.

For Valentino's mother, her deceased husband was the great love of her life; she remained faithful to his memory for the rest of her days, believing they would be reunited in Heaven. Although Valentino admired his parents' loving marriage, he was the promiscuous type himself. In the end, his family sent him to make his way in America. To get by, Valentino took turns being a gardener, a petty thief, a car washer, and a "taxi dancer"—a man who danced with rich women for tips. Often he found himself walking the streets hungry. At some point he became friends with Norman Kerry, who later became an actor in Hollywood and helped him along.

Before Valentino left New York, he was involved in his first scandal. He had been seeing a married woman he met in the dance clubs, Mrs. Jack de Saulles, but allegedly all they did together was dance the tango. Mrs. de Saulles, a native of Chile, was an heiress from a distinguished family, and Valentino had no intention of ruining her marriage. Shortly after he stopped seeing her, he saw her picture in the paper. She had shot and killed her estranged husband because she feared losing her only child in a torturous custody battle. Mrs. de Saulles was later acquitted of the killing. When she was in jail during the trial, Valentino made a point of visiting her there.

People kept associating Valentino's name with the murder, and dancing for a living in New York was not enough to bankroll the kind of life Valentino wanted to enjoy. On Norman Kerry's advice, he boarded the train for Hollywood. Ultimately, Valentino hoped to buy a farm, and California seemed like the right place for it, with its mild climate and sunny weather. Manhattan was cold in the winter, especially to the destitute.

In the beginning, Valentino found Hollywood as much of a scramble as New York, although he discovered a solid method of getting bit parts in movies as he followed Kerry into acting. Valentino would put in an appearance at the Alexandria Hotel bar every afternoon around five, when there were free sandwiches and people who might want to buy him drinks. D. W. Griffith hired him to dance in a stage show after spotting him there. Valentino, as he now called himself, was a definite crowd-pleaser. His chosen name came from di Valentina d'Antonguolla. Valentino means "sweetheart" in Italian. Valentino had added a touch of aristocracy to his own lengthy name, paring it down to a celebrity-style title.

At a Metro-Goldwyn-Mayer party he attended with his friend Dagmar Godnowsky, Valentino met four women who were to have a profound effect on his life. The first was Alla Nazimova, in whose honor the celebration was held. She had recently completed the film *Stranger than Death*, and Metro rewarded her by throwing a bash. MGM owned the smallest number of movie theaters compared to the other four major studios—Paramount, Twentieth Century-Fox, Warner Bros., and RKO—so it had to make its pictures desirable to outside theater owners. MGM did this by building a stable of top-notch stars. The firm's slogan was "More stars than there are in the heavens," although other studios believed the same of themselves.

Irving Thalberg, the studio's wonder boy, pushed for prestige pictures, much to the dismay of his boss Louis B. Mayer, and he was loyal to the stars who graced them. Since Nazimova was a star who brought a touch of class to the big screen (and made MGM a lot of money), the studio gave in to her every demand to keep her.

Nazimova was born in Russia. Although not a classic beauty, she knew how to portray one. Her dark hair was unruly, her smile much too wide, and she had a huge head balanced on a tiny body. Someone described her as having "gunboat feet." She was bisexual, so although she had a husband, she didn't shy away from girls. Her style was commanding and superior. When Dagmar Godnowsky tried to introduce Valentino to Nazimova, he was given the cold shoulder. "How dare you bring that gigolo to my table? How dare you introduce that pimp to Nazimova?" was the response.[2] Nazimova later altered her opinion of Valentino enough to let him play opposite her in *Camille,* in which his performance so outshone hers that she had his part edited severely.

Natacha Rambova also attended that fateful Metro party. As a very good friend of Alla Nazimova's, she did everything in her power to be like her. When Valentino later found himself in love with Rambova—who at that time worked as a set designer for *Camille*—he had to deal with the pesky problem of his continuing marriage to Jean Acker, another girl Valentino had met at the party.

Acker had been a favorite of Nazimova's and became her protégé. Just like Valentino, Acker was trying to get bigger parts. They seemed to have a lot in common. They married after dating briefly, but the story goes that Jean locked Valentino out of their bedroom on their wedding night. The relationship was never consummated, and nobody really knows why Jean acted as she did. According to some accounts, she was in love with someone else; others say it was Valentino's fault. Some reports say that he had picked up gonorrhea from one of his numerous partners and didn't tell Jean until after the marriage ceremony. This was the first of Valentino's nightmarish honeymoon nights. The second was due to a bigamy charge that came after he married Rambova. People teased Valentino about his knack for winding up in sexless marriages.

The fourth woman he met at the party had an impact as profound as the other three, although she and Valentino had a different kind of pairing.

June Mathis, a sharp-eyed Metro screenwriter, was scouting out actors for the novel she was adapting, *The Four Horsemen of the Apocalypse*. Mathis suggested Valentino for the lead, and she actually tailored the part to him. Valentino got to tango in that film, and it was the tango that sold him to the public. He became an overnight star after the premiere. Cast as the tragic Julio in *Horsemen,* Valentino had a charm previously unseen. He played to the woman on-screen as he flirted with the women in the audience, and he did it with ease. He had the ability to make every woman feel individually special, all at the same time. On-screen, he became the personification of masculinity. Biographer Emily Leider elaborates:

> Valentino was the first of his kind. He's a breakthrough figure. He was the first great screen lover. He was the first romantic lead with an olive complexion. He was always after stardom. He was always cast as an exotic. This was something new, too, because prior to Valentino, to look ethnic guaranteed you would be cast as a villain. So, the fact that Valentino was able to be cast as a romantic leading man indicates that film had matured and that audiences had matured and had been changed by World War I, which Europeanized American tastes and familiarized many Americans with what we would call cosmopolitanism and sophistication. And you didn't have to go to Europe anymore to taste those qualities. They were brought here and Valentino was the embodiment of Hollywood's idea of the exotic.[3]

After the success of his first films, Valentino started angling to get a date with Negri. His marriage to Rambova was coming to an end. His new contract with United Artists barred Rambova from the set, and even more so from interfering with the production. To pacify her, Valentino invested a large sum of money into *What Price Beauty?*, a movie she wrote and directed. The film flopped, and Rambova became hysterical. When Valentino insisted that they take a part in the production of *The Eagle,* she took off alone for New York. Valentino begged her not to go, but to no avail. Rambova believed in supernatural forces and was an enthusiast of the occult. She made all her decisions based on signs from extraterrestrial beings; for example, she thought she was receiving guidance from an ancient Egyptian prophet. She got readings from pebbles and rocks.

After the first encounter between Valentino and Negri failed to lead to anything, they saw each other for the second time at one of the famed San Simeon costume parties. That was when Marion Davies introduced the couple to each other again, this time with better timing.

Negri went to the party dressed as Catherine the Great, wearing a wardrobe piece from *Forbidden Paradise,* and Valentino was dressed in one of his toreador costumes from *Blood and Sand.* The two theatrical personalities couldn't help but attract each other with their mutual love of dressing up and putting themselves on display, as well as their love of dance. Their great skill as dancers was akin to a love elixir. Although he wasn't a trained dancer like Negri, Valentino was a striking dancer with great musical interpretation. Valentino was separated from Rambova at the time. Negri and he did not become officially involved until after his divorce.

It was Valentino who had been urging Davies to arrange a meeting with Negri. Davies kept setting up dates, but Negri backed out at the last minute time after time. Some claimed she was playing hard to get. She herself said she was not sure that she should meet him; she had an intuition that he was to be avoided. Valentino, on the other hand, was intrigued by each of her rejections, because such a reaction was novel to him. Initially, Negri turned down the invitation to the costume party Davies was giving in honor of William Randolph Hearst. Davies insisted that Negri attend, claiming that her absence would cause Hearst to be hurt. That argument persuaded Negri. She put on one of her *Forbidden Paradise* outfits, complete with gold-encrusted jacket, and came to the party knowing she would not be able to avoid meeting the legendary Valentino.

Valentino, svelte and masculine in his matador attire, stood a little behind Davies as Negri came through the door. He bent down to kiss Negri's delicate hand. Negri discovered that Valentino had a lilt to his voice. His words were soft and rhythmic, as he had lost most of his accent. He was a man, though also a boy. Where was the intensity that made him what he was on-screen? Negri could see no reason to fear him—until they danced the tango.

Soon after, Valentino traveled to Paris to divorce Rambova. It was Rambova who initiated their split. She never wanted to have children or give up her career and was surprised that her husband expected her to do so.

Valentino became a role model for young men. They grew sideburns, copied the outfits from his Spanish roles, and learned the tango. They copied his slicked-back hairstyle. Such an elegant man was something new for the American audience. Everything about him, such as his concern with custom-made shoes and suits, riding gear, and jewelry, aroused a great deal of interest. People copied all this but also mocked it. Some male journalists condemned Valentino for his extreme focus on his looks and considered him a negative influence on American men.

Valentino still wore a slave bracelet that Rambova had given him. He consulted with Dareos, a seer with a crystal ball, only to be told that the marriage to Rambova was indeed over. He became sullen and began spending a lot of time alone. Negri was his type—a raven-haired, ruby-lipped beauty with a commanding presence and a controlling nature, as masculine as she was feminine and appealing to both sexes. She was also an accomplished flirt and knew her way around the bedroom. Once she and Valentino tangoed, they were both smitten, and everyone saw it. Valentino was not the tallest man—he was said to be about five feet, eight inches. Asked about what attracted her to him, Negri answered: "It was the way he moved."[4]

"The unhappiness in you called out to the unhappiness in me," is what Valentino is supposed to have told her.[5] He had a somber nature, and there was an indefinable sadness to him. His mood swings that came and went for no reason seemed to feed the passion of his dance. Valentino didn't treat dancing as an art; he let the dance personify love and intimacy. With masculine firmness, he took charge of the woman before him. He was a fascinating, agile, and handsome man. In the tango, he brought the woman to him, bent her, curled her, and swept her head far back, all the while making himself the focus. As they circled one another, Negri lost track of the people around her. Valentino's matador suit heightened her awareness of his body. There was a readiness in his eyes. He looked like a hunter in the night, out to make a kill, stalking and waiting, knowing that the right moment would come.

Valentino's true strength, however, was in his sensitivity and gentleness. He knew how to pay a woman a compliment and accommodate female fantasies. He sensed that it is a woman's nature to want to be overpowered by a man. Valentino, physically confident and yet emotionally conflicted, could make any female yield to his desire. Her resistance would only create some delicious tension. Negri was strong enough to push back. Unlike Rambova, Negri had a sense of humor and could cajole Valentino into agreement.

Valentino had brought a date to the San Simeon costume party: Vilma Banky, one of his leading ladies. Banky pried Valentino away from Negri, interrupting their conversation and asking Valentino to take her home. With a hint of jealousy, Negri watched the two of them head out the door. Before he left, Valentino asked when he could see Negri again. Negri was horrified by the notion of having a real relationship with him, and she told herself that Valentino was only good for a dance. Something told her that, whether he meant to or not, Valentino would tear her life apart. She left for Europe thinking it best to avoid him when she returned. Meanwhile, the Hollywood gossip mill insisted that costars Valentino and Vilma Banky were lovers, but both denied the rumors. Banky later married Negri's former flame Rod La Rocque. La Rocque gave Banky the same diamond that Charlie Chaplin had given Negri and Negri had given La Rocque, but in a new setting. La Rocque and Banky stayed married for more than forty years, and Banky never knew where her ring had come from. Negri told the entire story only after La Rocque had passed away.

Moving rapidly from one film to another, Negri had enough work to keep her from an active love life. On her return from Europe, she gave a party for Michael Arlen, the well-known author of *The Green Hat*. There, at the Biltmore hotel where she was receiving guests, was Valentino, giving a party of his own.

Valentino didn't want to miss his opportunity, and he asked Negri to dance. The rotation of their bodies could not have been more fluid. Valentino was not one to obsess over form; he had little technical sophistication, but he knew how to entwine his partner. He went for what he wanted without being crude. He let her know that he was waiting, with no intention of waiting too long. Negri found herself entranced. When he said he would take her home, she stopped asking herself questions. She was in love the moment she lay down with him. Valentino was an unhappy person, a ball of anxiety, but seduction helped him escape from it. The popularity and adoration he was enjoying couldn't save him from the things he feared: sickness, old age, and death. Valentino wanted to believe that a beloved woman could protect him and shield him from the pain he sensed would come.

Valentino was an ordinary Italian guy who had managed to dance his way into feature films, and he knew that success was fleeting. To him, show business was just another way of selling yourself. He didn't have Negri's training and endurance; he just wanted to make his money and get out.

The similarities between the childhoods of Negri and Valentino are striking. They were each "the special one" out of three siblings, with Negri being the only survivor of hers. Both lost their fathers early in life. Both of their mothers delayed marrying until their early thirties, which made them treasure their children all the more, and both mothers felt they were cut from finer cloth. Valentino and Negri were both very lively and intensely physical children. They recognized their reflections in each other.

Negri had become the star that Hollywood wanted her to be. She owned a fabled house in Beverly Hills and her famous Rolls Royce with white velvet upholstery. She had impeccable taste and her own elegant sense of style, and she spared no expense on pleasures and gracious living. She wore white chiffon, black silk, or monotone velvets with matching tailored furs. Valentino now became yet another stage of her passionate, eccentric life.

As for Valentino, there was an urgency about the way he made plans. He behaved as if he knew he didn't have much time, as if he knew he would die young. Negri didn't have to wait for love to happen anymore. Their love was happening, and the momentum was speeding up. A. A. Lewis shares an intimate detail: "Pola told me about the first night of the consummation of their romance. Rudy arrived with his arms filled with roses. He stripped the petals off the roses and put the petals on the bed. And they laid on the bed, crushing the rose petals, the scent rising. It happened to be a scene in an old DeMille movie."[6]

14

Losing Valentino

The year 1926 found the lovers in peak form. They dined in front of an open fireplace and drank wine, and Rudy Valentino whispered loving words in French, their mutual language. Valentino had imagination and a great deal of style. Sometimes he was a charming and gallant gentleman, and sometimes, just to spice things up, he would act rough. Negri and Valentino created a world of beauty together—their own intimate universe. They stayed in bed whenever they could. Their love was pure togetherness, and neither of them wanted to break the trance. Former Paramount producer A. C. Lyles comments on the trend they helped to start:

> Our publicity department has always been very much alive, and Pola Negri and Valentino helped build it. She would be in her long exotic gowns, and he in his wonderful masculine outfits—what a team! They were a wow! The papers were full of their photographs. They were a studio's dream. Over the years we've had William Powell and Myrna Loy. You had your Jeanette MacDonald and Nelson Eddy. You had your Spencer Tracy and Katharine Hepburn. Rudy and Pola started that trend of putting people together that had tremendous chemistry. We owe them a lot for paving the way for romantic couples.[1]

Their romance became a gold mine for the press, as was later the case with Richard Burton and Elizabeth Taylor. Negri and Valentino were more like Mary Pickford and Douglas Fairbanks. They were equals, and their love became the number one topic for the press all over the world. "At the point where he hooked up with Negri, Valentino needed her more than she needed him," says Tony Villecco, author of *Silent Stars Speak.* "She was very big at that time, and he was sort of slipping a bit so he was not at the top of his game. But, then later he had a resurgence with *Son of the Sheik.*"[2]

One evening after dinner, Valentino's face lost all its color. Negri wanted to call a doctor, but Valentino wouldn't let her. He confessed that he was taking medication to prevent hair loss. A great lover with a bald dome would not be the Valentino of every woman's dreams, and he considered wearing a toupee. The cure for baldness had its side effects.

Men called Valentino a "powder puff," and worse, because he showed up in public in tights or fancy pants with an elaborate sense of masculinity. He was suave, and sometimes he pranced like a French poodle. He had that dainty way of holding a cigarette. Plus he wore lipstick and mascara on-screen.

The studio started looking for ways to correct that image of him; they wanted him to appeal to both sexes. Valentino was athletic, and he performed his own stunts. He could leap from a balcony or swing from a chandelier; he could also fight like a professional boxer. At last, male moviegoers began to see a side of Valentino that they could relate to. He wore costumes that showed the rippled muscles of his arms. He was able to look masculine even in a sheik's robe. He could gallop a horse across the desert to rescue some poor, misguided girl. Yes, Valentino had manicured nails and arm bracelets, but he could console a crying woman in a heartbeat. Valentino-to-the-rescue became the most romantic form of the Latin lover. Men began to realize that Valentino's seemingly effeminate mannerisms gave him an edge with women, who let down their guard and gave in to him easily. Valentino created a whole new style, and he eagerly showed it off. He proved that wearing jewelry could make a man more attractive to women. He was amused by his own appearance, and even his smiles were self-referential.

Negri continued to progress in her career. She was asked to star in *Hotel Imperial* with Mauritz Stiller in the director's chair. Negri was to play the unlikeliest of heroines—a floor-scrubbing chambermaid, a little person who finds her moment in the sun. Here was a film that would let her be an actress with a capital A. Paramount was coming through for her. Negri wanted to expose the turmoil inside the character. There were parts of Negri's personality that had not yet been shown on the screen, and it was time to uncage them.

The idea of doing a movie with Stiller enthralled Negri. Invited for dinner, Stiller brought the young Greta Garbo to Negri's house. Negri got a Lubitsch-type vibration from Stiller and knew they would work well together. Stiller was a homely man, a gentle giant with huge hands and an endearing manner. He was perceived as a bit of an eccentric with a sensitive nature, as well as a person who got things done. Stiller possessed enormous knowledge, and he used his unique understanding of the world behind the camera. Garbo was Stiller's Swedish protégé; Metro signed her up just so they wouldn't lose a good director. They paid her two hundred dollars a week but didn't give her any parts. Garbo was terribly shy and needed reassurance. Negri found her extraordinary to look at. She sensed that there was magic within her that most people missed. Garbo quietly asked Negri for advice on how to get into the movie business.

Negri advised her to leave timidity at the door. She told her to conquer her doubts and go in fighting. Garbo needed to speak up to get people interested in her beauty. Negri told her to open her mouth anytime, anywhere. Moviegoers were interested in actors who created a buzz. Garbo listened to Negri's advice. She lost weight, got her teeth fixed, and conquered her shyness. Garbo had once been Greta Gustafsson of Stockholm, Sweden, a poor girl who gave shaves in a barbershop. She never forgot why she came to Hollywood; going back home would mean returning to the stubble-faced lechers. Louis B. Mayer couldn't really see her as an actress. He tried to promote her as "the Norma Shearer of Sweden," to no avail. It was actually thanks to Stiller's camera work that Garbo finally proved herself with *The Torrent* in 1927. She went on to become one of the silent stars who found work in the talkies despite her accent. The irony was that Negri's accent was no thicker than Garbo's, but Negri, the one who had encouraged Garbo to talk, later found it almost impossible to get speaking parts in America.

Negri and Valentino were now fully integrated into each other's lives. Valentino did not want to grow old, saying he would be satisfied if he made it to forty. Negri was making long-term plans, hoping to change that. Valentino saw his body as his chief asset. Acting out the part of the virile male, he smoked, drank, and ate whatever he pleased. When he tangoed, though, he seemed like the healthiest specimen around. Negri was a social smoker and drinker, and she liked going out to clubs and restaurants. Negri knew how to keep up with Valentino, or even outdo him if she chose. She was not going to be left behind.

Negri had modeled her house in Beverly Hills on George Washington's Mount Vernon. Valentino's house on the hill was christened "Falcon Lair."

It looked like a fortress. Valentino and Natacha Rambova purchased it when they decided to join Hollywood's elite. Back then, Beverly Hills was a new neighborhood. Falcon Lair was built as a Spanish-style villa with stucco walls and a red-tiled roof. It had stables for Valentino's horses and kennels for his dogs. The property's namesake was *The Hooded Falcon*, a movie that got lost in disputes and was never produced—another project Valentino and Rambova could not see to completion. Rambova never spent a single night in that house.

Valentino had the place remodeled. Falcon Lair was to become Valentino and Negri's playground—their enchanted castle. Valentino designed some of the landscaping himself. He also went to Paris to get the necessary divorce. He wanted Negri, with a ring and a white dress. He wanted the house to be a safe and quiet haven for them. The man who had ricocheted from woman to woman was now ready for stability.

Negri was his sweet "Polita." They spent hours in bed together, loving and sleeping, lying in each other's arms. They made up tender words and murmured them into each other's ears. Over and over again, Valentino said he lived only for her. His childhood yearnings were finally being fulfilled; with Negri, he could behave like a man. Negri could now love him with no taboo, and Valentino took satisfaction in bringing her everything she needed.

Negri heard people say that Valentino still cried for Rambova and that she was just a distraction. Negri never believed those rumors because she knew how much the breakup had cost him. Valentino was crying from aftershock, Negri believed. He did not want to believe Rambova's view of him, and he could not bear the pain of having been used.

George Ullman, Valentino's business manager, thought Valentino was better off with Negri and told him so. After Ullman set up the successful Mineralava tour, Valentino asked him to become his manager. Ullman had his priorities straight, and he knew how to keep the money coming in. He made sure that problems were eliminated, but he had not been able to eliminate Rambova because she was a dictatorial wife, not part of the business arrangement. If Rambova had wanted what was best for Valentino, things might have been different, but her own artistic ambitions and her need to control ultimately doomed the relationship. There is no doubt, however, that she set Valentino on his path to superstardom. "From the very beginning of their relationship, Rambova molded Valentino into an effigy made to her liking," writes Michael Morris, Rambova's biographer.

"Under her spell, the well-groomed, muscular sophisticate emerged with his polished European manners and romantic bearing." Ullman agreed—he believed that Valentino was forever in her debt.[3]

Negri, even though she knew how to hurl abuse, was mostly warm and light-hearted. Most of all, she was not going to let Valentino's career get destroyed. She knew his power on the screen and his way of understanding the roles he played. Negri aspired to a happy life with Valentino, combining their artistic talents to support each other.

When Valentino had to take a trip abroad, he sent a telegram within hours of leaving the train station. It was in French, and he called Negri his "little lamb." He said he kissed her picture every night before going to bed. He was alone with his dreams and forever faithful, he promised her. Valentino signed himself *Querido* ("dear" in Spanish). Negri walked around rosy with the prospect of their marriage.

Negri's mother, Eleonora, was delighted when she came to visit. Rudolph Valentino and her daughter! She and Negri had come a long way from those Warsaw slums. Negri needed to keep Eleonora entertained. Her mother was fluent in Polish, Russian, and French, but she had not learned English. She had to have people to talk to, so Prince David Mdivani was invited to become Eleonora's bridge partner.

"Mdivani" was a name derived from the Persian word "divan." The name literally means "he who sits on the divan." David came from a line of ancient rulers. His father, Zakary, had married Elisabeth Sobolevska, a Polish girl. Together they had five children: Nina, Serge, David, Isabel Roussadana (Roussy), and Alexis. Allegedly, the older children remembered how much wealth the family had once had. The word among the European aristocracy was that before leaving Russia, the Mdivanis had possessed considerable wealth in Georgia, a country rich in oil wells and fertile fields. Georgia was also known for its silk mills. The family was highly popular in its homeland—so popular that after Georgia was proclaimed a republic, it was said that Prince Zakary was elected as military governor of Georgia by popular vote. Later he became Georgia's minister of war. Half of the aristocracy of Europe was acquainted with the Mdivani family. And even after the money was gone, Zakary's children were still looking to marry well. One of the daughters married Charles Huberick, an American who was a Harvard graduate. Brothers Serge and David wound up in America too, and they were not looking for regular jobs. They were well built, healthy, and handsome, and they thought their titles should be worth something. When Negri met them, they were straining their muscles in the Doheny oil fields at twenty-five dollars a week. David became a regular in her living room first, and Serge followed him later.

David took it upon himself to drive Eleonora around in one of Negri's cars, and he slowly insinuated himself into the household. Negri was grateful to him because her mother wasn't bored anymore. She now had a small circle of friends who spoke her language and enjoyed bridge.

David Mdivani benefited from the friendship as well. At one of Negri's parties, he met Mae Murray, a famous actress with bee-stung lips and peroxide blond "scrambled egg" hair. She had been making movies for quite a few years and had starred in two of Valentino's bit-player 1918 films, *The Delicious Little Devil* and *The Big Little Person*. Murray also knew Valentino from their early days as dancers in New York. At the time she met David Mdivani, Murray was doing *The Merry Widow* with John Gilbert, in the role that defined her career. She was wealthy and still attractive at forty-one. David sensed opportunity when he found her sleeping alone on a brocaded couch. Seeking a break from the party, she had slipped into a side room to nap. As she lay there with her eyes closed, another mouth touched hers. Leaping to her feet, she saw an athletic-looking man with curly blond hair. "In my country, this is how it is done," he told her. Before she could object, Valentino walked in and made the necessary introductions.

At first, Murray wanted nothing to do with David; something about his character repelled her. Refusing to take no for an answer, he came uninvited to one of Murray's parties, then hid in the closet to emerge before she was going to bed. Once he slashed his wrists, standing on her sidewalk, but Murray remained unmoved. Finally, he got her to go for a ride in his car, and eventually, Mae Murray did marry David Mdivani.

Valentino and Negri kept the heat rising in their affair, even though they were thousands of miles apart. Sentimental notes crisscrossed the ocean. Then one day, Negri read an item in the paper, a story about Valentino and a "Lady L." of London who was famous as well as beautiful, like all of Valentino's conquests. When other similar stories appeared, Negri decided there must be a kernel of truth to them. She stopped any communication with Valentino. When he cabled to ask what was wrong, Negri repeated the gossip about him having such a wonderful time. Valentino sent avowals of fidelity, but his French words were wearing thin. Negri started second-guessing their whole relationship, wondering if she was just another notch on the Valentino bedpost. Maybe he had been using her to advance his career after all.

As soon as he returned to the country, he rushed to her house, bringing numerous little packages, among them a diamond-studded, monogrammed onyx cigarette case. Overjoyed to see her lover again, Negri ran into his arms.

When Mae Murray and David Mdivani married, Valentino was best man at their wedding, with Negri at his side. In the wedding photos, all four of them look extremely happy. Even though each couple had different reasons to smile, for the moment their lives seemed headed in the same direction.

After the Falcon Lair remodeling was completed, Valentino took Negri on a tour of the house. Falcon Lair was a modest stucco house that Valentino had turned into a medieval castle. Terraces and picture windows made the house seem bigger than it actually was. There were open, sweeping views of hills and valleys. A Spanish gypsy, "La Gitana," gazed from a painting that hung over the bed. Valentino thought it resembled Negri. He had done everything to please her, hoping she would find the place to her liking. He still remembered Rambova's rejection of it.

Natacha Rambova loved modern art and clean, stripped-down lines. Now that Rambova was gone, Valentino was free to indulge his own tastes. He loved antiques and armor—anything connected to royalty and nobility. He had fantasies about his own heritage being aristocratic, and he identified with princes and kings.

Although neither Valentino nor Negri grew up wealthy or privileged, each of them possessed innate elegance. They now had the means to express it. Negri's house boasted damask walls, bear rugs, and gold-inlaid furniture. The Styka portrait of Negri hung over the fireplace. Negri's clothes were tailor-made for her in Paris and Vienna. Valentino's place was a museum of antique firearms. It also boasted a collection of Venetian and Bohemian glassware and sartorial extravagances from abroad, including a fur-lined Parisian bathrobe.

Despite his wealth and success, Valentino still had a self-destructive bad boy in him. Tortured by morbid premonitions and the horror of past experiences, he would drink too much or drive too fast. His vision suffered from his one lazy eye, but he was too vain to wear glasses. His hair was thinning and receding. Those signs of aging repulsed Valentino. No matter how many women he had slept with, he harbored doubts about his manhood. At times he was so depressed that he seemed unable to reach out to anyone. He told Negri he was a man so locked within himself that he felt paralyzed and could not move.

Negri and Valentino were always either passionately in love with each other or at war. They tossed around like two ships on a stormy sea. Negri kept spare clothes at Valentino's house but often kept her car and chauffeur parked outside of Falcon Lair in case she had an urge to flee in the middle of the night.

Despite Valentino's moods and the periodic explosions when she would stomp out, they had a great deal of fun together. They were right for each other, with all that they had in common. They went to openings and costume balls together. She threw a party for him at the Ambassador Hotel for his birthday and sailed with him on his yacht, *The Phoenix*. Unlike restrained and controlling Natacha Rambova, Negri was able to relax and enjoy each moment.

Valentino was overwhelmed by his own success. Paradoxically, he felt worse when things were going well. When his world was falling apart, Valentino seemed very much in balance—as if the mess outside him made the mess inside him bearable. Negri knew that these mood swings were not going to be without consequences. Life with Valentino could be very wearying, and Negri could not figure out why he was so inconsolable. She sensed that Valentino was not telling her everything about himself.

When Lady L. showed up at one of Valentino's parties, Negri took one look at her and knew that Valentino had been her lover. A fight hung in the air, but both women found it more cutting to be cool. They spoke politely, their smiles belying their intentions. Valentino was going to have to choose. He told Negri that he had already done so. Negri wanted to believe him, as she herself had been faithful to him for the long weeks he had been away. Negri hid in Valentino's bedroom to collect her thoughts. Then she saw that the photos of her had been removed from his dressing table, and she departed for home without so much as a goodbye. Valentino reacted dramatically, going over to Negri's house and imploring her until Negri took him back. She knew he had cheated on her, but he was taking a great deal of trouble to make her forgive him. She enjoyed crying and making up, but only after she had made him cry, too. Their need to be with each other had grown so strong that Valentino's philandering did not mean much anymore. The Lady L. dalliance was just an excuse for more high passion. A gleeful Valentino was always full of desire, and even more so when he was depressed. Other women could only dream of a lover like that, and now Negri had him all to herself.

Women who used to admire her beauty now hated her for it. Negri knew very well what jealousy could lead to. She didn't want any other woman to take Valentino away—she was still trying to figure him out. Negri liked doing things with Valentino's family: sitting with them by the poolside, playing with his nephew Jean. She also got along very well with Valentino's brother, Alberto, who treated her like a sister. Home movies show Negri with her hair down, a playful girl who was not a movie star. Hollywood would not allow her to do that often enough.

Valentino was also very serious about his cooking, which Negri always found hilarious. Negri was willing to try his concoctions, so he experimented in the galley of his yacht. He would not allow her to come below deck when he was mixing up specialties. Negri never tired of his meatballs and even learned the recipe. She was certain that none of the women he had slept with before had gotten that secret away from him. "I always enjoy his meat sauce," she told everyone.

They would also ride horses together up and down Beverly Hills. The area was just being developed, so there was room to roam. Valentino owned purebred Arabian steeds, and they rode like a dream. They also took part in tennis matches and diving competitions. Negri sensed that Valentino was the type of person who needed to stay busy. When he had too much time to think, his eyes became dark and sad. Maybe it was because he was having money problems. "Valentino was terrible with money," according to Valentino biographer Emily Leider. "Whatever he made, it was never enough. He was very self-indulgent, not a planner, not a budgeter, to put it mildly. Whatever he had was gone soon. He needed money always—just to pay his clothes bill and his bar bill and travel expenses. He was a spendthrift."[4] Valentino collected medieval and Renaissance art—a costly hobby for a man paying off two divorces. His house also needed a staggering amount of maintenance. And now United Artists wanted him to take a salary cut, since his last few pictures had not matched his earlier successes.

Negri came up with an idea. She asked her lawyer to phone the head of United Artists and hint that Valentino had been offered a contract somewhere else. The lawyer would refuse to be quoted, saying he was forwarding the information on the up-and-up. Because it was Negri's own lawyer who dropped the hint, the head of United Artists would think that Valentino was being solicited by Paramount, probably to costar with Negri.

The gambit worked, and Valentino received a pay raise plus a percentage of his pictures. Meanwhile, Negri offered him a hundred thousand dollars cash to pay off his debt. He took only fifteen thousand and treated it as a loan. She did not want to take his promissory note as guarantee of a payback, but he insisted, saying it would salvage his self-esteem.

When Negri was busy making *Hotel Imperial*, Valentino was working on *Son of the Sheik*. They got together on weekends and often sailed the California coast on Valentino's yacht, drifting slowly along. Aboard the boat, they didn't owe anybody anything. It was their time to relax.

Valentino owned a number of dogs. His constant companion was Kabar, a Doberman pinscher. Kabar was the only dog allowed to come inside the house; the rest of the dogs were kenneled on the estate. Kabar and Valentino shared an extraordinary understanding—the dog could read Valentino's mood and never made demands. He offered Valentino a selfless canine love. Other people did not exist for Kabar.

Valentino wrote poetry, and even published one full book of verse. Writing was his antidote to depression; he felt a need to pour his thoughts out on paper. As he wrote his poetry, Negri would often stroke Valentino's thigh or cuddle up with him. She desired Valentino in every way, both physically and spiritually. She assured him that she would not turn away from him, as Rambova had done.

Negri was feeling confident in her career and emotionally fulfilled, able to focus on Valentino instead of herself. Valentino's poems were said to be about Rambova, but it was Negri who was so often there at their inception. Most likely both women were written into the verses. Valentino considered himself a humble observer, dazzled by the beauty around him but forced to wonder if he was worthy.

Shooting *Hotel Imperial* took longer than expected. Director Mauritz Stiller and producer Erich Pommer were focusing on every detail—they wanted to prove they were men of merit. The movie was being shot in sequence in a large eight-room set, which had been constructed beforehand. Previously, the practice had been to assemble rooms as they were needed. Every scene that took place in one room was completed before the camera moved in, no matter where the scene occurred in the script. It was hard for actors to establish a mood in such a fragmented system. With the camera now following the action from room to room, emotional impact could be sustained. The composite set changed the course of Hollywood production. Negri learned to work this kind of set when it was still in its experimental stages.

Hotel Imperial opens with a scene of mass carnage. A title card informs the audience that even in a time of war, the Hotel Imperial still needs to be swept. Negri plays Anna, a menial housemaid trying to keep her spirits up as she attends to her chores. Anna is young and lovely but has little chance of rising in class status. As Russia wages war on Austria, a chain of events alters Anna's position. Lieutenant Paul Almasy (James Hall), an Austrian officer who has escaped the battlefield where most of his regiment was slaughtered, is hiding at the Hotel Imperial. He intends to return to battle. An intelligent young gentleman of wit and humor, Almasy is debonair and courageous.

Anna takes to Almasy immediately and decides to help him. The jovial old hotel manager rallies to her side. Among the tiny hotel staff of three, only Anna's rejected suitor seeks revenge and chooses to hurt where he can. He is a maintenance man at the hotel, and he thinks a chambermaid has a lot of nerve holding out for someone better.

The Russians take over the hotel. It is clean and comfortable and makes a good base in the city. Cooperation is expected from the staff, or else they will be shot. Anna and the hotel manager disguise their Austrian lieutenant as the hotel's only waiter. He lacks the proper documents, but Anna makes a plea to the overbearing Russian general: "How can we serve you if you remove our only waiter?" The general, fond of food and drink, thinks the waiter may be useful. He orders tea brought to his room. "Green tea, black tea, or TNT?" asks the "waiter" as he and Anna prepare the cups. Anna is bedazzled by this tall, upstanding man who is clever enough to make her laugh. She is not going to let him die.

The rejected suitor awaits his chance to expose the lieutenant without risking his own neck, but the Russian general is feeling romantic and sets his own sights on Anna. She has the power to protect the lieutenant, but her position is conflicted. A woman of virtue, she is a virgin who will never surrender her body to the enemy. She knows how to flirt, though, and uses her talent to keep the general at bay. He dislikes her straight-laced uniform, so he has boxes of fashionable clothes delivered for Anna. She models off-the-shoulder dresses and ruffled skirts for him. The general wants her right then and there, but Anna smiles and makes a game of being chased around. At that point, a Russian spy arrives to give the general his reconnaissance. Before he can do so, the waiter-lieutenant dispatches him with a bullet to protect Austrian secrets. The murder is discovered, and the waiter is called to testify before the general. Where was he when the fatal shot was made? The waiter has no alibi. Anna rushes forth to say he was in her room—a confession that could get her killed on the spot.

The Russian general fumes and threatens to tear off the clothes he bought her. Anna immediately takes off the expensive gowns and changes back into her old, torn clothes. The general spills an ashtray on the floor and orders her to clean it up. Anna drops to her knees to scrape up the debris without a whimper. The rejected suitor is enjoying it, thinking, "Maybe she will have me now if I still want her!"

Austria is victorious, thanks to the bravery of the waiter, who saved thousands of lives, and he is honored with a medal and a parade. Anna, dressed like a lady, watches him from the crowd. She is tearful over losing him but glad that he is alive. He spots her from afar and brings her to stand beside him—the unsung heroine. Anna finds she is not forgotten after all. Her good deed has been rewarded, and justice prevailed.

Negri believed this role would allow her more full-bodied expression. A courageous character, a woman free of greed, false pride, and sinful thoughts, sacrifices herself as a patriot; Anna's ingenuity helps other brave Austrians avoid trouble. She serves her nation with honor. With this movie, Negri finds herself on Mary Pickford's turf, as the gutsy heroine who surpasses expectations.

Negri hoped that playing such an unimpeachable role would show that she was capable of so much more. *Hotel Imperial* has a classical Hollywood theme: Everything turns out right in the end if your heart is pure and uncorrupted. The production showed the subtleties of that philosophy more than any role Negri had been given before.

"A first-rate Negri in a first-rate picture makes a conjunction that is auspicious for the future," said *National Board of Review Magazine*. "A wartime story, part romance, part thrilling adventure, swiftly moving and expertly told in the language of the camera, gives us back the Pola Negri we have known of yore and effectively wipes out the stigma that had become attached to her of a good actress gone wrong. . . . It has little of the spectacular about it; she does not burst upon us in a glittering, overwhelming role which dwarfs the picture."[5]

It seemed that at long last, her relationship with the studio was becoming what she had hoped for from the time she started working in Hollywood. Not only was she offered materials that rose above typecasting, but she was also surrounded with the very finest production artists available. If this continued—and there was no reason to suppose that it wouldn't—Negri's American career could be long and prosperous. At the same time, it seemed that Valentino was regaining his old self, thanks to her support. In *Son of the Sheik,* he again played a passionate man of character. At the long-awaited premiere, Negri held Valentino's hand. They were now the couple who turned up together everywhere, to the joy of all their fans and the fan magazines.

The setting of the premiere was truly exceptional—United Artists did not want the film to slip past the critics. The producers had full confidence in Valentino. *Son of the Sheik* featured Valentino in dual roles, as both father and son, and he was equally attractive as both—handsome, slender, and muscular. He could be the object of affection for young girls but also for their mothers.

The film had been recut and edited several times to polish its weak spots. The final version was considered strong enough to open at Grauman's Million Dollar Theatre in Los Angeles, the Oriental palace on Hollywood Boulevard, home of the stone Heaven Dogs and other artifacts imported as originals from China. Nobody needed to travel abroad to see fine Asian architecture; Grauman's showplace resembled a Far Eastern pagoda.

For the premiere, held in June 1926 at the palatial theater, Negri wore a "close-fitting silver sheath gown for the occasion, with diamond tiara and a pearl necklace."[6] Her eyes were shining bright—she was a rainbow of iridescence. This was Valentino's hour, but Negri was his reason for being there. Joseph Schenck was glad that Negri brought his star favorable publicity. Other Hollywood VIPs were in attendance: Mary Pickford, Douglas Fairbanks, Mae Murray, Louella Parsons, Marion Davies, and Charlie Chaplin, who was a friend of Valentino's. Everyone was out to pay Valentino homage for being the man who had achieved "great lover" status—by Hollywood standards, no less.

Chaplin was not averse to making money for United Artists, as that was still his favorite studio. Marion Davies was on the premises; so was Mae Murray, who once had a crush on Valentino when he was her leading man. Her husband, David Mdivani, escorted Murray. Everyone present knew each other in and out of the business, as intimates as well as coworkers, which made them even more of a cohesive group.

Premieres were becoming a chance for everyone to connect with their fans. The actors knew they were there to woo the crowds. Movie people seldom badmouthed each other at such events, but Louella Parsons was there just in case any argument should arise. Negri took care of everything—she was supporting Valentino and working the crowd. She had an eight-foot floral arrangement set in the Grauman's lobby. Red roses made a frame around the white ones, which spelled out Valentino's name. The card read: "To Rudy, good luck from Pola." It was an excellent move because, at the same time, she was advertising her own film and publicly backing her man. Valentino held her tightly as they took their seats.

All his life, Valentino was accident-prone. After the screening, he got up to speak to the audience. A large ceramic planter was on the stage with him. While he was talking, the planter began to tip, and it almost fell into the audience. Valentino stopped it in the middle of the fall, but unfortunately he was carried into the orchestra pit by the planter and was knocked out. When he came to a few minutes later, he got back on the stage and reassured the audience that he wasn't hurt. The screening after-party was held at the Coconut Grove, where Negri and Valentino celebrated the movie's release surrounded by their colleagues, employers, and friends. This was their last date.

When they saw how audiences warmed to the movie, United Artists was anxious to cash in. Valentino was to make a tour of personal appearances, starting in San Francisco and ending in New York. Negri knew she would miss him desperately, but she was happy about the critical acclaim. She hoped the trip would help reestablish his former star status. Naturally, Valentino told her he would telephone every night. As he stepped out of her car on the day of his departure, Negri had an unsettling sensation that Fate, which had brought them together, was about to overturn the cart.

Negri drove Valentino to the train station in her famous white car and kissed him goodbye. Increasingly, Negri sensed that Valentino was headed for a different world. She cried, despite her mother's reassurances. Valentino had four more days on the east coast when Negri heard his voice for the last time. He phoned in the evening to tell her how wonderfully he was doing. People lined up for blocks to see him; he could not have asked for a better reception. He was the beloved star of audiences across the country. His tone carried so much gusto that Negri berated herself for sounding a false alarm. Valentino's trip was almost over, and he assured her that he was taking care of himself. Negri's fears were appeased and she enjoyed a good night's sleep. Unfortunately, there were some things that Valentino neglected to mention.

For some time now, he had been suffering from abdominal pain, but he did not want to see a doctor. Still shaken by his divorce, he had been partying with abandon, not sleeping, drinking more than he should, eating too much greasy food, and chasing the ladies. When he went out, his fans tore the buttons off his coat, scratched his face, and mussed his hair, and he joked that he was being "loved to death." Although his health was declining, he chose to ignore it.

On top of this, he had been the target of a hateful editorial that raised doubts about his masculinity. The *Chicago Tribune* ran a piece entitled "Pink Powder Puffs" that cut him to the bone—it blamed him for the introduction of automated powder puff dispensers in men's bathrooms. "A powder-vending machine! In a men's washroom! Why didn't someone quietly drown Rudolph Gugliemi, alias Valentino, years ago?"[7] Valentino was extremely offended at being so publicly maligned, and the pugnacious Italian in him emerged. He challenged the offending writer to a fight, but the coward didn't want to reveal himself. Instead, Frank "Buck" O'Neil, the boxing columnist for the *New York Evening Journal*, came forward and offered to fight Valentino.

Valentino had been taught to spar during the making of *The Cobra* and had been coached by Jack Dempsey, the champion boxer. Dempsey found Valentino's punches to be more than adequate. "He was no creampuff, that fellow. He could hit you with a good punch and take a good one, too, without folding," was how Dempsey put it. Dempsey warned O'Neil about Valentino, but O'Neil thought he was pulling his leg. The bout was scheduled to take place on the roof of New York's Ambassador Hotel.

Reporters and photographers arrived to document the bloodshed, but that thirst was not quenched. Valentino countered a punch that missed his jaw with a headshot that sent O'Neil sprawling to the floor. O'Neil shook Valentino's hand at the end of the match, having learned that Dempsey had not been kidding.

Valentino continued burning the candle at both ends after that, staying out late and refusing to rest. On August fifteenth, he collapsed in the lobby of the Ambassador Hotel, clutching his stomach and moaning. Valentino had an undiagnosed gastric ulcer and appendicitis. He was taken to the hospital, where surgery was performed. Even in that era of medicine, the procedure typically had a successful outcome; it was not considered a life-threatening condition. At a physical less than a month before, he had been pronounced perfectly healthy.

Negri wanted to get on the next train to be at his bedside, but she was in the middle of filming *Hotel Imperial*, and her absence would have been costly for the studio. She called the hospital constantly, awaiting news. Valentino was in no condition to talk after the operation, but his doctors were marking his progress. A week after he was admitted to the hospital, he took a turn for the worse. He incurred a massive infection and died on the twenty-third of August.

Before Negri could even be notified about what had happened, a reporter called to ask how Miss Negri was taking the news of Valentino's death. Negri had answered the phone, saying she was the maid. Marion Davies rushed to Negri's house, and together they drove out to Falcon Lair. There, Negri tottered from room to room, calling out Valentino's name until she had no breath left. Davies hugged and consoled her, but Negri was hysterical. She would collapse and then cry some more, claiming that she was cursed. Every man she became attached to was torn away from her. It was cruel. She believed she was destined to have no one, condemned to stay alone.

The world and Negri were in shock. The unthinkable had happened. Valentino had been the picture of health; nobody had ever considered such an outcome. Negri moved into the Ambassador Hotel; her house had too many memories of Valentino. At the Ambassador, she received a letter delivered by Mary Pickford, from Valentino's doctor, Harold D. Meeker:

> Dear Miss Negri,
> I am asking Mary Pickford, an old friend and patient of mine, to deliver this message to you. . . . About four o'clock Monday morning I was sitting by Rudolph alone in the room. He opened his eyes, put out his hand and said, "I'm afraid we won't go fishing together. Perhaps we will meet again—who knows?" This was the first and only time he realized he would not get well. He was perfectly clear in his mind. He gave me a message for the Chief, Mr. Schenck, and then said: "Pola—if she doesn't come in time, tell her I think of her." Then he spoke in Italian and went into his long sleep. I feel an obligation to get this message to you.[8]

After Valentino's death, Negri needed a doctor herself. She was prescribed barbiturates to lessen the shock. Her premonition had been correct. She and Valentino were a perfect whole, and now she felt as if she had died as well. She had lost the man she loved and their wonderful future together. He was only thirty-one.

Negri managed to avoid the press at first, but it would be impossible to avoid them at the funeral. They were sure to follow her everywhere, nagging her and asking questions. All she wanted was a chance to mourn her lover in private. The studio issued instructions for her train trip to New York. Adolph Zukor is supposed to have said, "Get her first-class accommodations, a doctor to travel with her and, of course, a good publicity man."

Negri was able to attend Valentino's first funeral in New York. She dressed in black widow's clothes. After New York, his body was taken by train to California for a second funeral at the Hollywood Memorial Cemetery (now called Hollywood Forever). She attended the second funeral as well. Many of Valentino's friends and associates and the press thought she cried so hard at the service in New York that she distracted the mourners' attention from the ceremony. Negri's reputation in the United States never fully recovered from the negative publicity connected with her tremendous outpouring of emotion at Valentino's funeral.

Negri always defended herself, saying, "It is difficult for a foreigner coming to America. . . . I had been told so much what not to do. It was particularly difficult for me, a Slav. My emotion seemed exaggerated to Americans. I cannot help that I haven't the Anglo-Saxon restraint and the tact."[9] But people accused her of acting as if Valentino's funeral were a Pola Negri premiere and of wanting the spotlight on her and her grief. Jean Acker, Valentino's first wife, was also part of the ceremony. Valentino's second wife, Natacha Rambova, was not present, but there were a million female fans who felt as if they had lost a lover. Emily Leider tells of the "woman in black": "The tradition of the Lady in Black, the grieving woman at the crypt where Valentino is buried, originated with Pola Negri. She was the first one. She was the woman in black, the veiled figure weeping at the crypt where Valentino is entombed. For evermore there has been a lady in black, a grieving woman, and the press loves this. That's one of the reasons the myth is sustained, there's always a photographer to take a picture."[10] Negri was wearing the most stylish mourning clothes—filmy black stockings and a dress expensive enough to ease the chill of loneliness—but she couldn't stay on her feet. She needed to be supported from both sides as she walked. The newsmen took pictures of her keeling over.

Valentino's fans wanted to view the great star one last time. Crowds lined Broadway to get a glimpse of his face, viewed through the unbreakable glass of his ten-thousand-dollar silver-and-bronze coffin. The mob pressed forward, knocking over anyone who tried to stand in its way. Horses trampled several onrushers, and up to a hundred people were hurt. People fainted from the crush of the crowd, but no one wanted to leave; they were determined to have their one last glance at their beloved actor.

Some women laughed as they exited the viewing chapel, presumably at Valentino's made-up, waxen face. The entrepreneurial spirit descended upon the crowd, with men selling sandwiches and umbrellas, or even their places in line. Finally, owing to the concern about riots and to prevent instances of disrespect, the body was removed from view.

Negri sent two thousand dollars' worth of flowers to the funeral—blood-red roses with "Pola" spelled in white blossoms across the middle. Valentino's and Negri's fans were not accustomed to such overt public displays of emotion at a funeral, but it was not out of the ordinary for someone like Negri, who was only expressing the huge pain inside her. She claimed that her reaction had been spontaneous and honest. She could not understand why people were so offended. The public had always asked that she share her true self, and yet when she let them peer into her heart to see true grief, she was accused of showing too much and behaving falsely. "If you people know what was in my heart, how I loved Rudolph, you would not be so cruel to me," she told an interviewer. "You would not think my trip across the country was for anything except a tribute to my love. And I want you to know that Rudolph loved me as I loved him."[11]

Officially, Valentino died of peritonitis on August 23, 1926. Several women committed suicide upon hearing of his death, and all of America seemed to go into mourning. In Hollywood, ten thousand people crammed themselves into the Hollywood Memorial Cemetery, where he was laid to rest, Rambova's slave bracelet still adorning his wrist. Before the tomb was sealed, Pola Negri kissed Valentino goodbye by kissing the tomb. The last person to say goodbye to the great actor was Valentino's brother, Alberto.

Until a more impressive mausoleum could be built, Valentino was temporarily placed in a vault that belonged to his friend and discoverer, June Mathis. However, plans for a grand monument were later abandoned, and Valentino still remains in the borrowed vault: Crypt No. 31205. Ironically, Valentino had visited the site many times in his life as he accompanied Mathis on visits to her mother, who reposes just below Valentino to this day.

Over the years, Negri never lost her affection for Valentino, but she was not the famous woman in black who appeared at Valentino's grave every anniversary of his death, well into the 1950s, to lay a rose. That woman was never identified. According to Negri, people began to write to her to encourage her to buy Valentino's house and make it into a shrine. She was not interested in becoming a high priestess of any kind of Valentino cult.

Undoubtedly, Negri missed Valentino desperately, and she cried a river over her unfulfilled dreams. She sank into despair after his death. After both funerals, Negri returned to Falcon Lair. Kabar, Valentino's Doberman, saw her and thought his master was soon to arrive. Negri tried to take the dog home with her, but he ran away. Later she learned that he had died of loneliness after waiting and waiting for Valentino to come back. Nobody could take Valentino's place, as Negri discovered for herself. She had other kinds of love after that, but she was never again to experience the passion that she and Valentino shared. Although they never had the chance to make a movie together, their love was cinematic.

Valentino's brother, Alberto, was good-natured, but he had none of Valentino's physical appeal. After Valentino died, Hollywood called on Alberto to try to reinstate the legend in the flesh. Alberto remained in town to settle Valentino's complicated affairs, which took some time to untangle. Movie agents told Alberto that he was perfect for the job of Valentino replacement—all he needed was a nose job, and the camera would take care of the rest. It would be wrong of him to refuse to perpetuate the Valentino myth, the agents said, and he could help fans ease their grief.

Negri had grown close to Alberto, who treated her like a sister, but she knew he was not movie material. Valentino had a hypnotic way of moving, but Alberto was a businessman—and no camera could change that. Alberto became swept up in the notion that he, too, could be a great movie star, but countless nose jobs, done and redone, could not help him put on a passionate lover's face. Alberto finally gave up and went back to a desk job; he had a family to support.

Negri was very fond of Alberto, and she did what she could to give him a fresh start. Her lawyer had counseled her to collect the fifteen-thousand-dollar debt Valentino owed her and to make a claim against the estate. Negri did not want to pursue it, because she viewed the loan as a heartfelt gift, but in the end she did collect the money to simplify things in the estate proceedings. Alberto's wife and son moved to California with him. Later he became the head of accounting at Fox, and his son Jean became a motion picture sound engineer.

Three other Latin types were nominated to fill Valentino's shoes: Ricardo Cortez, Ramon Novarro, and Antonio Moreno. Cortez was handsome, but he lacked Valentino's intensity. Moreno, who had starred with Negri in *The Spanish Dancer*, had ability and sex appeal, but he was intimidated by women. Ramon Novarro met all expectations and went from silents to talkies with success.

Baffled by the way the public reacted to her after Valentino's death, Negri retreated further from the Hollywood social scene. She rented a beach house in Santa Monica so she could plan for the future while she finished *Hotel Imperial*. Working helped her translate her real-life pain into her on-screen character's emotional demands.

Edwin Schallert, drama critic of the *Los Angeles Times* from 1919 to 1958, was one of the few people who did not view Negri's grief as excessive. "Pola brought with her to Hollywood the European cult of the artist," he wrote in 1928. "The Valentino episode, particularly, placed her every action under the magnifying glass."[12] He believed that Negri's temperament was better suited to the world of theater or grand opera than the film world. He defended her behavior as very much in character:

> She might, to be sure, have taken the whole affair more restrainedly, but after all, she could hardly have sat twiddling her thumbs at the studio. Once Pola Negri threw herself into anything, that was *finis!* She has a peculiar type of concentration, which seems to cause her to work herself into a frenzy over anything on which it happens to center. . . . To become more and more distraught and disturbed over the death of Valentino for every mile of rail pounded East was, for her, a perfectly logical evolution. Doubtless, she felt everything that she expressed herself as feeling. It was all part of the event, and of her own reaction piling up in a natural, dramatic climax. These things are not, however, always understood in America.[13]

15

Paramount Pictures, 1927

When Max Reinhardt came to Los Angeles after his successful new production of *The Miracle*, Pola Negri had become everything he knew she would, proving that he had an eye for spotting talent. Negri arranged a private screening of *Hotel Imperial*, and he was very impressed. "I would give half my life if I could produce and direct a picture like that one," Reinhardt told Mauritz Stiller. That was a huge compliment for the director of *Hotel Imperial*, and it meant the world to him.

Stiller passed all the honors to Negri for working under "unendurable agony" and completing the picture after Valentino's death. Negri knew that Stiller's emotional state had been comparable to her own. Garbo had shattered Stiller's heart when she turned her attention from him to John Gilbert. Negri and Stiller often consoled each other, having become good friends.

Ironically, Gilbert's main screen rival had been Valentino. Gilbert became the king of heartthrobs in 1926 after the success of *La Bohème*. In this movie he fired the passions of Lillian Gish—which was an achievement, as she wasn't known for exuding sex appeal. *Flesh and the Devil* paired him with Greta Garbo. That was when the two of them discovered they couldn't get enough of each other. The erotic tension in the movie let the public in on their offscreen romance. Garbo called Gilbert "Tacky," and he nicknamed her "Flicka," the Swedish word for girl. MGM tried to capitalize on the romance by giving Garbo and Gilbert a movie called *Love*, but by that time, Garbo had already had enough of Gilbert.

Meanwhile, Stiller was sinking into depression and his health was failing. MGM fired him from *The Temptress*, Garbo's second American film, even though he had completed most of her scenes and knew that the picture would make her a star. Stiller was lucky to make it through *Hotel Imperial* with Paramount behind him. The studio was even willing to try him again on *Barbed Wire,* but ultimately Rowland V. Lee replaced him. Saddened by the loss of Garbo, Stiller returned to his native Sweden and died not long afterward.

Gilbert and Garbo were paired on-screen as a romantic couple again in 1928 in *A Woman of Affairs.* Gilbert was between marriages at the time, after recently divorcing his second wife, actress Leatrice Joy. Rekindling a romance with his leading lady offscreen was on his mind. He almost got Garbo to marry him, but at the last minute she left him at the office of the Justice of the Peace. Gilbert went on to marry two more actresses, Ina Claire and Virginia Bruce.

Like so many others, Gilbert lost his money in the stock market crash of 1929, and he became an alcoholic. His career fizzled as the demand for talkies grew. His voice in *His Glorious Night* sounded thin and whiny. Some say it was because L. B. Mayer had ordered the sound engineers to play around with the sound and boost the treble, because the two disliked each other tremendously. Mayer did everything in his power to get Gilbert out the door, but the actor had an ironclad contract.

On March 20, 1934, Gilbert took out an ad on the back page of the *Hollywood Reporter* that read: "Metro-Goldwyn-Mayer will neither offer me work nor release me from my contract." After that, Garbo helped him get the lead opposite her in *Queen Christina.* The movie became one of Gilbert's more popular talkies.

Gilbert's career never really revived. Having grown used to the adulation of the crowds, he couldn't come to terms with not being a star anymore. Despite heavy drinking, he kept his looks. He had a brief affair with Marlene Dietrich, who tried to rehabilitate him and his career. He thrived for a while but then stumbled again. One of his drinking buddies was his neighbor John Barrymore, another former matinee idol now on the path of self-destruction. Another drinking partner was Ina Claire, whose nasal voice—people called it a "Bronx honk"—banned her from the talkies. Barrymore and Claire drank as much as they could, as fast as they could. Nothing but death would stop them. Barrymore succumbed first. He died at home in 1936, officially of a heart attack. Bleeding ulcers and chronic insomnia, along with bouts of unconsciousness, had marked his final years. Being away from the movies simply broke his heart.

Negri invited Max Reinhardt to stay in Hollywood, assuring him that she could talk Paramount into letting him direct her next picture. Reinhardt was dedicated to the theater, however, and he avoided taking a Hollywood

Pola Negri and Jean Hersholt in *The Secret Hour,* directed by Rowland V. Lee, Paramount, 1928.

Pola Negri's plaque at Grauman's Chinese Theatre in Los Angeles, April 2, 1928.

Pola Negri with Warner Baxter in *Three Sinners,* directed by Rowland V. Lee, Paramount, United States, 1928. Courtesy of Photofest, New York.

Pola Negri in *Three Sinners,* directed by Rowland V. Lee, Paramount, United States, 1928.

Pola Negri with Paul Lukas in *The Woman from Moscow,* directed by Ludwig Berger, Paramount, United States, 1928.

Pola Negri with Hans Rehmann in *The Way of Lost Souls,* directed by Paul Czinner, England, 1929.

Pola Negri in *A Woman Commands*, directed by Paul L. Stein, RKO, United States, 1932. Courtesy of Photofest, New York.

Pola Negri and Roland Young in *A Woman Commands,* directed by Paul L. Stein, RKO, United States, 1932. Courtesy of Photofest, New York.

Pola Negri and Basil Rathbone in *A Woman Commands,* directed by Paul L. Stein, RKO, United States, 1932.

Pola Negri arriving in Los Angeles by train after her vacation in Europe, 1932.

Pola Negri with Professor and Mrs. Albert Einstein at Palm Springs, California, 1932.

Pola Negri and Pierre Richard-Willm in *Fanatisme,* directed by Tony Lekain and Gaston Ravel, France, 1934.

POLA NÉGRI et RICHARD
WILM dans FANATISME, une
production Via-Film éditée par
PATHÉ-CONSORTIUM-CINÉMA.

Cover of *Cine-Miroir,* May 4, 1934, France.

Pola Negri with Franziska Kinz in *Mazurka*, directed by Willi Forst, Berlin, 1935.

Pola Negri in *Mazurka*, directed by Willi
Forst, Berlin, 1935. Courtesy of George
Schönbrunn.

Pola Negri with Gustav Diessl in *Moscow-Shanghai,* directed by Paul Wegener, Berlin, 1936.

Cover of *Filmwelt,* April 25, 1937, Germany.

Film playbill for *Tango Notturno,* 1937, Germany.

Pola Negri with Ferdinand Marian and Aribert Wascher in *Madame Bovary*, directed by Gerhard Lamprecht, UFA, Germany, 1937. Courtesy of Brother Alexis Gonzales.

Pola Negri publicity photo, Hollywood, 1930s. Courtesy of Photofest, New York.

Pola Negri publicity photo, Hollywood, 1930s.

(*Above*) Pola Negri with Martha Scott in *Hi Diddle Diddle,* directed by Andrew L. Stone, United States, 1943. Courtesy of Photofest, New York. (*Below*) Director Sam Wood, Pola Negri, and Gary Cooper at a Los Angeles party, 1944. Courtesy of George Schönbrunn.

Pola Negri and Adolphe Menjou at a Beverly Hills Hotel party, 1944.

Pola Negri and Dennis O'Keefe at lunch at the Beverly Hills Hotel, California, 1948. Courtesy of Photofest, New York.

Pola Negri with her mother, Eleonora Chałupec, as they arrived on the American export liner *Excalibur*, New York, November 8, 1948.

Left to right: Sterling Holloway, Pola Negri, Hedda Hopper, Loretta Young, and Ricardo Montalbán, on the radio show *Hedda Hopper's Hollywood,* 1951.

Pola Negri in her home in Bel Air, California, 1954. Courtesy of Brother Alexis
Gonzales.

George Schönbrunn (*left*), Pola Negri, Margaret West, and an unidentified guest at the Beverly Hills Hotel "Polo Lunch," 1955. Courtesy of George Schönbrunn.

George Schönbrunn and Pola Negri on New Year's Eve, 1957, in Palm Springs. Courtesy of George Schönbrunn.

Pola Negri's star on the Walk of Fame, Hollywood.

Pola Negri and Eli Wallach in *The Moon-Spinners,* directed by James Neilson, Walt Disney, United States, 1964. Courtesy of Photofest, New York.

Hayley Mills and Pola Negri in *The Moon-Spinners,* directed by James Neilson, Walt Disney, United States, 1964. Courtesy of Photofest, New York.

Pola Negri publicity photo for *The Moon-Spinners,* directed by James Neilson, Walt Disney, United States, 1964. Courtesy of Photofest, New York.

Pola Negri receives an award for enriching American culture in San Antonio, 1968, at the Hemisfair, Saint Mary's University. Standing with her are Father Louis Reile, *far right,* and Brother Alexis Gonzales. Courtesy of Brother Alexis Gonzales.

Pola Negri at the Museum of Modern Art for a screening of *Woman of the World,*
New York, 1973. Courtesy of Photofest, New York.

job until 1934. Meanwhile, Negri spent time with old friends and sought new diversions. She had a fling with Russ Columbo, a handsome crooner who had a startling resemblance to Valentino.

Columbo, whose real name was Ruggiero Eugenio di Rodolpho Colombo, started out as a poor child in San Francisco, but his fortunes changed when he was recognized as a musical prodigy at age twelve. A few years later he moved to Los Angeles, where he played in nightclubs and picked up some extra money playing the violin on the Paramount studio sets. It was common practice to have mood music in the background. After Columbo played on the sets of Negri's films, they became intimate. She introduced him to her circle of friends, including Gloria Swanson and Ramon Novarro, and helped him get bit parts in movies. According to Columbo biographers Joseph Lanza and Dennis Penna, "A legend surfaced shortly after Valentino's burial. Negri supposedly anointed Columbo . . . by presenting him with an opal ring that Valentino had supposedly regarded as a talisman. Hollywood mythmakers would later speculate that the ring was cursed."[1] By all accounts, the relationship didn't last long, but Columbo and Negri crossed paths again a few years later in Hollywood and New York.

Negri starred in *Barbed Wire* on the heels of *Hotel Imperial*. Again, she plays a good girl whose very natural longings—the desire to love and marry—are thwarted by politics and prejudices during wartime. In *Barbed Wire*, a movie with a universal, timeless theme of peace and antiwar sentiment, Negri's character, Mona Moreau, falls in love with an enemy soldier. The film contains beautifully eloquent moments that illuminate how war is not the solution to problems. It demonstrates how all human beings are dealing with issues of love and friendship and how war tears lives apart. In the end, Mona's brother, who has been injured, returns to the village and expresses this to the people. It is a great plea for tolerance. Even today, the scene is relevant and moving. The film is as fresh today as it was then because of Negri's performance.

Negri's performance in *Barbed Wire* makes the audience's heart bleed. World War I and its social climate leave the girl hemmed in, forced to find a path to freedom when it seems that she has none. Mona, who has never been off the family farm in France, is a milkmaid and lives in tune with nature, kissing the newborn calves and harvesting grain by her own hand. Caretaker to her father and brother, she works hard from dawn through dusk.

While she is indulgent to her father and brother, Mona can also be uncompromising. She takes a hard line about the invaders of her country and wants them to suffer. Mona condemns the Germans, indignant that her dear brother has been drafted to defend France. Then her own farm is co-opted by the French and turned into an internment camp for captured Germans. Barbed wire encircles Mona's home, fencing in the enemy soldiers.

Now that they are disarmed, the Germans are congenial men. Mona sees them daily, but she can't forgive them for starting the war. Even when an acrobatic prisoner takes a flying leap to please her, she doesn't crack a smile. Four prisoners are selected to help Mona's family bring in the harvest. When one of them becomes ill, another German prisoner, Oskar Muller (Clive Brook), comes to the field to work.

Having worked in Paris, Muller can speak French, and Mona is suddenly in contact with a German who can speak her language. He treats her with respect, and his sincere, steady eyes offer his condolences. He explains that he has things to accomplish in his life and that he has to follow orders against his will. Mona realizes she loves the German, despite the news that her brother has been killed in action at the hands of German soldiers. Muller has been taught to silence his heart as a soldier, and he does not force the affair. They engage in seemingly neutral conversations, but the girl is obviously not indifferent to him.

Mona still wants the intruders to be driven out of her country, but now her heart has gone over to an enemy soldier. When a sly French officer tries to take advantage of Mona, Muller punches him in the face. For doing so, he is brought before a French military court, where the French officer lies to protect himself. When Mona courageously comes forward and tells the truth, her neighbors denounce her as a traitor to France. As she walks the road back to her home, the German POWs remove their hats and give her the respect she is due as an honest and brave woman, while her own village people turn against her. Even with her life falling apart at the seams, she holds her dignity and the power of her love.

Mona's brother, who has been presumed dead, surprises everyone by returning home. He lost both his eyes in battle, but he refuses to be blind to injustice. Even though peace has been declared, Mona's neighbors still consider her a traitor. Mona and Oskar have chosen to marry, but they will not be tolerated in France or in Germany. With her father dead, the farm is bequeathed to Mona, but the neighbors wave sticks and pickaxes to expel her and her German husband from her property. Fortunately, Mona's brother steps in, and the people start to listen. He has survived much suffering and has become a peacemaker. He learned firsthand the horrors of war, but he also experienced unparalleled kindness. As machine guns raged on the battlefield, a German saved his life. The young soldier now regards this German as family. The neighbors walk away, embarrassed.

Some critics were put off what they considered pro-German sentiments, but most viewers recognized *Barbed Wire* as a deeply moving story. A committee of the Hollywood Women's Club passed a resolution commending the film and calling upon the women of America to support it, calling it "the greatest single blow against international intolerance that has ever been struck."[2] Negri received rave reviews for her beautiful depiction of a woman with a conflicted heart, torn between the love she has for a man and that she has for her country.

In 1928 Pola Negri was asked to add her hand and footprints to the Walk of Stars at Grauman's Chinese Theatre, an invitation extended to only the most memorable performers. That year, only Negri and Chaplin were honored. The timing was coincidental. Charlie's square was No. 10 and Negri's was No. 11—although Charlie's square was later moved when his leftist political views caused it to be vandalized repeatedly. Negri's ceremony was on Aviators' Night, with Sid Grauman's own aerial squadron, the Black Falcons, flying overhead. "Dear Sid, I love your theatre," she wrote alongside her dainty shoeprints and handprints. She had come to Hollywood and made it to the top, and now her contribution was immortalized in cement.

After *Barbed Wire*, Negri made five films for Paramount: *The Woman on Trial, The Secret Hour, Three Sinners, Loves of an Actress,* and *The Woman from Moscow.* None of these brought her the fanfare of her previous movies. *Loves of an Actress* and *The Woman from Moscow* were seen by hardly anyone. Her audience began to dwindle after Rudy's death, for several reasons.

Americans were now looking for homegrown talent; the European mystique was wearing off. The studio had molded Pola Negri to play shallow and showy women, rather than nurturing the spontaneity and passion her earlier work demonstrated. Profits from Negri's pictures were steadily declining in America but were still strong in Europe, which continued to make her bankable for the studio.

Also, Negri was feeling weary and mentally exhausted. Gone were the days when she put out four or five films a year. Ever-fickle Hollywood was always on the lookout for fresh new faces. It didn't matter that the young candidates for tomorrow's stars had never attended drama school or taken a single dance lesson. All they needed was a photogenic face and an appealing body—the camera would do the rest. Negri was beginning to realize that her acting no longer enraptured the audience. Also, the gypsies and czarinas that she played were out of style. Women were entering the workforce and modernizing the country, and they wanted to see more of their true selves on the movie screen, to build their confidence and inspire them. To such women, Negri no longer seemed so liberated. Film historian Jeanine Basinger reflects in an interview:

> When you get to the end of the 1920s and you move over into the 1930s, you get a different kind of star emerging. It's a new decade. We're going to have gangsters, we're going to have downtrodden shop girls. It all turns very realistic and tough. They just wanted new stars, different stars, and Pola was associated with something more eloquent, something glamorous in the 1920s tradition. That decade of stardom is very different from the thirties, and she was also getting older. Her time had passed. Not very many women stars ever last more than a decade. She lasted a long time, and she created an image that was locked into her decade. I don't think it was sound that took her out of it. I think it was age. Changing times.[3]

Perhaps the biggest reason for Negri's box-office slump was a startling decision she made six months after Valentino's funeral. When her engagement to Prince Serge Mdivani was announced, the same people who thought she was grandstanding at the funeral for publicity purposes criticized her for betraying the memory of Valentino by marrying so soon. The movies were changing, and Negri was changing too.

16

Princess Mdivani

Back in happier days, Negri and Valentino had attended the wedding of David Mdivani and Mae Murray. Mdivani's brother, Serge, had a Latin look to him, while David was more Nordic-looking. Cheerful and full of energy, they both liked visiting Negri's house in Santa Monica for a swim in the ocean. They had a tradition of visiting her every Sunday.

When Mae Murray came back from her tour, David Mdivani stopped visiting Negri, but Serge continued to visit alone. Negri viewed him as a happy man with a touch of mystique, and they became friends who brightened each other's day. The gossip columnists kept sniffing around for something juicy.

Before Murray and David got married, Negri tried to warn Murray that David was only interested in her money, but to no avail. Negri had thrown a wedding party for them, which was how she met Serge. She had no interest in him at the time—she was still involved with Valentino. But from the moment Valentino died, Serge started courting her. It was around the time when David was leaving Mae Murray. David received a sizable amount of money from Murray, then soon afterward met an even better candidate to marry—a Standard Oil heiress.

Serge was in a hurry for an engagement. Just like his brother, he wanted to marry a movie star. When Negri went to France to see her mother, he appeared on Negri's train to New York and on her boat to France. He knew how to impress a woman: he took care of everything, and he was thoughtful and diplomatic. He even managed to get Negri through French customs smoothly; it had been a trouble spot for her in the past. Serge also kept the reporters at bay. And his family's good breeding was an undisputable asset.

Negri met the Mdivani family in Paris. The Mdivani women were much more interesting than the Mdivani men. One of the sisters married

Sir Arthur Conan Doyle's son. Another sister married José Maria Sert, a well-known painter, who created the mural on the international building in Rockefeller Center. His work covered up the original Diego Rivera murals, which John D. Rockefeller considered too left-wing. Sert eventually sculpted a bust of Negri.

Negri didn't suspect, however, that the Mdivani family had gathered in Paris for her engagement to Serge. Serge had already told columnist Louella Parsons a story about an elopement to France.

Friends warned Negri that marrying Serge Mdivani would be a mistake, but she paid no attention. Distinguished guests attended lavish parties throughout Paris to honor the engaged couple. The studio ordered Negri to neither confirm nor deny her intentions, because back in the States, she had been voted Hollywood's most popular movie star. To avoid the press, she hid out in her French château. De Hulewicz had a cottage on the estate and still managed the farm and adjacent lands.

One day, Serge came to the château door urging Negri to announce the engagement. He also asked friends to persuade Negri that he was a suitable match for her. He was handsome and titled and from an influential family. Serge's family brought around their many elite friends in the arts: the composer Maurice Ravel, the dancer Matilda Maria Kchessinska, and the painter Pablo Picasso. This was all impressive to Negri, but she had become attached to the American way of life and the many colorful people in her adopted country.

Serge's sister Roussy was a free spirit, even eccentric. To the amusement of all Paris, she walked the streets regularly with two monkeys dressed in jewel-encrusted Oriental brocade. She took Negri under her wing, introducing her to a circle that included the writer Sidonie-Gabrielle Colette.

One evening, following a party where Negri had flirted with Serge, he started insisting that they set a wedding date. Irritated, Negri countered that she felt led by the nose and that she had never been consulted about the announcements. She told Serge to leave before she made a scene. The next day, congratulating herself on her broken engagement, she went to visit her mother and give her the news. Eleonora had already been worked on by the Mdivani family, who had done everything to make Serge appear the perfect prospective son-in-law. Eleonora urged Negri to reconsider. Roussy arrived next to speak on behalf of her brother, and she persuaded Negri to agree to one more meeting. Serge arrived, contrite and devoted. Finally, Negri gave in and a wedding date was set. Still, de Hulewicz insisted on a prenuptial agreement to keep Negri's property safe. Serge did not like being mistrusted, but he signed it, bitterly.

The ceremony was modest, officiated by a local mayor. Sert served as best man. Since the location of the ceremony had somehow been leaked to the press, the town square filled with reporters and spectators. Eleonora arranged a champagne buffet for the couple. The newlyweds had to delay their honeymoon cruise along the coast of Normandy, however, because Serge lost himself in the casino next to their hotel for days. He ran a credit line to cover his losses, and Negri was presented with a new bill every morning. She had no intention of covering her husband's debts, but Serge felt that her money was his to spend, nonetheless. For him, living an extravagant lifestyle was part of the marriage package.

The marriage made all the headlines. No one could understand why she married this short-legged man who, despite having classic Hollywood good looks, was not known to be bright.

When they arrived back in California, Serge saw no reason to return to the oil fields—he wanted to scale the Hollywood heights. Not only did he not work; he put a big dent in Negri's earnings. *Barbed Wire* was doing well until word of the marriage got out, and fans turned on her for abandoning her love with Valentino. Abusive letters replaced her once-positive fan mail. Apparently, moviegoers could not accept her new relationship.

Nevertheless, Negri was offered another role. Her new movie, *Rachel,* which was later renamed *Loves of an Actress,* was a struggle from the beginning. It was built around Negri and required expensive Napoleonic-era sets and costumes. Negri vied with the studio for control of the script, pleading for production changes. She experienced discord on the set and unhappiness at home. Serge acted as if he owned her, stalking her on the production lot and fuming with jealousy at her love scenes. He bristled whenever someone addressed him as "Mr. Negri."

To buy some peace, Negri set Serge up in an office on Wilshire Boulevard to deal with real estate investments. Real estate was a booming business, but Serge was always backing some wildcat scheme and losing more of Negri's money.

Loves of an Actress was the last movie Negri made for Paramount. The first talkie was made in 1927, and the silent-movie era in America was about to end. Paramount only recouped the production costs of *Loves of an Actress* when it began to play in Europe. Meanwhile, Serge gave Negri a string of diamonds, emeralds, and pearls, and bought himself two large rubies to decorate his Rolls Royce. He put the entire purchase on Negri's Cartier account for her to pay.

When Negri's contract came up for renewal, the studio offered her a reduced salary. Serge insisted that she should not take the cut but hold out for better terms. Then Negri discovered she was pregnant. She had always wanted a baby. Now, pregnancy reordered her priorities; she needed Serge. Their focus turned to home and hearth, and Negri fell in love with the prospect of becoming a mother.

They decided to move to the château in France, leaving behind the studio, the contract, and her career—it was all to be forgotten. They wanted to raise the child together; nothing else mattered. Negri had enough money put aside to retire for life, and Serge supported the idea.

The studio paid off Negri's contract too easily, leaving her unsettled. The last days at Paramount were full of conflict. Negri shared a soundstage with Clara Bow, and there was a mutual dislike between them. As Pola Negri's musicians started up a somber violin concerto to get her ready for an emotional scene, Clara Bow's musicians fired up a peppy Charleston. The two actresses—the drama queen and the new sex symbol—exchanged some words and the situation got worse. The studio had to order Bow and Negri not to get within three feet of each other. After Negri left, she was dismayed to learn that the studio had bequeathed her fabulous and personally decorated dressing room to Bow.

David Gasten, the author of the website polanegri.com, describes Negri's life at the château:

> Living at the château in France to raise a family was probably the happiest time in Pola's life. She thought she was forever finished with films and thought that she was leaving on a high note. She was going to have a baby and be a mother. To pass the time, she wrote a book reflecting on her times as an actress. And she only pressed two hundred of those, I would assume to give to friends. It was just wonderful—a little memory of her, looking back at her triumph as a star and happily retiring to take on a domestic life.[1]

Eleonora was going to be a grandmother, and the Mdivani clan was ecstatic at the idea of having a blood tie to a famous actress. Both families urged Negri to put aside her ambitions for domestic bliss.

She still had offers from film companies all over the world. The head of Gaumont-British visited, insisting Negri was too young to retire. A British producer wanted to make movies with her after the baby was born, but Serge overheard the conversation and rudely cut the man off short. Negri was going to stay home, and that was that.

She busied herself writing *La vie et le rêve au cinéma* (Life and dreams in cinema), about her experiences in film. In the booklet, Negri warned would-be actors of the hazards of the industry. Her first and utmost recommendation was: "Be simple, be natural." She acknowledged, however, that this was the most difficult thing to do. She also reflected on the role of the director: "Very few directors possess the supreme aptitude for capturing the human spirit and adapting it into film. These 'Princes of the Art' possess, along with intense erudition and talent, extreme patience. Their number is limited. The cinematic director's role is to translate a dream into reality while simultaneously expressing the dreamer's vision. This is his mission; his quest; his sacred obligation. However, most directors fail to accept these obligations honestly; rather, they tangle the tapestry with twisted threads of illogical mysteries."[2]

During the pregnancy Negri also started taking better care of her health: better food, no alcohol, and regular exercise. One afternoon she was walking with Serge when a storm broke out. Thunderstorms had frightened Negri all her life. They sought shelter under a large elm, Serge shielding her with his body. He held her, telling her everything would be all right. The sky calmed, and Negri relaxed and looked up. At that moment, lightning struck a nearby tree, and the current seemed to pass right through Negri. She could barely stand, let alone run. Panic engulfed her, and then she felt pain. Serge carried her back to the house, but the damage was already done. The happy dream was over.

The miscarriage was a huge blow to Negri, to Serge, and to their marriage. She grieved over the loss of her child and felt like a failure. Overweight and depressed, Negri floated aimlessly around the house. Serge and Eleonora brought friends to the house to provide affection and support, but Negri didn't want to see anybody. She began to drink alone.

One day Serge persuaded her to go horseback riding with him. A motorcycle spooked her horse, causing it to throw her. While Negri lay on the ground with internal injuries, Serge had to walk miles for help. She got to the hospital and was out of danger in thirty-six hours, although the newspapers reported that "death was feared." Serge quickly sought relief from his guilt in an all-night revelry.

The marriage, which had never had a strong foundation, floundered. Negri and Serge had no more to say to each other. They began living separate lives long before they stopped sharing a house together.

Negri packed Serge off to America to set things in order on one of their real estate investments. While he was away, Negri received another film offer: *The Queen's Necklace,* based on the Alexandre Dumas novel *Le Collier de la Reine.* Eleonora considered the French movie proposal God's way of showing Negri the light at the end of a very dark tunnel in which she was getting further and further lost. Negri knew her mother's words were true. She stopped drinking and started to exercise to get back into shape. The movie was to be a period piece similar to the Du Barry movie.

Serge returned to Europe as production was beginning on *The Queen's Necklace.* He was surprised and unhappy to find Negri resuming her career. There was a scene in the script where Negri's bodice was to be torn off. Negri did not mind the partial nudity required in the film as long as it served the plotline. The director even offered to film the scene from behind. Serge became irate, insisting that Princess Mdivani was not to "strip in public." He demanded that Negri give up the film. She had to pay 1 million francs to break her contract.

Negri withdrew into her own private hell. Her home was beautiful, with spectacular grounds, but there was no intellectual stimulation for her. Serge, on the other hand, enjoyed living the life of the idle rich. A new film proposal arrived from the Gaumont-British group, which would allow her to select her own material to take to the screen. Eleonora insisted that Negri accept the offer, and if Serge interfered again, she should leave him. Negri liked her husband's family, but they were not worth putting up with him. She went to London, happy to be on her own.

After arriving in London, Negri rented a house and wrote to the famous playwright George Bernard Shaw to see if he had any properties for her. They met, and he thought she would be perfect for playing the "Egyptian vixen" in *Caesar and Cleopatra.* Negri was intrigued, but Shaw's asking price was too high. When she asked him if he would sell her a play, he responded that his shop was always open, though nothing ever came of it.

17

Working in Europe

Feeling suspended in a void after her separation from Serge, Negri went sightseeing in London, but she wasn't drawn to the shops. She spent time at the museums instead. She tried not to think about men at all and decided she wanted to give her heart a rest. When she read in the papers that Serge had a girlfriend, an opera singer, Negri was relieved to think her marriage might finally be over.

One night Florence de Pena, a London socialite and hostess, assigned Negri a dinner partner who turned out to be a handsome navy commander and pilot named Glen Kidston. Florence gave Negri the following description: "He is rich, blasé, cynical, spoiled rotten, and completely adorable; a risk-taker and a daredevil. Half the women in London are mad about him—and the only thing that saves the other half is that they haven't met him."[1] The commander was late for the party because of a forced landing miles away.

Kidston was sometimes called "the man who cannot be killed." As a fifteen-year-old naval cadet, he survived the torpedoing of first his training ship and then the ship that rescued him. During the course of various races, he survived two plane crashes and was piloting a speedboat when it broke in two.[2]

Negri received orchids from Kidston the next day. He also called and invited her for a boat ride down the Thames. He admitted he was having trouble with his wife, and Negri told him of her position with Serge. Kidston joked that he and she were in the same boat.

Negri, although taking her time, now had an exciting suitor, a man exhilarated by what he was doing and going out of his way to make time for her. Kidston would fly himself out to wherever Negri was filming. When on location in a small coastal village, she outlined a field with white bed sheets so he could land.

One day Kidston decided to put on an aerial stunt show above Negri's film shoot—loops and barrel rolls, flying upside down—and suddenly his motor went dead. The watching crowd froze in panic. At the very last minute, the plane's engine started up again. Terrified, Negri choked back the tears. This man had just entered her life, and he was already dancing with death. It was as if she was jinxed.

Now she had to face the divorce with Serge. The French courts ruled that both man and wife had to appear before a judge upon the breakup of their marriage. The judge alone would assess whether the vows had been breached. Negri and Serge's judge believed in everlasting love and told them it was never too late to repair a marriage. Divorce would be a big mistake if there was still even a trace of affection. Serge wanted a chance at reconciliation, and Negri was willing to try. Serge seemed suddenly genuine. She phoned Glen to tell him about the situation. With typical British reserve, he telegrammed his congratulations and offered to meet Negri and Serge as a couple when they were in town.

Negri returned to the château for another attempt at domesticity, but the old problems still lingered. Sleeping together was not enough to make their marriage work. They had conflicting ideas about everything, even about how their day should go. When the New York stock market crashed in 1929, Negri lost millions. Serge went to America to check on what was left of her fortune. He came home with the news of a nearly total wipeout. The crash had taken about everything she owned, so Negri decided to return to work. She had received an offer from the United Kingdom from Charles Whittaker Productions. Serge would have to understand that it was necessary that she do so, especially if he didn't want to change his exorbitant spending habits. Now that his wife was broke, Serge didn't try to dissuade her from working again—or from pursuing divorce once more. This time, Negri claimed they were temperamentally incompatible. Serge's lover, international opera star Mary McCormic, took him back willingly and married him when the divorce was final.

The French château went on the market, and Negri gave Eleonora a small house on the grounds. De Hulewicz would wait for a buyer and move on. It was one cost-cutting measure after another. Divested of her house, her husband, and her fortune, Negri needed to hold on to her career.

The film she returned with was to be her last silent film. It featured the sound of Negri whistling, but it was not a talkie, which was now the genre that the studios and audiences preferred. *The Woman He Scorned,* also known as *The Way of Lost Souls* and *Street of Abandoned Children,* never got the full recognition or attention it deserved at the time, but many historians consider it her best silent film. The great German director Paul Czinner directed it in 1929. It tells the story of a Marseille prostitute transformed by the love of a decent man. Negri plays tough, cynical Louise, who drinks, smokes, and lets a man fondle her if she thinks she can gain a customer. The world holds nothing for her until she encounters John (Hans Rehmann), a law-abiding sailor with strong convictions.

The sailor refuses to be yet another client of hers, but Louise is incorrigible. She wraps her feather boa around him and sits in his lap, but the stranger pays no attention to her. He chews his sandwich and gulps his drink, brushing her hands off him as she offers new enticements.

Although he won't succumb to the bar girl, John still helps her when she is in danger. On the dance floor, Louise is robbed by one of her regulars. The thief has just lost at cards, and he knows where Louise keeps her money—inside her cleavage. John jumps to the rescue, leaving the offender cut and bleeding. Touched that someone would defend her, Louise follows John from the bar, but he wants nothing to do with her. He just did what was right and now wants to go about his business. Louise can't return to work, having caused such a disturbance, and realizes that she has no one to turn to.

Louise knows she lacks the human dignity her rescuer has, and she doesn't deserve him. The sailor intends to leave her forever, then reconsiders and decides to marry her. That suits Louise very well, even though John is slow to show his feelings. She adjusts to provincial life, trading her high heels for work shoes and wiping the rouge off her face. She cooks and irons, slowly turning her reluctant husband into a tender, loving provider.

Underneath all her toughness, she is a girl hungry for kindness and affection. With quiet pride, Louise tells her husband she is expecting. But even though she has changed her ways, the odds are stacked against her. The wounded gambler who had tried to rob her is now on the run for a more serious crime. He sneaks back into Louise's life, hiding in the house one night when her husband is gone. After the police force the gambler out into the daylight, Louise's husband learns that the gambler was alone with his wife.

Louise swears by her marriage vows, but John refuses to believe that she's been faithful. His blind righteousness leaves no room for excuses.

Louise ends up alone in a rowboat on a stormy sea, and the image depicts her whole existence. Louise's mouth tightens as she considers her position. She is pregnant by a man who has just disowned her. Louise tosses her oars overboard in the raging storm, accepting death as her destiny. Once again, Negri plays the hard-hearted girl, beholden to no one. Louise tried to have a different life and lost through no fault of her own.

The Way of Lost Souls served Negri well at this juncture in her career, for it led to a 1931 British stage debut appearance at the famous London Coliseum. Containing over two thousand seats, the Coliseum was designed in 1904 by architect Frank Matcham and was the brain child of impresario Oswald Stoll, who wanted to create a "people's palace of entertainment of its age."[3] It showcased variety programming until 1931, when it began staging full theater productions.

Negri's engagement at the Coliseum was billed as "An All-Star Variety Programme including Pola Negri and Company in Playlet 'Farewell To Love' and High-Class Varieties." At first, Negri found it a challenge to return to the theater, especially with three performances a day. The twenty-nine-minute vignette *A Farewell to Love* (originally named *The Last Tango*) was written by Max Frantel and Pierre Lagarde and adapted and produced by Norman Loring. It was set in a nightclub in Paris and featured a cast of four. Negri handpicked her leading man, Reginald Tate, to play Pierre opposite her Nadia, a sad nightclub singer whose lover is being sentenced to a lifetime in prison. Negri's performance of the song "Farewell, My Gypsy Camp," accompanied by gypsy guitarist Boris Golovka, was later recorded with "Black Eyes" and pressed to wax.

Because Negri was to act and sing in English, this venture was going to be a very important step in getting the world and the film industry at large to recognize Negri as a viable talkie actress. It also helped give her the confidence she needed to know she was ready to accept another contract from Hollywood. But the questions still remained: Would her voice be acceptable? Would her accented English work? She was staking the future of her career on the Coliseum engagement. If it failed, she could wind up out of work and out of money.

During her engagement at the Coliseum, she was given Sarah Bernhardt's dressing room. Bernhardt's reflections on her career in acting corresponded with Negri's view: it was a long, lonely struggle. Bernhardt's portrait on the wall seemed to offer silent encouragement. Negri loved being in London, and the London press and her silent-film fans welcomed her warmly. Although the shows were sold out and the audiences rose to their feet each night, when the reviews came, they were not altogether favorable—either for the one-act play or for Negri herself. The *Evening Standard* was the most acerbic, calling her performance a disappointment: "Her movements are slow, and stilted, her voice monotonous, and her expression (ineffably sad) never changes. Away from the screen she is not a great actress."[4] The *Daily Mail's* review was titled "Pola Saved by Kiss—Audience Escapes Boredom by One Minute," but it also reported on the twelve curtain calls she had to take.[5] The fans still loved her and were thrilled to see her perform live. Negri had not received such an immediate reaction for many years, and she was grateful for her fans. *News Chronicle* reported: "The prolonged applause at the end was evidently more a tribute to the actress than to the play. Pola Negri had to take eight curtain calls and then made a speech of thanks."[6]

Negri was encouraged to know that people still wanted to see her perform, and the lukewarm reviews did not curb her determination and ambition. Numerous papers reported her speaking with much authority of a film contract being offered to her from Hollywood to perform in the talkies. At first, she didn't offer specifics, because there weren't any offers. She was spinning her own story in order to lay the bait for the press. After all her years in Hollywood, she knew how to make the press and her fans wait on pins and needles. *Motion Picture* magazine reported: "Pola Negri is staging a real gamble for new fame and new fortune. For three years, she has been turning down all sorts of foreign picture offers, biding her time, improving her English, waiting to get back to Hollywood."[7]

The questions remained on everyone's mind: Would her voice and her accent be accepted? Would her dark alto voice translate well to screen? Attitudes were changing in Hollywood regarding accents, and perhaps Hollywood's ear was being retuned to more varied and exotic sounds. The *Daily Express* suggested: "From a revenue point of view, there were worse things in the world than English spoken with a guttural mid-European accent."[8] It was not just Dietrich and Garbo who were on the screen with non-American accents. Elissa Landi, Maurice Chevalier, and Lupe Valez were also working under talkie contracts, so "Why not Pola?" asked *Motion Picture* magazine in August 1931 when musing whether Negri's comeback would threaten the thrones of Dietrich and Garbo. "Who knows? The experimental contract may work!"[9]

Edwin Schallert, writing in *Picture Play*, had always felt that Negri was miscast and misunderstood in Hollywood: "Pola, I feel, did not ever have just the right guiding hand during her career. . . . Pictures she has made, that were in the proper key, have too often lacked background. They were conventional, trite stories of marital difficulties. They seldom gave her the chance to disclose the greater sweep of her talent. . . . No fan who has watched her work fails to realize that it has nearly always been a battle between her and the screen environment in which she was placed." Always appreciative of Negri's temperament and European artistry, Schallert expressed optimism about Negri's renewed Hollywood career and hoped that her voice would not be a setback: "I personally believe in the future of Pola. The screen needs her type—and what she can give of her vibrant and vibrating personality. That she has endured some terrific setbacks would not amount to a snap of the finger if she came forth again in some rightly contrived picture."[10] Despite the flurry of publicity, Negri still lacked an official offer. She was getting offers from companies in Europe, but she was waiting for Hollywood. Finally, she received offers from Warner Bros. and RKO. She decided to test for RKO, since they were offering more money.[11]

Before leaving for her screen test, Negri set her affairs in order in Europe in preparation for her return to Hollywood. On a side trip to France, Negri bought her mother a villa on the Riviera to share with de Hulewicz. They were both growing older and needed companionship. Out of everything Negri owned back in France, Negri kept just one possession: an Isotta Fraschini, a deluxe limousine that Valentino had ordered before his death. Negri had purchased it for herself.

When she said her goodbyes to Glen Kidston in England, she made him leave with a promise. After his many near misses in airplane, motor-cycle, speedboat, and even submarine accidents, Negri felt that his luck was running out and wanted him to promise there would be no more rac-ing. Instead, Kidston promised that he would stop after just one last flight. When he escorted her aboard her ship, she had a premonition it would be the last time she would see him. In April 1931, while returning home from completing his record-breaking trip from the United Kingdom to South Africa, he crashed his de Havilland Puss Moth airplane into the Drakensberg Mountains during a dust storm and was killed. Negri was loveless once again, but by now she had given up on finding lasting love. She expressed it this way: "When all is said and done, love is not the main reason for our existence. Each of us has a central aim in life, which must be fulfilled. And the motive of my life has always been that of making myself a great actress."[12]

18

First Talkie

When Negri returned to Hollywood, there was plenty of buzz about her comeback, but she still lacked a contract; nothing was signed with RKO. She took a gamble and won. RKO had promised they would give her three pictures if the screen tests went well. Once they saw them, they signed her for three years—a real victory for Negri.[1] She was once again front-page news, especially after announcing that the studio had granted her the right to choose her own screenplay—a rarity in the industry—and that she would be presenting a new personality. Critical of her earlier work, she told a reporter: "I do not consider those pictures personal failures because they were not *my* failures. They were the mistakes in judgment of the men who selected my stories. I suffer from them, yes. I am not a Talmadge, a Pickford, even a Garbo. I cannot be fit into their patterns. I am Negri—I have my own place. People have not forgotten me."[2]

Upon arriving in Los Angeles, careful not to share the same train as Marlene Dietrich in order to maximize the attention from the press, she said, "I am so happy to be back. I want people to like me, to say that there has never been anyone for them like Pola." The article that quoted her goes on to say, "*Picture Play* has heard her speak—her voice is lovely. Let's all cheer the return of a queenly exile!"[3] Writer Herbert Howe describes her comeback in an article called "The Prodigal Daughter Returns": "Pola says she has returned to us a different woman. Which means that she has rewritten Negri. The Countess came in '23, departed The Princess in '27, comes back the Prodigal Daughter in '31 and is served a nice fat contract for three years."[4]

Negri was back, but now she needed to find the right script. To help her select her self-appointed comeback vehicle, Negri hired Estelle Dick, Valentino's former secretary. She knew that Estelle had done an excellent job for him. When they discovered a young German writer living in

America, Thilde Forster, and her screenplay *A Woman Commands,* they knew they were onto something. Based on the life of Queen Maria Draga of Serbia, it had all the makings of a classic that would let the world hear Negri's singing voice for the first time in a picture.

A Woman Commands tells the story of Maria (Negri), who loves a captain named Alex (Basil Rathbone). Maria sacrifices their relationship when she learns that Alex has bankrupted himself to win her favor. After she becomes a famous cabaret dancer, King Alexander (Roland Young) falls for Maria and risks starting a revolution in order to marry her. Eventually, the army storms the palace and the king is assassinated.

Negri wanted Laurence Olivier, then a young upstart who had just had a hit on Broadway, to play Alex. Olivier first came to Hollywood to play opposite Greta Garbo in *Queen Christina,* but Garbo insisted they use John Gilbert, her former silent-film costar and lover. Negri knew that Olivier—young, handsome, romantic, and a wonderful actor—would be perfect for the part. At the same time, Basil Rathbone was being considered. He was married to Ouida Bergère, ex-wife of director George Fitzmaurice from Negri's first two Paramount films. Bergère lobbied hard for Negri to take Rathbone. In the end, fate intervened—Olivier came down with severe jaundice and had to bow out, and so the role went to Rathbone. Some critics believed the film would have been far more successful with Olivier in the lead. Negri felt awful that Rathbone did not work out. He couldn't do the part justice, despite his best efforts. Roland Young played King Alexander with more success, but the cast never came together as one.

The movie faced production problems from the very beginning. The set seemed cursed with many other illnesses and accidents. During Negri's routine prefilming medical exam, she was diagnosed with an inflamed appendix. She elected to postpone surgery until the movie was completed, not wanting to delay the project. During shooting, a horse-drawn carriage went out of control as a stallion bolted under the glare of a reflector light, and it careened into a crowd of extras. Negri and Roland Young were inside the carriage, and Negri had a baby on her lap. As the baby's mother shrieked from the sidelines, Negri held the child close. A brave bystander seized the horse's reins just as the carriage started heading toward the bridge, and, luckily, serious injury was avoided.

Only days after the movie wrapped up, Negri collapsed on the set of the RKO studios. She was rushed to Santa Monica Hospital where the outcome of her condition, an acute intestinal obstruction, was declared by her physician Dr. Leo J. Madsen as "doubtful."[5] She had neglected her health, and now her condition was critical. News of her impending death spread quickly. A priest was called in to administer the last rites, but Negri pulled through. She recalled in her memoirs that though her life hung in the balance, her only recollection of the ordeal was the sound of carolers singing "Silent Night."

Negri decided to convalesce in Palm Springs, where Albert Einstein had the bungalow next to her hotel. They met and reminisced about Berlin before Hitler, and Einstein played his violin for her. Negri found that his music soothed her. The *New York Times* reported on her recovery: "Pola Negri, the Polish film actress, who is recovering here after her recent operation, and Dr. and Mrs. Albert Einstein, on a brief vacation, met today and talked in German for more than forty minutes. 'Have you ever met Hitler, the German Fascist leader?' Miss Negri disclosed she had asked. 'No, but I have seen his photographs,' the German physicist replied with a wink, 'and they are sufficient.'"[6]

Negri wasn't completely recovered when *A Woman Commands* premiered in New York, but she made it to the festivities supported on the arm of Mayor Jimmy Walker, a longtime friend. She wore a gleaming white gown with a jeweled tiara. Mobs pushed through the police cordon, and the mayor and Joseph Schenck had to spirit Negri away to safety.

Although her part was well received, Negri's performance could not offset the movie's shortcomings. Critics praised her but panned the movie—especially the script, which they found lacking. "What a pity that Pola Negri should return in such a trite, impossible and worn-out theme," said *Photoplay*. "If she had anything to do, she would have done it well. Her bright spot is singing in a cabaret. The gal has a luring voice which records gorgeously."[7] The *Time* reviewer reported that Negri had "a warm soft voice" but didn't think the part was a good fit: "This curious little picture—a combination of comedy, romance, mid-European melodramatics, court intrigue and fictionized history—does not suit her so well as the vampire parts she used to play in silent films."[8]

No one could deny, however, that the film was still a huge success for Negri. It marked her singing as well as her speaking debut, and both were pronounced an unprecedented success. Nacio Herb Brown wrote the film's theme song, "Paradise," specifically for Negri's vocal range and timbre. Sensuous and haunting, her singing voice is reminiscent of Edith Piaf or

Greta Garbo. Negri's recording of "Paradise" was the highlight of the film and became an international hit, playing in multiple languages years after the picture had its run.

Film historian Jeanine Basinger comments on Negri's voice: "She's an excellent actress. After all, she came from theater. She knows how to deliver dialogue. Yes, she does have an accent, and it is a bit heavy, but it's not unintelligible. It wasn't sound that changed things for her as much as it was the era."[9]

Negri soon found employment on the vaudeville circuit with a sketch written around the song "Paradise." Audiences accepted her with enthusiasm. Negri had a way of reaching out to people, and the support of the die-hard fans always lifted her morale. She performed with Milton Berle and George Jessel, who introduced her to a new favorite: kosher delicatessen food.

Russ Columbo, the young Valentino look-alike who had distracted Negri shortly after Valentino's death, reappeared in Negri's life around the time of the premiere of *A Woman Commands,* and they resumed their relationship. Billed by NBC as the "Romeo of Radio," Columbo had achieved national success as a crooner and a bandleader. Columbo's song "You Call It Madness (But I Call It Love)" was a national hit, and at one point the press viewed Columbo and Bing Crosby as neck and neck in "The Battle of the Baritones." His good looks and singing ability had scored him small roles in several Hollywood films, and the press eagerly followed his romantic exploits with various singers and actresses, including Dorothy Dell of the Ziegfeld Follies. The press had also paired Columbo with Greta Garbo, but whether it was a real affair or a publicity stunt is hard to tell.

All went well for the two lovers, and they both appeared on a playbill for a "George Jessel Variety Review" in February 1932. On the poster, Negri gets top billing and Columbo is described as "Radio's Romeo of Song." Another singer replaced Columbo shortly before show time, however. On June 13, Negri sent Columbo a telegram ending their relationship: "EVERYTHING MUST HAVE ITS END BUT SO MUST OUR ROMANCE IT WAS BEAUTIFUL STOP I WILL BE LISTENING TO YOUR SONGS ALWAYS = GOODBYE = POLA." She sent him a two-word letter two weeks later from her suite at the Ambassador in New York: "Forget me."[10]

Columbo soon recorded the mournful song "Paradise" himself, making it a staple at his performances. During the next two years, his life was on an upward swing: continued musical success, three feature films

(*Broadway through a Keyhole, Moulin Rouge,* and *Wake Up and Dream*), and a promising relationship with Carole Lombard. Fortune didn't smile upon him long, however. In 1934 he died suddenly at age twenty-six when a Civil War pistol a friend was examining accidentally went off and shot him in the face.

In 1933 Negri got a stage role in the touring play *A Trip to Pressburg,* but she gave only a few performances before her health declined—she had an inflamed gall bladder—and the show had to travel on without her. Sadly, hopes were dashed, and everyone felt short-changed as the show wound up in arbitration. The *New York Times* reported: "Despite a private settlement agreed upon by Les Shubert (producer) and Pola Negri, just before an arbitration hearing, the production has been called off by mutual consent. Mr. Shubert had requested $25,000 for alleged damages and Miss Negri wanted $4,000 due for her salary. Although considered a Continental success, the play, written by Leo Perutz, has encountered several obstacles."[11]

In 1934 Pola Negri left the United States for Paris, where she embarked on a new challenge. She was engaged to star in a talkie in French. Titled *Fanatisme,* the film was directed by Tony Lekain and Gaston Ravel. Again, Pola Negri looked ravishing on the screen. The story line included several dance scenes that highlighted Negri's talent. The film was released throughout Europe and was well received by Negri's fans and the press alike. The public hoped Negri would make more French movies, but this was not to be. The film survives at La Cinémathèque française and is screened periodically still today at film festivals.

When Negri returned to the United States after production was finished, she was offered a theatrical stage tour around the country. Three performances a day kept her in touch with her audience and earned money to pay her bills. As far as Negri knew, she was back in America to stay. But her life changed yet again when she was approached by UFA, the German production company with which she had worked before.

19

Return to UFA

Universal wanted to put Negri under contract and do a film in Berlin with UFA, one of its affiliate studios, but Negri had no interest in returning to Germany. Among other things, she remembered Einstein's descriptions of Hitler as a menace. The head of Universal begged Negri to read the script for *Mazurka* before she gave him a definite answer. Author A. A. Lewis describes the film's background:

> *Mazurka* was really *Madame X* under a different name, but the director was the great director at UFA at the time, Willi Forst. The head of Universal, Carl Laemmle, was handling the deal and he said to Pola, "Do it. It will be a great success and Hollywood will come after you. They will want you to make an American film of *Mazurka* and you'll be back on top." So she went to Germany. She did the film and it was indeed a great success worldwide. Hollywood did indeed buy the rights to make an American film, but the American film was made with Kay Francis. It was not a hit for Warner Brothers, who made the film.[1]

Mazurka tells the story of a woman who commits murder to save her estranged daughter from a cruel heartbreaker—the same man who had ruined her own marriage. Pola, wearing a blond wig and playing the wretched mother, shoots the predator who had seduced her many years ago, when she was drunk. Decades later the same man is making a play for her daughter, although he has no way of knowing that the two women are related. *Mazurka* lets Negri portray many sides of the character in different phases: a lively young wife, a famed cabaret singer, and an aggrieved, aging mother who is on trial for a murder she had committed to protect the daughter she was forced to abandon at birth.

Negri asked the head of Universal to shoot the movie in America. Unfortunately, as required by its producers, *Mazurka* had to be made in Berlin. Negri really wanted the part, and she also needed the money. This role would pay only twenty-five thousand dollars, much less than she was used to, but she had no other firm offers. It was not a sum to be frowned upon for someone who had tax trouble. In 1929, the *New York Times* reported: "Three liens have been filed in Federal Court against Apolonia Mdivani, whose screen name is Pola Negri, seeking a total of $68,680.30 in alleged unpaid income taxes for the years 1924, 1925, and 1926. The lien charges that the actress claimed too many exemptions, and failed to list certain income in her reports for those years, stating that she received large sums for working in pictures and profits from business enterprises."[2]

Negri never did recover financially from her disastrous marriage to Serge Mdivani and the crash that decimated her stock investments. She now owed plenty of people money. The court permitted her to travel outside the country, but the trip didn't begin well. On her way by plane to New York to catch the boat for Germany, a blizzard caused a forced landing in Amarillo, Texas. The passengers had to ride a train to Kansas City and transfer to another plane there. It was New Year's Eve, 1934. Negri always celebrated her birthday on that day, and this time she was spending it in a caboose attached to a cattle train. She sent a fellow passenger out to buy champagne, but all he could find was some cheap rye whiskey. "We sat on our suitcases and made a banquet table out of my trunks," she wrote later. "It was about as gay a New Year's Eve and birthday I had ever spent."[3]

If Negri was apprehensive about her new role, her employers were a little nervous, too. Director Willi Forst was not sure how Negri would fare with the German language. They, too, thought of her as a silent star and weren't convinced about her voice. Negri was used to making up her own dialogue in any language—Polish, German, French, English, or Russian— that was appropriate to where the film was being shot. Even though they had no written dialogue, the actors in silent films still spoke to each other during their scenes, and audience members tried hard to read their lips. Actors made up their own dialogue to fit the scene and the characters' story line. All through Europe, silent-film actors were speaking either in their own native tongue or in the language of the country where the film was being made, and accents and delivery had never mattered. But now, with scripts to memorize and microphones recording the dialogue, actors needed to sound convincing.

The producers were also concerned about Negri's age. At thirty-eight, still unquestionably beautiful, she was perhaps more suited to playing wives and mothers than seductresses. Trude Hesterberg, the Russian actress Olga Tschechowa, and the unknown Hilde Krahl, whom Willi Forst later directed in *Serenade,* had all been considered for the *Mazurka* lead, but only Negri was sent a script. After a flurry of telegrams back and forth, Negri was asked to take the next boat over, paid for by the producers. She arrived on the ship *Bremerhaven,* wearing a flowing lilac gown that dramatized her dark hair and luminous makeup. She looked like a true thespian queen, ageless and of another world.

Willi Forst reported that he was relieved by the way Negri carried herself. At their first meeting in her luxurious cabin aboard the ship, he noted traces of white powder (which he assumed to be cocaine) on her upper lip, but she didn't use anything of the sort during the film shoot. She openly drank champagne all the time from a silver chalice, but it never seemed to cause any adverse effects. She loved champagne and felt she could afford it.

Mazurka took a long time to complete. Ingeborg Theek, who played the part of the daughter, became seriously ill during the shoot. When the film finally made it to the theaters in November 1935, it was hailed as a crowning glory—not just for Negri, but for all those who participated. Forst asked everyone who saw it not to give away the plot, which was based on an actual newspaper story.

The core of *Mazurka* is Negri's unforgettable portrayal of a nightclub chanteuse. She sings songs that are fraught with memories, seemingly fueled by her own personal struggle to keep things from unraveling. Certain that her audience still wanted her, she had no intention of leaving her profession, even if she was getting older. Critic Sydney Carroll summed up Negri's role in *Mazurka:* "Every pert little miss who fancies herself an embryo star should, in a spirit of awed humility, take this opportunity of studying the methods of an artiste whose passions come from the heart, whose voice is vibrant with feeling, and whose emotions are expressed with every fiber of her being."[4] Even though Negri's soprano numbers were mostly dubbed—she herself was a contralto—she easily created the correct facial expressions to be convincing. Hilde Seipp's voice is intercut with hers whenever a song hits a high note. Peter Kreuder, the film's composer, remembered afterward that Negri's contralto sounded quite good but that she was unable to sing the higher notes in the song.

Negri's vocal tone was full of melodrama and passion. In the past, she had had only her body and her face to help portray her unappeasable erotic temperament, but now she had her voice to shake the world. Negri's costar in *Mazurka*, Albrecht Schoenhals, remembers that when they rehearsed their big seduction scene, she told him, full of feverish emphasis, "Albrecht! The scene must get much more erotic! Much more sexual! We are the most erotic couple in Paris! In all of Europe!" Albrecht considered Negri a "magnificent colleague." He said he could listen to her for hours. When she told him humorous stories with her dark and cracked voice, the truth was not always confirmable, but, he said, "she lived out the richness of her emotions and continuously presented herself in the most enchanting manner."[5]

For all the critical acclaim *Mazurka* brought her, Negri almost didn't get the role. Not long after she arrived in Germany, she was blacklisted for supposedly "being a Jewess." Dr. Joseph Goebbels, Hitler's chief of propaganda, accused her of having a Jewish grandparent, which would have disqualified her from working in Germany at the time. Goebbels announced that her father was Slovak, and the Third Reich persecuted Slavs. Also, Negri had hired her old friend Paola Loebel as her secretary, which particularly offended Goebbels. He equated it with having pro-Jewish sympathies. Negri was not used to having other people comment upon or choose her friends. She and Paola had a long history, and her many Jewish contacts in the business, from Ernst Lubitsch to Ben Blumenthal, had been part of her career from the early days.

Negri was not pleased to find herself pilloried again. Forst showed her a letter written by Goebbels that prohibited her from practicing her craft. Upon seeing it, she went to her private bar and poured herself a triple shot of whiskey. That same day, she secured an appointment with the minister of state, although no one is quite sure how she managed that. In *Memoirs of a Star*, Negri says that she phoned the Polish ambassador and threatened to leave Germany, knowing that it would be an embarrassment to everyone if a world-famous actress protested in this fashion. The *New York Times* reported: "Pola Negri, the Polish motion picture star, who was intended to play the leading role in a proposed German film, was informed today by the Propaganda Ministry that she would not be allowed to act in Germany. The actress was told that this Ministry had received numerous anonymous letters accusing her of anti-German activities abroad."[6]

Adolf Hitler eventually signed his permission for her to work in the country. Negri's story made the front pages. "Everyone knows I'm a Catholic," she announced. Investigators labeled her Polish-Aryan to save face. The *New York Times* set the record straight with the headline "Hitler Removes Ban on Pola Negri Film: Actress Is Cleared of Charges of Working against Germany and Being of Jewish Descent." The paper reported: "After a two-day struggle, which involved the intervention of the Polish Ambassador, Pola Negri triumphed over Dr. Paul Joseph Goebbels, Propaganda Minister, and the ban against her re-entry to German film production was removed on orders from Chancellor Hitler."[7]

According to composer Peter Kreuder, it was very fortunate she got a reprieve, because the film was inconceivable with anyone else. Pola Negri became Hitler's favorite actress, and there was a rumor she was under his "special protection." Later, it was reported that Hitler was a fan of *Mazurka* and watched it two or three times a week, crying with emotion. Negri found it unsettling that her name was being associated with the Reich chancellor. Goebbels noted in his diary that *Mazurka* was "virtuously made, and Negri acts breathtakingly." That did not prevent him from making life difficult for her later.

Uncomfortable in Germany, Negri went to Cannes to be with her mother whenever shooting was interrupted. And every time she was called back to work, she tried to ignore the political environment. Peter Kreuder recalled:

We had no difficulties with Pola Negri. She was generous, warm-hearted, and candid. Whenever I came to her room for music rehearsals, she let the champagne flow and received me with such cordiality that I quickly felt I had known her for many years. Despite Jurgensen's [her tutor's] best efforts to teach her the German language, she continued to talk in her peculiar mixture of Polish, English, Yiddish, French, and German. She also continued to receive a silver chalice each day on the set, discreetly covered by a serviette, which contained pure whiskey. At first we were afraid that, with such heavy drinking, Pola Negri would spend the shoot tumbling through the sets, but if you didn't know, you couldn't guess that she had been drinking. One bottle of whiskey each day contributed to her well-being. However, at least during the shoot, she didn't use any more cocaine.[8]

Director Willi Forst started his career as an actor. In 1927 he appeared with Dietrich in *Cafe Electric*. On-screen, he was as suave as Cary Grant, but he became better known for his work on the other side of the camera. Two of the films that he directed were later remade by Hollywood, duplicated scene for scene: *Masquerade*, renamed *Escapade*, in 1935, with Luise Rainer taking the place of Paula Wessely, and *Mazurka* in 1937, now titled *Confession*, with Kay Francis reprising the Negri role. It is *Mazurka* and his film *Die Sünderin* (The sinner) that show Forst's penchant for melodrama. Offscreen, he is said to have had a cruel, almost sadistic streak. He understood how a woman could find it in her power to be hurtful, and he knew how to bring that out in Negri.

After *Mazurka*, Negri was hoping to make a triumphant return to the United States. The film reminded Irving Thalberg and Louis B. Mayer, the heads of MGM, of Negri's range, magnetism, and star power. They came to Berlin to bring her back to Hollywood and make *The Good Earth*. By that time, UFA was making very little money on anything other than Pola Negri's movies. They were not about to release her from her contract to go to Hollywood—they knew she would never come back. *The Good Earth* would have been a good vehicle for Negri, but she lost it because of contract logistics. A. A. Lewis reflects that hers was "a career of things she could have had by being less of what she was. Which was more than anybody else. Some of which were beyond her control. But, it was a career that ended too soon because of a series of flukes that were not of her doing. Pola was really Wednesday's child."[9]

Events in Europe continued to drain Negri's energy. Some of them were personal and some were political. Her secretary, Paola Loebel, finding herself more and more restricted in Germany for being Jewish, decided to leave the country. Negri gave her the money and assistance to start a new life in Holland. Her old friend Casimir de Hulewicz succumbed to cancer. He did not want Negri to learn of his disease while she was in the middle of a film shoot. Gallant and considerate to the end, he looked out for Negri and her mother until the day he died.

The success of *Mazurka* surpassed all expectations. Critics called it the best German talkie ever. Unfortunately, not everyone who took part in it fared well. Gregory Rabinowitz and Arnold Pressburger, the movie's producers, were told that they could no longer work in Germany. They left quickly, hoping that the film would procure jobs for them elsewhere.

Negri found this all very dispiriting. She wanted to get out from under the Third Reich—all she wanted to do was to practice her art. However, there were a few compelling reasons why she didn't pack up and leave. She had a fragile, elderly mother, and she had de Hulewicz's funeral to pay for. She decided she had to stay and continue working.

UFA now offered her an extremely attractive new contract: 175,000 marks per picture, half of it payable in Swiss francs to her account in Switzerland. The company was making an effort to keep her in Germany. Goebbels himself would not release her from her contract. As minister of propaganda, he considered Negri a strategic commodity for his campaigns. She never participated in any Nazi propaganda films, but she stayed in Germany and was unhappy.

Negri was not looking for the company of the Nazi dignitaries. The first one she met was Hermann Goering. He immediately made sure to tell her he had seen her years before in *The Yellow Ticket,* in which she played a persecuted young Jewish woman determined to be educated. Goering claimed that Negri had acted her role so convincingly that she must have drawn on her own experience. At the funeral mass of the Polish state leader Marshal Pilsudski, held at St. Hedvig's Cathedral in Berlin, Negri was shocked to see Hitler. He was accompanied by Goebbels, Goering, Rudolph Hess, Heinrich Himmler, and others. She realized that the German enemy was formidable and that her home country was in grave danger.

These same dangerous Germans also loved listening to Negri's songs that had become hits. David Gasten explains: "*Moskau-Shanghai* [*Moscow-Shanghai*] and *Tango Notturno* both feature Pola singing, and she does a wonderful job. *Moskau-Shanghai* was directed by Paul Wegener, who appeared with her fifteen years prior in *Sumurun,* interestingly enough. The "Tango Notturno" song is probably some of her best singing in German films, even though the movie itself is not as good as *Mazurka.*"[10] Negri's version of Peter Kreuder's song "Wenn die Sonne hinter den Dachem versinkt" ("When the Sun Goes Down behind the Roofs") is still sold on CDs. Actress-singer Camilla Horn made another recording of the song in 1936, when it was used in Karl Anton's anti-Soviet melodrama *Weisse Sklaven–Panzerkreuzer Sebastopol* (White slaves: Battleship Sebastopol).

Restrictions in Germany were becoming increasingly oppressive.

Negri attended some government banquets, which was considered a prudent thing to do. At one of them she found herself seated next to Emil Jannings, who in 1918 had pretended to stab her at the top of the stairs in *The Eyes of the Mummy Ma*. She had not seen him since they had worked in Hollywood together. He had become the top male star of the Nazi government and now held a position in its Ministry of Culture. Negri wasn't surprised to find that he was as obnoxious as he had always been.

After *Mazurka*, Negri starred in *Moskau-Shanghai* (1936), *Madame Bovary* (1937), *Tango Notturno* (1937), *Die fromme Lüge* (The secret lie) (1938), and *Die Nacht der Entscheidung* (The night of decision) (1938). The films had sophisticated sets but did not equal the first production. Some critics thought Negri's acting was overly emotional. *Tango Notturno* stands apart from the other movies because Negri gives a milder performance; her face has a softer appeal. She inhabits the role of Mado Doucet, a well-known singer who turns to cocaine to soothe the pain after the death of her beloved son. The film was said to be intended for Marlene Dietrich if she ever returned to Germany. Ironically, Dietrich was back at Paramount making *Song of Songs*, a remake of one of Negri's silent films, and was scheduled to do a talkie version of *Hotel Imperial*, although that was never completed.

Tango Notturno has certain plotlines that are similar to *Mazurka*. Again, Negri plays opposite Albrecht Schoenhals. The movie tells the story of a married woman who reconnects with a former lover, only to find that her life has been ruined in so many ways that she will never recover. The story is told in flashbacks, so the audience is constantly reminded of how far the main character has fallen.

Aside from her movies, Negri watched hard-luck stories unfold in real life. She learned of Serge Mdivani's new marriage to Louise Astor Van Alen, a Newport heiress who had already divorced Serge's brother Alexis. Not long afterward, Serge had a polo accident in Palm Beach and died from his injuries. Mae Murray, who had been married to David Mdivani, also fared badly. David left Murray after she lost her fortune in the crash. One night she was found sleeping on a bench in New York's Central Park and was arrested for vagrancy. Murray was later provided for by Gretchen Young, Loretta Young's daughter, whom Murray had helped raise. Negri's circle of female Hollywood stars came through for each other after their men abandoned them.

After Negri finished working on *Tango Notturno*, she discovered that the film was having trouble getting approved for distribution to German theaters. Censorship was rampant. By Goebbels's orders, Negri's right to choose roles and scripts, granted to her in the contract, was canceled. Goebbels felt that art was the enemy of the state and was creating an "absolutely anti-intellectual" Germany. Forbidden books were being burned in the public squares.

Goebbels placed publishing houses and universities, as well as movie studios, under Nazi control. He now controlled all movie production, and nixed every story that she offered: Ibsen's *A Doll's House*, Zola's *Nana*, and anything narrative or creative. Finally, permission was granted for *Die fromme Lüge* (The secret lie).

After *Die fromme Lüge*, the government was eager to do another Negri film, but she was suffering from exhaustion and sought refuge in a Dresden sanatorium. Once released, Negri wanted to go to Switzerland. Stopping in Bayreuth along the way, she came down with typhoid and had to undergo quarantine. Rumors flew that she had been poisoned by one Frau Winifred Wagner, a woman thought to be in love with Hitler and jealous of his admiration of Negri. The truth was nothing so dramatic—Negri had drunk unpasteurized milk from an infected cow.

She was hospitalized for weeks. With the next movie already on her schedule, she desperately wanted to leave Germany. The country frightened her. One day, while shopping in Berlin, Negri suddenly heard air raid sirens and saw the city bathed in a fiery red light. The fire department had been called out. Hours later, people were informed that this had been a dress rehearsal, a test of how the city would respond in a real attack. Germany was priming itself for war.

While in Germany, Negri rehired Paola Loebel as her assistant. Although Loebel was Jewish, Negri and Loebel traveled together around Europe. Negri knew the van Dijk family and stayed with them in Holland. J. G. M. van Dijk, who was a young child at the time, remembers Negri bringing Loebel and her brother to Holland. After staying with the van Dijk family, they made their way from Holland to England. According to van Dijk, Negri claimed that she was being followed and watched by the German police because she had helped the Loebels leave Germany.

Negri started shooting *The Night of Decision*, but halfway through the movie, all the studio workers—including grips, cameramen, electricians, and editors—were ordered to report for military service. The people who replaced them could barely do their jobs. Negri was thankful that her leading man, Iván Petrovich, was Yugoslavian and not eligible for the draft.

Tanks soon took possession of the streets, and soldiers could be seen everywhere as men and equipment were being mobilized. "Today Germany—tomorrow the world!" became a resounding slogan. Production on *The Night of Decision* was held up for three days while the Treaty of Munich was signed. It gave Hitler control over Czechoslovakia, but Negri knew that would not be enough for him. When her film was finally completed, she got permission to vacation in France for her usual hiatus. She packed one suitcase and left everything else behind, knowing they were watching her. She left most of her jewels, her furs—almost everything. She was signed to UFA for three more pictures, so she had to give the impression she was coming back.

In Nice she joined the Polish Red Cross when she found out that her home country had been invaded. When the Italian bombardments laid waste to the French countryside, Negri and her mother stayed in the house, holed up in the basement until the armistice was declared. No strangers to falling bombs, Negri and Eleonora believed God was there to keep them safe from harm.

The sensational tabloid press found a new topic: Pola Negri's alleged affair with Hitler. She was made to look like a Nazi sympathizer. She sued *Pour Vous,* the French magazine that printed the story, and received 10,000 francs as compensation, but the damage was already done. In America many people believed she had been Hitler's mistress. Now that the United States was about to go to war with Germany, the idea did not sit well. In an article titled "Pola Negri Wins Suit," the *New York Times* reported: "Pola Negri today won her libel suit against the French review, *Pour Vous,* but obtained only 10,000 [francs] damages instead of the 1,000,000 she asked. The court held she failed to prove material losses of movie contracts she claimed to have missed because of untrue statements that she had been friendly with Nazi leaders and later confined to a concentration camp. The court awarded her 10,000 francs for moral prejudice."[11]

Agnes Grunstrom, Negri's former wardrobe mistress, had the last word on speculations about any possible relationship with Hitler: "Miss Negri herself is a dictator. She would not stand for taking orders from Hitler. They could not get along ten minutes together unless Pola is very much changed."[12]

20

Escape from Germany

UFA sent word for Negri to return to Berlin, but she had resolved that the Third Reich would not make any more money off of her. She also knew that any new story lines would contain blatant pro-German propaganda.

Negri advised the Polish consul in Nice of her situation and was told to stay put and wait for his instructions. When she told UFA that she was physically ill and could not withstand the strains of production, it sent a representative to check up on her story in person. Negri was prepared with falsified evidence: a doctor's certificate stating that she was in no condition to work. When the UFA representative arrived at her door, Negri sat wrapped in a blanket with a nurse at her side, entirely confirming the doctor's opinion. UFA threatened to hire another actress, and Negri said she could only agree to that.

Negri realized that unless she did something, her financial resources would soon be depleted. The property she owned required maintenance, and she had other financial obligations to attend to. France and England were no place to find a job—Paris had fallen to the Germans, and England faced a battle of its own. Negri felt that America could still tap her potential, even though she had been away from Hollywood for so long. After making sure that her mother would be comfortable in her absence, she took a train through Spain to Portugal. With Europe torn by war, long delays were common. Refugees from every country invaded by Hitler were all pushing for a new life in America.

There were flights and ships from Lisbon headed for the States. Negri could not get a flight, but she managed to get a reservation on a ship, the *Excalibur*, that would depart in four weeks. She stayed in Lisbon and kept to herself, sightseeing alone and staying clear of social obligations.

The *Excalibur* was not designed or equipped to carry such large numbers of passengers, but nobody complained. The passengers were thankful for a chance to pursue freedom. Negri could finally breathe a sigh of relief. The tiny cabin was a far cry from the luxury liners that she was used to, with their private baths and polished railings. She was returning to her humble beginnings and having to get used to living with less. All that mattered was reaching the country where people were not persecuted. What she had seen in Europe petrified her—she could easily have ended up in a concentration camp. America was her asylum now.

When Negri landed back in America, there were no bands to serenade her—only the ship's photographer to mark the return of the now tired and disheveled star. Negri was detained on Ellis Island, because she had been gone from the United States for more than six years and her visa had expired. Her entrance was secured by officials from both embassies, which issued her the correct documents to be allowed entry as an American resident. Only a handful of reporters and fans showed up. One kind woman handed Negri a parcel of food, assuming that the actress must have endured extreme hardship in Europe, and Negri was touched by her sympathy. She was being treated as a war victim. But the reality of this didn't strike her until later.

In the United States she was suspected of collaborating with the enemy, although she was never formally charged. Several unflattering newspaper stories about her had insinuated the worst. Negri made it a point to tell the real story to every journalist who came her way. She loved America. She had spent some of the best years of her life here, and believed she could reestablish herself. She had made twenty pictures for Paramount. She was hurt by all the false allegations.

Paramount finally called her with an offer for the role of Pilar in Hemingway's *For Whom the Bell Tolls*. Negri knew she was all wrong for the part, and declined. She busied herself selling war bonds and looked for more appropriate roles. After a year of living modestly, she was given the part of a stylish, temperamental opera singer in the 1943 film *Hi Diddle Diddle*, a United Artists screwball comedy in which the characters chased each other in circles. Adolphe Menjou played the husband of Negri's character. He was still the suave gentleman he had always been and as handsome as ever in a tuxedo. Negri loved working with her old friend again.

"The highlight of *Hi Diddle Diddle* is the return to the U.S. movies, in a comedy role, of Pola Negri, fabulous vamp of the Rudolph Valentino era," said *Time*. "Negri plays a Wagnerian diva married to Adolphe Menjou.

Clothed in sumptuous black and white, Pola is as vivacious and comely in comedy as she was as a glamour girl."[1]

She executed the role with such flair that she was offered more jobs in the same vein. She was not keen on doing low-end comedies, however. Negri was still dreaming of a more ambitious repertoire, but Hollywood was not her kind of town anymore. In 1944 she found herself back in New York. Hearst Publications offered her $7,500 to write about her life and added a $3,000 bonus for the highly satisfactory materials she provided. Unfortunately, Negri did not do well in the snowy, brutal New York winters; she needed a respite—her sensitive lungs required a warmer climate. That was when Marion Davies invited her to Santa Monica to stay in her guesthouse, free to do as she pleased. The sunny beach was just what Negri needed. It restored the joy in her life.

She was offered a two-week nightclub engagement in Boston, which led to more offers of the same type, but Negri didn't think she had the stamina for it and rested instead. She then returned to New York, where she rented a small apartment on East Ninetieth near Park Avenue. She suffered from depression, owing in part to having no contact with her mother. The Germans had seized control of France, and there had been no word from Eleonora for more than a year. Her mother was over eighty, and Negri worried about her. According to A. A. Lewis, "After *Hi Diddle Diddle*, Pola came back to New York, and she was really in dire straits. Her doctor told me that she had attempted suicide. Pola never told me that. Certainly, as the devout Catholic she was, she would never admit to having thought that was a way out of her despair."[2]

Once the war was over, Negri planned to return to France to oversee her mother's care and manage the investments she had left behind. She also hoped she might find more dramatic work there. In the United States, she was sent only silly scripts with small parts. She couldn't get permission to travel abroad, however. Only military personnel and people involved in European reconstruction were being allowed to travel there. With her finances tight and her prospects grim, she moved into a lower Park Avenue residential hotel. To survive, Negri started selling off her famous jewelry. She parted with her Hapsburg and Hohenzollern pieces—royal treasures she had kept for over twenty years. She had no steady income, and anything she might be able to recover from Europe would take time.

Negri was learning the hard way that New York was a big, exciting city only for the wealthy. To the poor, the old, the hungry, and all the actors looking for work, it was cold and hostile. Negri, the great star, was now on the same level as all the average players looking for their next paycheck. Hitting it big certainly didn't guarantee a solid retirement, and past successes did not necessarily promise future rewards. Paired with the reality of her advancing age, Negri's financial situation was increasingly precarious and painful. The future was uncertain for this aging star who had already lived three lifetimes.

21

Life with Margaret West

Pola Negri was in debt, with no income, when she accidentally ran into the retired radio hostess Margaret West. The women quickly became the best of friends, having met briefly years before. Margaret was the first person to bring country and western music to network radio. She was wealthy with family money. Her family had been prominent in Texas and had a forty-thousand-acre ranch. Margaret was childless and married to a man she soon divorced. According to A. A. Lewis, "Margaret rescued her. Truly rescued her." Negri's close friend and confidant George Schönbrunn said: "I think Margaret, like Dietrich, slept with other women and certainly she liked men. I don't think there was much going on with Margo and [Pola], but since she had a horrible time in New York, and was getting older making it harder to get any pictures in Hollywood—she didn't want to go back to Europe—what could she do? When I met her she was forty-two, and now she was forty-eight years old."[1]

Margaret invited Negri to come live with her. She found her lively company, and they had a lot in common. They headed back to Hollywood together. Negri was enough of a realist to know that her career would probably now consist of character parts, not the sexy female leads of her youth, but she didn't mind. She just wanted to work. Not much came of her return to Hollywood, though. Negri was offered roles here and there but turned them all down. The two friends, however, became art collectors and Hollywood hostesses who were the talk of the town with their fabulous parties. They sponsored a wonderful young German singer named Gretta Keller, who sang at all the parties.

During this period, Margaret used her considerable influence to get Negri's mother out of Europe and into the United States. Negri and Margaret bought Eleonora a house. In her advanced years, she was still a

187

ball of energy. She became very active in the Polish community and acquired a pet project: the building of a proper Polish church in Los Angeles. This was also the dream of Father Krzeminski, who unfortunately died before the church was built, but Eleonora lived to see it through. The Holy Mother of Czestochowa Church was erected thanks to Eleonora's tireless fund-raising efforts through concerts, sales, and bazaars. It was Eleonora's crowning achievement and, in addition to her daughter's success, the pride of her life. Two bronze plaques were later added to the entrance of the church. One is dedicated to Father Krzeminski; the other to "Eleonora Chalupiec—the Mother of Pola Negri." George Schönbrunn recalls: "Pola was a very good Catholic—went to church every Sunday and celebrated Easter. That's one thing she took seriously, otherwise she did everything the Catholic Church doesn't want you to do. Her friend Margo West converted to Catholicism. I went to church with her. She took communion. They mentioned the mother several times. All the Polish people made a great fuss when Pola came. They kissed her and knelt down and she enjoyed it."[2] Negri's mother died in 1954 of pancreatic cancer, not long after the church was completed. Eleonora had done everything she wanted to accomplish, and Negri had helped her live out her dreams. Mrs. Chałupec was buried at the Calvary Cemetery in Los Angeles in a mausoleum, with a space reserved for Negri.

When Margaret West's health started failing because of a heart ailment, she yearned to return to her hometown of San Antonio, Texas—and she wanted Negri there to take care of her and keep her company. Negri could always make Margaret laugh, and the two indulged gleefully in Hollywood gossip. There was much speculation as to the nature of their friendship, but mostly, they were thought of as two mature women who bonded for the purpose of keeping themselves entertained and not being alone. In 1957 Negri and Margaret moved from Bel Air, California, to live out the rest of their lives in Olmos Park, a tree-shaded area of San Antonio.

Margaret West had entered Negri's life when the star could see no future in front of her. Their encounter in New York had been a happy accident resulting in a close friendship that benefited them both. Brother Alexis Gonzales, drama and film professor at Loyola University and a good friend of Negri's, commented on their relationship: "Who cares what they did? Margaret helped Pola. That's the part I got. That she really helped her financially when Pola had been forgotten and had nowhere else to go. Margaret gave her a place to go."[3] After helping countless people in times of need in previous years, Negri was now the recipient of goodwill and generosity. When Margaret died in 1963, she left Negri financially comfortable for what turned out to be the next twenty-five years, the rest of her life.

Like most people, Negri had regrets as she neared the final chapters of her life. One was not having had children. When she was younger, she took the idea of having children for granted. Now, she perceived the lack of family as a missed chance in her life. She also felt she had lingered in Germany too long, especially once UFA was restructured to suit the needs of the Third Reich. Negri was in a very precarious situation at that time, and her excuses for staying with UFA didn't make sense anymore. Having had Hitler as a putative employer had definitely cast Negri in a bad light.

Her extended stay in Germany was not the only career choice that haunted Negri through her later years. Her decision in 1950 to decline the role in Billy Wilder's *Sunset Boulevard* is still a topic of speculation and debate. According to the accounts of witnesses reported in fan magazines, when Negri was approached for the role, she promptly chased director Billy Wilder from her house. Film historian Jeanine Basinger explains: "There has always been much speculation as to just whom Norma Desmond was modeled on, but it was probably no one actress. She's most likely a combination of the ego of Negri, who always knew what she was doing, and the genuinely crazy Mae Murray, who apparently never knew what she was doing. Having Gloria Swanson play the part verifies the character, and in fact gives the entire story a credibility it might not otherwise have had."[4]

According to A. C. Lyles at Paramount, Negri met with Wilder and read an early draft of the screenplay for *Sunset Boulevard*. That version was not the final film known to audiences. It was proposed that Negri would act opposite Montgomery Clift. Negri knew the story—as then written—and the casting would not be right for her. Additionally, she had just recently been reunited with her mother and wanted to share time with her. Negri was comfortable financially and did not feel obligated to take the role of Desmond, a reclusive, bitter, and eccentric actress. Negri also knew that Mary Pickford and Mae West had turned down the part.

When Gloria Swanson played Norma Desmond, she was only fifty-one. Even though she guest-starred on TV and appeared on Broadway in her later years, for most people she remained Norma forever: an aging, delusional diva who believes she is still queen of the movie lot, waiting for her close-up with Mr. DeMille.

The specter of Swanson's Norma Desmond, aging and undesirable, was terrifyingly real for actresses like Negri who had also paid the price for fame and fortune and were now mostly forgotten. Negri was still a living legend, but she was quietly slipping into film history. *Sunset Boulevard* brought Gloria Swanson a well-deserved Oscar nomination for her brilliant performance. Whether based on protecting her ego, preserving her image, or fear of ridicule, Negri's decision to pass on Norma Desmond leaves us forever wondering about the potential result of her taking the role, which surely would have been equally magnificent.

When Negri became a U.S. citizen in 1951, it was the consummation of her long love affair with the country. She had been a woman of the world in many different circumstances in many different countries, but she had always wanted to find shelter in the safe arms of the country that made her a star. Margaret threw a big party to celebrate the occasion. From the streamers to the table linens to the cake shaped like a flag, the whole house was done up in red, white, and blue. George Schönbrunn recalls: "They had classes for Europeans who wanted to be citizens. I called up the teacher and I asked if he would like to come over and teach Pola. She learned the amendments and passed the citizenship class, and I was one of her witnesses. So, there she was—the great American. She even appeared on the radio broadcast with Hedda Hopper to tell how happy she was to become an American citizen. She did seem very proud."[5] Schönbrunn remembers that at a party he and Negri attended for presidential candidate Richard Nixon, Negri approached Nixon and said, "I am one of 500,000 Poles that stand behind you, and maybe you will be the next President of something." They were then photographed together.

A few years earlier, Negri had attended a reunion party aboard the *Excalibur,* the ship that had brought her and other refugees back from Europe during the war. "I definitely belong in America," she said when she traveled back from France. It was nice to travel, but even nicer to come home. "She was very proud of becoming an American citizen," remembers Negri's friend Brother Alexis Gonzales.

By 1963, Margaret's health was precarious. But when Disney offered Negri the role of Madame Habib in *The Moon-Spinners,* Margaret managed to persuade Negri to take the role. The studio offered Negri every enticement to come out of retirement. Sadly, Margaret died as the movie was about to go into production. Walt Disney himself offered Negri his condolences and let her know that every allowance would be made. David Gasten of polanegri.com comments:

> Both *Hi Diddle Diddle* and *The Moon-Spinners* are a lot of fun to watch because they are both respectful sendoffs of Pola's feisty wildcat roles from the silent days. You really get a chance to see her real-life persona to some degree. One interesting thing about *The Moon-Spinners* is that Walt Disney was just elated to have Pola out of retirement, so he gave her the red carpet treatment and let her steal that movie, which she does completely. He was so glad to be able to return a favor that she had done for him when he wasn't feeling so well in the twenties. He was so grateful that he jumped at the opportunity to return her kindness and did so several times during the filming of *The Moon-Spinners.*[6]

Negri only has a total of thirty minutes of screen time in *The Moon-Spinners,* but she is the most memorable member of the cast, which included Hayley Mills and Eli Wallach. Madame Habib is a jewel thief who drapes herself in furs and finery, lives on a yacht, and is always eager for more.

Some of the scenes in the movie seem borrowed from the star's own tumultuous life. In one memorable shot, the camera focuses on the back of Madame Habib's hand while she polishes her gemstones with precision. A cheetah lounges nearby on its own fancy pillow. The script originally called for Madame Habib to have a housecat. Negri felt that something more was needed to spice up her part, and the cheetah was her suggestion. This pet perfectly exemplified her persona: proud, graceful, and temperamental.

Actor Eli Wallach, who plays the thief Stratos in the film, remembered Negri's handling of the animal in their big scene: "She said, 'You have the jewels?' and I said, 'Yes, I have the jewels.' She said, 'Come here,' and she sounded wonderful, with real power in her voice. On a large ottoman was sitting a cheetah—a live cheetah. So, I walked towards her with my jewels that I had stolen, and as I walked near the cheetah, the cheetah went 'Grrrr,' and I stopped. And she said to the cheetah, 'Quiet, Shalimar.' Now, every time my wife and I have a fight, she says, 'Quiet, Shalimar!'"[7]

In the opening of the film, before the story begins, we see Madame Habib walking a cheetah. This is more amusing for any viewer familiar with Negri's history of owning exotic pets before it was fashionable. She is also seen washing her jewelry in a glass of champagne. When the camera finally reveals the face connected to such eccentric behavior, the audience sees Pola Negri, and the entire montage makes for a charming self-reference, merging elements of Negri's on-screen and offscreen personas—references that are playful without making fun of the great star. Negri inhabits the character truthfully, which makes it even more comical. Near the end of the film, when her conquered villain states that stars never lie, Negri informs him that everyone lies if it suits their purpose, even stars. Then she goes on to deliver the perfect self-referential quote: "I have survived two wars, four revolutions, and five marriages." The writers of the film provide a perfect vehicle for Negri to reveal her understanding of the business and her own self-awareness. She had great integrity as a star until the end.

Negri's young costar Hayley Mills, who played Nikki Ferris, comments:

> Movie stars have changed since Pola Negri's day. There's far too much attention paid to the private lives of actors and actresses, as if it's important in the great scheme of things. In Pola's day, she and people like her felt a responsibility to the public, and as a result many times what the public was told about the stars wasn't true at all. They would create a persona that fit the image of the star, and that was it. They were given a fantasy. They were the days of great magic—movies in their infancy. They all had a luster that is not there today. There's a lot to be said for being able to identify with the boy or girl next door. In the days of Pola Negri, they gave people something to aspire to.[8]

Negri's scenes for *The Moon-Spinners* were filmed on a London soundstage where she was treated like a queen, at Walt Disney's insistence. Walt and Negri had met in 1927. At the time, he was a struggling artist who had submitted some sketches to Paramount, only to be rejected. Negri liked his work and saw that he had genuine talent. Two nights later, she invited Walt Disney and his wife to a party at her house. Disney never forgot her kindness. Despite being sixty years old, Negri still grabbed attention. Hayley Mills, who was eighteen at the time, found her amazing to look at:

> I first met Pola Negri off the set, in the corridor outside the makeup room. It was a very brief meeting because it was early in the morn-

ing. She arrived that morning as she did every morning, swathed in a black cape and with a black fedora hat pulled down over her eyes and an enormous pair of black glasses. I didn't really get much of an image of what this mysterious diva, this wonderful silent movie star looked like. She went into the makeup room, and the door was shut and locked and nobody was allowed in until she was ready. Then the door was opened and out she came, looking like Cleopatra with that wonderful Cleopatra hair. That's my memory of it—wonderful hair and immaculate makeup and looking beautiful.[9]

Eli Wallach was surprised by Negri's self-assurance:

I thought, my God, she hasn't made a movie in twenty years and here she is—secure. There's a Greek legend where the men tied themselves to the poles because as these women, these sirens, went by they would seduce the men. So, I think she was one of those seducers. When it came to sirens, there was no one like Pola Negri. She was the Marilyn Monroe of her time. I did the last film with Marilyn; I danced with her in that movie. I wish I had a chance to dance with Pola Negri. In all the advertising, the posters they made, she was always in the center giving that glazed look of seduction. I heard stories about all the men she was with.

Pola had dark, big brown eyes, and the clothes she wore always signaled that she was vulnerable but in command. That mixture is what made her a real sex symbol. Pola had that magnetism when you watched her on-screen.[10]

22

Final Days

The Moon-Spinners made a big splash and could have revived Negri's career, but she didn't want to do any more movies. She simply didn't have to work that hard anymore. When she went to London for the premiere, she was well received by the media and felt appreciated among the fans. She decided it was the best moment to withdraw from professional life and leave on a high note. William Hall from the London *Evening News* reported:

> It was in its fantastic, colossal, unbelievable way, a moment of utter glory—the descent of Miss Pola Negri upon her doting public at noon today. Pola Negri, queen of the vamps, temperamental empress of film passion, petticoated cyclone of the twenties— whose heavy-lidded sex appeal caused male audiences to faint in their seats—was in town making a comeback. We waited breathlessly, and Miss Negri did not fail us. A stir in the crowd outside the Dorchester's Gold Room, a gasp, and Miss Negri swept in with a friend. "Friend" being a three-year-old cheetah straining at its steel chain.
>
> Pola Negri, in black satin, black lace elbow-length gloves, her jet-black hair swept under a black turban, did not flinch as the cheetah lashed out with its claws. "Stop that, darling, you will frighten the gentlemen."
>
> To the adulators, the adorers, the admirers thronging the Gold Room, Miss Negri brought the dear, dead, golden days of Hollywood back for one sweet moment.[1]

Tempting as it was to continue, Pola stepped out of the public eye, doing very little self-promotion and immersing herself in her charities instead. Brother Alexis Gonzales explains her involvement:

Pola was very generous to everybody: to the church, to any poverty program. When I told her there were young children and students who wanted to learn something about drama or see some film, Pola always said, "I will donate something for this group," and she always did. Pola would send a check.

I think she was sincere. She was very honest and down to earth. Pola was not the prima donna that the press sometimes made her out to be. She had been a hard worker—a lot of that is in the Polish character. You don't get anything for free; you work for it, and you take pride in what you do—and Pola always did. When Pope John II was elected and she realized he was Polish, she was absolutely delighted.[2]

Negri was content with her present life situation. She liked San Antonio, although Margaret West's death had hit her hard. Because Negri was provided for in Margaret's will, she could have taken up residence anywhere, but she chose to stay in San Antonio. The West family looked after her and tended to her affairs. She had a supportive group of friends and strong association with her church and the priests there. The clear, dry air of San Antonio probably aided her weak lungs. Local children often saw her in the garden among her beautiful flowers, wearing white silk slacks and a broad-brimmed hat. Negri was always kind whenever they approached her. She even let little girls try on her rings. Her skin was still white as fine porcelain, her hair very black with some threads of gray. Negri's gentle smile told everyone that she was at peace.

In 1968, at the Theater of the Performing Arts, Negri received the keys to the city of San Antonio. She was the first person to be honored in this fashion. Her life became deliciously simple. She had a bungalow-type condo at the Chateau Dijon and was attended by a chauffeur and a maid. Sometimes she took part in various civic affairs, but mostly she worked on her book and just enjoyed the luxury of letting life flow by.

When Liza Minnelli was preparing for her award-winning role as Sally Bowles in *Cabaret,* her father, director Vincente Minnelli, urged her to study Pola Negri. In 1974 Vincente Minnelli approached Negri to appear in the film *A Matter of Time* with Liza, but Negri could not accept the role because of her failing eyesight.

Up until the time she turned seventy-seven, Negri traveled to New York twice a year. She made appearances at the Museum of Modern Art when retrospectives of her films appeared there. She was invited to speak at a Rudolph Valentino festival but wasn't able to attend. People applauded when her name was mentioned in connection to Valentino. Negri was a great lady in her final years, forthright and community-minded. She was always smartly dressed in hats, capes, and heels and remained sharp-witted. She smoked long cigarettes until late in life and lived into her nineties. Unlike the Norma Desmond character from *Sunset Boulevard*, she did not live in an apartment full of memorabilia from days gone by.

Negri prayed and attended church regularly, even when it became painful for her to walk. She maintained a close friendship with Father Louis Reile, who was professor of film studies at Saint Mary's University in San Antonio, Texas. She found comfort and guidance in their conversations. Negri was also active in the Republican Party. She understood that people did not work just to support themselves. She had always shared her income with her many friends and her beloved mother, and she was indebted to the country that had made it possible. She was invited to Ronald Reagan's presidential inauguration but was unable to attend.

Writer A. A. Lewis became a close friend of Negri's. He remembers how they first met:

I met Pola Negri through Doubleday. Larry Ashby at Doubleday wanted to do a book about Pola. They were looking for a writer. I had written many plays and a great deal of television, but I had never written a book. My agent called me and said Doubleday wants someone to work with Pola Negri on her memoirs, and they made an offer that I couldn't refuse.

So, I met Larry, and we went to the Plaza Hotel in New York, to what was then the Edwardian Room, and there in the corner, near a window, but shrouded by the curtains, sat Pola Negri. She was quite attractive, certainly did not look her age, or rather what I thought was her age. Larry warned me: "Remember, when she says Rudy, she means Valentino, not Vallee." That was his only warning. . . . She was a genuinely warm, nice woman when one got beneath the mystique, the image, and the legend, which she did so much to promote. I mean, she lived her legend. For instance, in that first meeting, she said to me that it was difficult for her to go shopping at Saks Fifth Avenue because all the people she knew were looking at her and wanting to approach her. It was always this image of this still glamorous, great movie star—a sort of Norma Desmond at that point—but only in public. In private, she was real.[3]

The result of A. A. Lewis's collaboration with Negri was the book *Memoirs of a Star*. It was eventually translated into many languages and remains one of the few sources of information about her early life.

In 1964 Negri was awarded the German Film Prize for "long and extraordinary achievement in the development of German film." She received another distinction in 1968. Saint Mary's University in San Antonio put together a film tribute to Negri, along with a citation for "enriching American culture." In the 1970s, numerous Polish organizations in the United States honored her with awards. Finally, Pola Negri had found her place in history. Her work was in the archives, forever valued and preserved.

Although poor and declining eyesight often kept her at home, she continued to support the arts. For years, Pola Negri remained on the Board of Directors of the San Antonio Symphony and the San Antonio Theater. Bringing culture to the public became one of her pet causes.

Every now and then, reminders would surface of how large Negri's world used to be. One day, she heard from Gloria Swanson, who suggested they should get together and sift through their memories. The press would be so much kinder to them now, since they were off the screen. Gloria had expanded her career to include other ventures: clothing designs (Gowns by Gloria) and health food lectures. She was a walking example of the power of good nutrition. Gloria was also a doting grandmother, having had three children of her own. Unfortunately, she died before the two stars could reunite.

Pola Negri outlived many of her contemporaries. In the end, on August 1, 1987, she died from a brain tumor. She had also been undergoing treatment for pneumonia. Before passing in her sleep, she had one last Hollywood moment. A handsome young doctor read her chart but didn't seem to recognize the name. Negri spoke in a weak voice but with a dramatic tone: "You don't know who I am?" She made it plain that his ignorance was inexcusable.

"Fade to Black" was the *San Antonio Daily News*'s comment in posting her obituary: "Whether she was leading a tiger on a leash, draping herself over Valentino's coffin, or merely painting her toenails red, there were always plenty of cameras in attendance." Jeanine Basinger summarized her life: "Pola Negri is an ideal woman because she's impassioned and fiery and exotic and mysterious on one side, she's down to earth and ordinary and practical and capable and funny on the other. The woman who could get both of those is the woman who leads the best life of all."[4] George Schönbrunn adds: "She was really glamorous. I think she hated white, but she always wore black or white—very rarely any other color. She always said makeup makes you look very old, but she wore false eyelashes and lipstick. She had beautiful skin, which she covered from the sun, and never put any rouge on."[5]

Some people remembered Pola Negri kindly. Others thought she was hard at the core. She mingled with scholars and artists. She married a count and a prince but never needed royalty to play the part of a queen.

Negri donated her personal library to Trinity University in San Antonio. To Saint Mary's University, the oldest and largest Catholic university in the Southwest, she gave a large collection of memorabilia, including several rare prints of her early films. A large portion of her estate also went to Saint Mary's University, which established a scholarship fund in her name.

Nothing remains of Negri's Hollywood home at 610 North Beverly in Beverly Hills. Producer Hal Roach bought it in 1987 and sold it for $4 million in 1988. The new owner had the mansion bulldozed for new construction.

Falcon Lair, Rudolph Valentino's home, was auctioned off after his death to help cover his debts. The new owner paid $145,000 and never moved in. The place stood empty for eight years and was later sold to conductor Werner Janssen and his wife, actress Ann Harding. Gloria Swanson rented the home in 1953. Later, tobacco heiress Doris Duke bought it.

There is a place where the footsteps of Negri, Pickford, and Fairbanks are still visible in Hollywood. Along the front walk of Sid Grauman's world-famous Chinese Theatre, beneath the pagodas and skylights, are the imprints of those original silent stars—stars who knew how to make use of a purely visual medium. They appealed to the audience and could speak volumes in a single gesture. The audience watched for their signals, awaited their cues. Their faces told the story and their images set the trends. Image was all silent stars had to offer, and those images were expertly crafted—larger than life, but never too large for the screen.

Acknowledgments

When I moved to America in 1998, I was surprised to find that Pola Negri had all but slipped into obscurity. The modern-day film buff would be astonished to discover the plethora of press attention to Negri during her lifetime. She was every bit a paparazzo's dream and was followed everywhere she went. Her face decorated magazine covers in more than a dozen countries.

With this in mind, I am very grateful to all the collectors and preservationists from whom I have obtained original articles and magazines featuring Pola Negri. This book is the result of my intensive research, starting in 2002, for my first documentary feature film, titled *Pola Negri: Life Is a Dream in Cinema.* I have been able to study materials from the United States, Poland, England, France, Spain, Brazil, the Netherlands, Russia, Colombia, Germany, and other places. I am also thankful for Negri's generosity in bequeathing much of her own collection and possessions to Saint Mary's University Library in San Antonio, Texas, where Brother Robert Wood was the curator during my research. I would like to thank him for keeping the door open and welcoming my requests to dig deeper and come to know her better.

I am grateful to the following people for giving generously of their time and expertise as I sought out the best interview subjects for the film: Hayley Mills, Eli Wallach, Jeanine Basinger, Scott Eyman, David Gasten, Alexis Gonzales, Emily Leider, Allan Alfred Lewis, A. C. Lyles, George Schönbrunn, Anthony Slide, Howard Mandelbaum, Greg Barrios, and Tony Villecco. These contributors' combined stories and accounts helped paint a colorful portrait of the subject.

For allowing me to view the films Negri made and for access to other research materials, I would like to acknowledge the Lincoln Center Library for the Performing Arts in New York, the Museum of Modern Art in New York, La Cinémathèque Française, Filmoteka Narodowa, the Academy of Motion Picture Arts and Sciences in Los Angeles, and Towarzystwo Kulturalne in Lipno, Poland. It is in seeing Negri's work that one truly grasps the importance of her contribution to the early development of film, especially in Europe. I am grateful for institutions that are tireless in their attempts to find and preserve lost works and make them available to researchers and the public.

The Muzeum Kinematografii in Łodź, Poland, has shown continued dedication to Pola Negri's career; my thanks go especially to Krystyna Zamyslowska and Mieczyslaw Kuzmicki for allowing me access to the museum's unique and precious collection.

When my documentary film about Negri was released in 2006, it had the honor of premiering at the Polish Film Festival in Los Angeles. To Charles Silver and the Museum of Modern Art in New York, which also maintains a body of work by Negri, thank you for allowing me access to it. I also appreciate their giving me the opportunity to have the New York City premiere of my documentary film at their Negri retrospective.

Many drafts of this book have been developed over the years. I would like to thank the following people for their contributions: Elizabeth Kanski, Lynn Moran, Wendy Wheeler, Lea Rosa Garcia, Brian Burrowes, Naomi Emmerson, and Austin Davison.

When my earlier book was published in Poland in 2011, it was due to the faith and hard work of Anna Derengowska and Iwona Pacholec at Proszynski Media. I thank them for guiding me through the process and putting together a beautiful book. Special thanks go to Anna Palka-Boyet for her meticulous translation work from Polish to the English text and to Regan Brown, my editor, whose enthusiasm for the topic was most appreciated.

Most important, I have unending thanks for the editors and staff at the University Press of Kentucky, particularly Anne Dean Dotson, Bailey Johnson, Ila McEntire, Richard Farkas, Blair Thomas, Cameron Ludwick, and copyeditor Linda Lotz. They are the ones who recognized a need to add this book to the field of research on Negri and have devoted countless hours to bringing the book to fruition.

Finally, I would like to thank Pola Negri, who was a true legend and star, dedicated to her work, mysterious, smart, and innovative. May we all strive to be the same.

Chronology

1892   Jerzy Chałupec and Eleonora Kelczewska are married July 10 in Lipno, Poland.

1897   Pola Negri is born Barbara Apolonia Chałupec on January 3 to Jerzy and Eleonora Chałupec in Lipno, Vistula Land (present-day Poland), which at that time was under Russian rule. She was the youngest of three children but grew up as an only child, owing to the early deaths of the other two children. Felicia, her older sister, died of whooping cough in 1899.

1903   Pola's father is arrested for revolutionary activities against Russia and is sent to Siberia. Negri and her mother sell all their possessions in Lipno and move to Warsaw.

1911   Pola is accepted into the Imperial Ballet of Warsaw and begins training as a ballet dancer.

1911   Makes her first public performance at the Imperial Opera in Warsaw as a baby swan in the Baby Swan Chorus in Tchaikovsky's *Swan Lake*.

1911   Begins private acting classes with renowned Polish stage actress and professor Honorata Leszczyńska.

1912   Is accepted into the Warsaw Imperial Academy of Dramatic Arts. The director, Casimir de Hulewicz, becomes her mentor.

1912   Makes her acting debut at the Small Theater in Warsaw on September 2 in Aleksander Fredro's play *Śluby panieńskie* (Maiden vows).

1913   Performs a solo role in the Saint-Léon ballet *Coppélia*. She falls ill with tuberculosis and enters a sanatorium, where she is advised to stop dancing. A poetry reading inspires her to take up acting instead, and she takes on the pseudonym Pola Negri after the Italian poetess Ada Negri.

1914   Graduates from Warsaw Imperial Academy of Dramatic Arts. Her graduating performance is as Hedvig in Henrik Ibsen's *The Wild Duck*. The performance results in offers to join a number of prominent theaters in Warsaw. She performs at the Grand Theater, the Small Theater, and the Summer Theater.

1914   Writes, directs, and performs in the first-ever Polish feature film, *Niewolnica zmysłów* (Slave to her senses), which she sells to Alexander Hertz for fifty dollars. She becomes part of his film company, the Sphinx Film Company.

1915   Continues to perform in films by day under the direction of Hertz and on the Polish stage at night.

1915   Director Ryszard Ordynski of Max Reinhardt's Deutsches Theater Company in Berlin brings *Sumurun* to Warsaw and hires Pola Negri. Reinhardt discovers her on opening night.

1917   Reinhardt's Deutsches Theater troupe hires Negri for his production of *Sumurun* in Berlin, which launches her career in Germany. She meets Ernst Lubitsch.

1917   Signs with independent German film studio Saturn-Film and performs in six films with it.

1917   Signs with UFA, Germany's largest film studio, at the end of the year.

1918   Negri's first UFA release, *Mania,* directed by Eugen Illés, is released at the beginning of the year. (The film was lost for many years. In 2006 it was found, and over five years it was restored and rescored with music by Jerzy Maksymiuk. In 2011, the film had a five-city European tour with live music, in a project organized by Filmoteka Narodowa as part of the Polish presidency in the Council of the European Union.)

1918   *Die Augen der Mumie Mâ* (Eyes of the mummy Ma), directed by Ernst Lubitsch and costarring Emil Jannings, is released, followed by another collaboration with Lubitsch, *Carmen* (*Gypsy Blood*), costarring Emil Jannings.

1918   The German-made UFA film *Der gelbe Schein* (The yellow ticket) is released. Negri plays a Jewish university student in Warsaw during the time of the Russian occupation in Poland. This is the first film to deal with the subject of anti-Semitism. (Later in Negri's career this caused controversy with Joseph Goebbels, who objected to the story line.)

1918   Negri purchases property for her mother in Bydgoszcz near Lipno, where Negri was born, in order to keep her mother close to the family. (Today, a commemorative plaque marks the building.)

1919   Marries Count Eugene Dombski at the Catholic Church Wniebowziecia Najwietszej Marii Panny in Sosnowcu, Poland, on November 5.

1919   UFA releases another five films featuring Negri: *Das Karussell des Lebens* (The carousel of life), *Vendetta* (Blood revenge), *Kreuziget Sie!*

(The woman at the crossroads), *Komtesse Dolly* (Countess Dolly), and *Madame Du Barry.* The latter film is another Negri-Lubitsch collaboration, and it becomes an instant international success. It is released in the United States as *Passion.*

1919   At the premiere of *Madame Du Barry* in Berlin, Charlie Chaplin is introduced to Negri. (Later, in his book *My Trip Abroad,* he said one of the most beautiful things in Europe was Pola Negri.) Negri receives a letter from an adoring fan, an unknown film extra named Rudolph Valentino.

1920   UFA releases four Negri films: *Die Marchesa d'Armiani* (The Marquise of Armiani), *Das Martyrium* (Intrigue), *Arme Violetta* (The red peacock), and another Lubitsch-directed film, *Sumurun,* which is released in the United States as *One Arabian Night.* It is based on the stage play *Sumurun,* which first gave Negri her start in Germany (1915) and was the vehicle that brought Lubitsch and Negri together.

1920   Negri separates from Count Dombski and begins a relationship with German industrialist Wolfgang George Schleber.

1920   *Madame Du Barry* premieres in New York as *Passion* at the Capitol Theatre. It opens on a Sunday and sells 21,000 tickets. One thousand people are turned away. On the first day, the film grosses $12,000. In the first week, the box office takes in $55,000. In the full two-week run, three hundred thousand people see the film. Because of the American ban on German films, it is initially advertised as an Italian film. Its huge success results in a lift of the ban, opening the door for many of Negri's other films to be introduced to the U.S. market.

1920   Negri's father, Jerzy Chałupec, dies.

1921   Producer Ben Blumenthal signs an acting contract with Negri to be fulfilled in the United States.

1921   Negri appears in Lubitsch's expressionist film *Die Bergkatze* (The mountain cat) and in the contemporary costume drama *Sappho* (Mad love).

1922   The final Negri-Lubitsch collaboration in Germany, *Die Flamme* (The flame), is filmed. Negri plays the character of Yvette. This is also the final German silent for Negri, and it is the final German picture for Lubitsch. (It was heavily censored in the United States and was released in 1924 by Paramount as *Montmartre.*)

1922   Jesse Lasky, founder of Famous Players–Lasky in California, goes to Berlin and buys Negri's contract from Ben Blumenthal.

Chronology

1922   Negri divorces Count Dombski.

1922   Famous Players–Lasky licenses Negri's German films, and First National starts to release them in the United States; included are *Carmen, Sumurun, Die Flamme,* and *Sappho.* She is signed to a two-year contract.

1922   In Paris, Negri sits for the world-famous portrait painter Tadeusz Styka.

1922   Arrives in New York City September 12 on the *Majestic* with fellow passenger Mabel Normand and is greeted by Mr. and Mrs. Adolph Zukor.

1923   In Del Monte, California, Charlie Chaplin and Pola Negri announce their engagement.

1923   Negri's first American silent film, *Bella Donna,* is released by Paramount. She appears in a remake of *The Cheat* with Jack Holt and makes a cameo in the all-star film *Hollywood.* She also stars in the epic film *The Spanish Dancer* with Antonio Moreno and Wallace Beery. These films become big successes and establish Negri as a Hollywood celebrity and star.

1924   Negri becomes good friends with Marion Davies, the mistress of William Randolph Hearst, and spends time at San Simeon Castle.

1924   Films *Shadows of Paris, Men,* and *Lily of the Dust.*

1924   Lubitsch and Negri reunite for another Paramount Picture release, *Forbidden Paradise,* their only American film together.

1924   Negri breaks her engagement to Chaplin and establishes a relationship with Rod La Rocque, her costar in *Forbidden Paradise.*

1925   Renews her contract with Paramount Pictures for three more years: $7,500 per week for the first year, $8,500 per week the second year, and $10,000 per week the third year.

1925   Marion Davies officially introduces Rudolph Valentino to Negri at a private costume party. Valentino and Negri, dressed as Cleopatra, dance together to the popular tango "La Cumprasita."

1925   Negri appears as a Eurasian character in *East of Suez,* directed by Raoul Walsh, and as a Mexican character in *Flower of the Night,* directed by Paul Bern. She also appears in two partial comedies, *The Charmer* and *A Woman of the World.* She leaves Rod La Rocque.

1926   Sells her property near Łodź and purchases the Château le Rueil-Séraincourt in Vigny, France.

1926   Appears in *The Crown of Lies* and *Good and Naughty,* two more Paramount pictures.

1926 Valentino goes to Paris to finalize his divorce with Natacha Rambova and returns to Negri in Los Angeles. They become engaged and she gives him fifteen thousand dollars to help him purchase Falcon Lair. (Upon his death the money was returned to her from his estate.)

1926 On June 27 Negri is the maid of honor to MGM actress Mae Murray and Valentino is the best man to Prince David Mdivani. It is at the wedding that Negri first meets David's brother Prince Serge Mdivani.

1926 On July 9 Rudolph Valentino and Negri attend the premiere of what would be Valentino's final film, *Son of the Sheik,* at the Egyptian Theater in Los Angeles.

1926 On August 23, at age thirty-one, Valentino passes away suddenly in New York. Negri is told the news while filming *Hotel Imperial* in Hollywood. The film is put on hiatus as Negri takes a train to attend the funeral in New York. She becomes the first "woman in black." A second funeral is held in Los Angeles. Valentino now rests in the Hollywood Forever cemetery.

1927 *Hotel Imperial* is released and breaks box-office records.

1927 Negri marries Prince Serge Mdivani on May 14 in France.

1927 Appears in *Barbed Wire* and *The Woman on Trial,* both directed by Mauritz Stiller.

1928 Writes the novelette *La vie et le rêve au cinéma* (Life and dreams in cinema). Only two hundred copies are printed. (It was later published in Russian.)

1928 Appears in *The Secret Hour* and *Three Sinners* (as a blond) and then in *The Woman from Moscow* and *Loves of an Actress,* both silent films with soundtracks.

1928 Negri, expecting a child with her husband, decides to return to Château le Rueil-Séraincourt in Vigny, France, and retire from film. Her contract is not renewed with Paramount. Talkies are increasing in popularity.

1928 On April 2 Pola Negri places her hands and feet in front of the famous Grauman's Chinese Theatre, becoming the eleventh star on the sidewalk.

1928 Sculptor Joseph Marie Sert completes a bronze bust of Pola Negri. (She later bequeathed the bust to the National Museum in Warsaw.)

1929 Negri miscarries her baby and falls into a deep depression. Encouraged by her mother to return to making films, she travels to London and meets with George Bernard Shaw and Gaumont

Productions to discuss a film version of *Caesar and Cleopatra*. When the rights prove to be too expensive, an original story by the project's director, German Paul Czinner, is adopted instead. The film is released by Warner UK and Charles Whittaker Productions under the title *The Woman He Scorned;* it is Negri's last silent film.

1929   Gaston Ravel and Tony Lekain offer Negri a role in the French film *Le collier de la reine* (The queen's necklace). She didn't make the film.

1931   Negri divorces Serge Mdivani on April 2.

1931   Performs in a stage production of *The Last Tango* at the Coliseum in London, where she sings gypsy songs in Russian. Her chosen leading man is Reginald Tate. These tremendously successful performances lead Victor Records UK to record her singing with guitar accompaniment by Boris Golovka and a chorus of gypsy singers. The songs are recorded over the course of a two-day session in March, and the singles "Black Eyes" and "Farewell, My Gypsy Camp" are released from these sessions in May.

1931   Sells the château in Vigny and moves to Nice, France.

1932   American Film company RKO–Radio Pictures signs Negri to her first talkie film, *A Woman Commands,* opposite Basil Rathbone and Roland Young. She returns to the United States. The theme song from the film, "Paradise," sung by Negri, becomes an international hit. The success of "Paradise" prompts a hugely successful vaudeville tour for Negri. She and singer Russ Columbo, who also recorded "Paradise," become romantically involved.

1932   The New York premiere of the film *A Woman Commands* is held at the Mayfair Theater on Broadway. Negri is escorted down the red carpet by New York mayor Jimmy Walker.

1932   She convalesces from an illness in Palm Springs and develops a friendship with Albert Einstein.

1933   Negri is scheduled to appear in an extended touring stage production of *A Trip to Pressburg* but falls ill, is only able to perform one show, and defaults on her contract, which later results in a well-publicized lawsuit.

1933   Records a French-language version of "Paradise," which is released as a single by Ultraphone and becomes a huge success.

1933   Is romantically linked with Chicago millionaire Harold McCormick.

1933   Is contracted by Pathé France to appear in the film *Fanatisme,* in which she acts and sings in French. It is released in 1934.

Chronology

1934   Returns to Hollywood. Carl Laemmle, the head of Universal Pictures, approaches Negri with the German screenplay *Mazurka,* to be directed by Willi Forst in Germany. The Reich minister of propaganda, Joseph Goebbels, bans Negri from re-entering Germany, calling her a Jewish gypsy. Hitler later lifts the ban, causing much controversy on both continents. The American industry falsely accuses Negri of sympathizing with the Nazis and participating in propaganda films.

1935   *Mazurka* is filmed in Germany and is released in Europe; it becomes a top-grossing film. Songs from *Mazurka* are released as a single by Odéon Records in Germany.

1936   The head of MGM, Louis B. Mayer, and Irving Thalberg see the film *Mazurka* and offer Negri a role in *The Good Earth.* She has already signed a six-picture contract with the German company UFA and cannot be released.

1936   Negri's film *Moskau-Shanghai* (Moscow-Shanghai) (UFA) is released in Europe. Director Paul Wegener previously appeared as an actor with Negri in *Sumurun.* American rights to *Mazurka* are purchased by Warner Bros.; the original is suppressed from release in America and remade scene-for-scene as the Kay Francis vehicle *Confession,* released in 1937.

1936   A single featuring English-language versions of the songs from *Mazurka* is released on Parlophone in the United Kingdom. Two German-language singles, one featuring music from *Moskau-Shanghai,* are released by Odéon.

1937   Negri's films *Madame Bovary* and *Tango Notturno* are released by UFA. *Madame Bovary* is the only 1930s German Negri film to be released in the United States. Songs from *Tango Notturno* are released as a single by Odéon. The French magazine *Pour Vous* circulates a rumor that Negri is having an affair with Adolf Hitler; she sues the magazine and wins. *Pour Vous* is required to pay her 10,000 francs in damages.

1938   *Die fromme Lüge* (The secret lie) and *Die Nacht der Entscheidung* (The night of decision) are released. Songs from *Die Nacht der Entscheidung* are released as singles by Odéon.

1941   After the Nazis take over France, Negri finds their oppression too difficult to bear and emigrates back to the United States via Lisbon, Portugal. She sails on the ship *Excalibur* and lands at Ellis Island.

1942   Is considered for the role of Pilar in *For Whom the Bell Tolls,* but the role instead goes to Greek actress Katina Paxinou. She turns down a role in the movie *Claudia,* which then goes to Olga Baclanova. Negri goes on a tour to help sell war bonds for the American war effort.

1943   Is offered the role of Wagnerian Genya Smetana in the United Artists–distributed comedy *Hi Diddle Diddle.* The film is directed by Andrew Stone and costars Adolphe Menjou, Martha Scott, and Dennis O'Keefe. While filming, she lives at Falcon Lair.

1943   Tours the United States on the supper club circuit, singing a repertoire based on "Paradise."

1944   Becomes reacquainted with Margaret West, whom she met in New York a decade prior, and the two become best friends.

1944   Turns down numerous offers to rehash her *Hi Diddle Diddle* character in other films. After continuing to do more supper club appearances, Negri decides to retire from show business altogether. Thereafter, she is supported financially by and lives with her friend Margaret West in Los Angeles.

1948   Returns to Europe to sell her property and bring her mother back to live with her, first in New York and then in Los Angeles. Over the years they have addresses in Bel Air, Santa Monica, and Beverly Hills.

1948   Is approached by Billy Wilder to appear in *Sunset Boulevard* as Norma Desmond, opposite Montgomery Clift. She declines because the script is not ready and the character is not right for her. She also has more interest in developing her family life and caring for her mother. The role goes to Gloria Swanson instead.

1951   Becomes an American citizen in Los Angeles.

1952   Negri and Margaret West donate money toward building the Stations of the Cross in the Holy Mother of Czastochowa on West Adams street in Los Angeles.

1954   Negri's mother, Eleonora Chałupec, passes away.

1957   Negri and Margaret West move to San Antonio, Texas. Their residence is in Olmos Park.

1960   Negri is granted a star on the Hollywood Walk of Fame for her contribution to motion pictures.

1963   Margaret West passes away.

1963   Negri agrees to come out of retirement to appear in the Walt Disney film *The Moon-Spinners,* costarring with Eli Wallach and Hayley Mills. Negri films her role in London.

1963   Moves from Margaret West's home to a three-bedroom apartment at the Chateau Dijon on Broadway in San Antonio, where she lives for the rest of her life.

1964   *The Moon-Spinners* is released in London. Negri stays at the Dorchester Hotel. During the press engagements, she makes appearances with a cheetah on a leash, creating a sensation.

1964   Receives award from the German film industry for her "long and extraordinary achievement in the development of German film."

1968   Receives Hemis-Film award at San Antonio's Hemisfair. Saint Mary's University hosts a special film festival of Pola Negri films to acknowledge her for "enriching American culture."

1968–1970   Works with Alfred A. Lewis at the Plaza Hotel in New York to complete her autobiography, *Memoirs of a Star,* published by Doubleday.

1972   Attends the screening of *Carmen* at the Witte Museum in San Antonio.

1973   Attends the screening of her film *Woman of the World* at the New York Museum of Modern Art—an event held in her honor.

1973   Is made an honorary citizen of Los Angeles.

1975   Director Vincente Minnelli brings Negri to Los Angeles to discuss the role of Contessa Sanziani in the film *A Matter of Time.* She is unable to accept it because of her failing health. The role goes to Ingrid Bergman instead.

1978   The title character of Fedora in the Billy Wilder film *Fedora* is based on Pola Negri.

1980   Negri appears in *Life Magazine*'s cover story "Where Are They Now?" which follows up on the whereabouts of many classic film actresses. It is her final high-profile media coverage.

1987   Negri dies on August 1 in San Antonio, Texas, at age ninety. She is buried in Calvary Cemetery, Los Angeles, next to her mother, Eleonora. She leaves most of her estate to Saint Mary's University and Trinity University in Texas, including several rare prints of her films. She donates money to establish a scholarship in her name.

Filmography, Discography, and Stage Works

Films

Polish Silent Period

Note: All of the films in this period were directed by Alexander Hertz and produced by the Sphinx Company.

Niewolnica zmysłow / Der Sklave der Sinne [Slave to her senses] (1914). Poland's first feature film. Released in the United States as *The Polish Dancer.*

Żona [Wife] (1915).

Czarna ksiązka [The black pass] (1915). An early version of *Der gelbe Schein* [The yellow ticket].

Studenci [Students] (1916).

Bestia [Beast] / [Bad girl] (1916).

Tajemnica alei Ujazdowskich [Mystery of Uyazdovsky Lane] (1917). Part of the *Tajemnice Warszawy* [Mysteries of Warsaw] serial.

Pókoj Nr. 13 [Room no. 13] (1917). Part of the *Tajemnice Warszawy* [Mysteries of Warsaw] serial.

Arabella (1917).

Jego ostatni czyn [His last gesture] (1917).

German Silent Period

Nicht lange täuschte mich das Glück (1917). Director: Kurt Matull; Saturn-Film AG. Negri plays a dual supporting role as a nun and as a cabaret dancer.

Zügelloses Blut (1917). Saturn-Film AG.

Küsse, die man stiehlt im Dunkeln (1917). Saturn-Film AG.

Die toten Augen (1917). Saturn-Film AG.

Wenn das Herz in Haß erglüht [When the heart burns with hate] (1917). Director: Kurt Matull; Saturn-Film AG. This film survives and has been shown at La Cinémathèque Française in Paris and at the Museum of Cinematography in Łódź, Poland.

Rosen, die der Sturm entblättert (1918). Saturn-Film AG.

Mania: Die Geschichte einer Zigarettenarbeiterin [Mania: The story of a cigarette girl] (1918). Director: Eugen Illés; UFA; set designer: Paul Leni.

Die Augen der Mumie Mâ / The Eyes of the Mummy Ma (U.S. release title) (1918). Director: Ernst Lubitsch; UFA; costars: Harry Leidtke, Emil Jannings. The first Negri-Lubitsch collaboration.

Der gelbe Schein [The yellow ticket] (1918). Directors: Victor Janson, Eugen Illés, and Paul Ludwig Stein; UFA; costars: Harry Liedtke, Victor Janson.

Carmen / Gypsy Blood (U.S.-release title) (1918). Director: Ernst Lubitsch; UFA; costar: Harry Liedtke.

Das Karussell des Lebens [The carousel of life] / *The Last Payment* (U.S.-release title) (1919). Directors: Victor Janson, Eugen Illés, and Paul Ludwig Stein; UFA; costar: Harry Leidtke.

Blutrache [Blood revenge] / *Vendetta* (1919). Director: Georg Jacoby; UFA; costars: Emil Jannings, Harry Liedtke.

Dämmerung des Todes (1919). Director: Georg Jacoby; UFA.

Kreuziget Sie! [The woman at the crossroads] (1919). Director: Georg Jacoby; UFA; costars: Harry Liedtke, Victor Janson.

Madame Du Barry / Passion (U.S.-release title) (1919). Director: Ernst Lubitsch; UFA; costars: Emil Jannings, Harry Liedtke.

Komtesse Dolly [Countess Dolly] (1919). Director: Georg Jacoby; UFA; costars: Harry Liedtke, Victor Janson.

Die Marchesa d'Armiani [The Marquise of Armiani] (1920). Director: Alfred Halm; UFA.

Sumurun / One Arabian Night (U.S.-release title) (1920). Director: Ernst Lubitsch; UFA; costars: Ernst Lubitsch, Paul Wegener, Harry Liedtke, Jenny Hasselqvist. A film remake of the Max Reinhardt theater production, which also featured Negri and Lubitsch in their same roles. This is the only time the two appeared on-screen together and the last time Lubitsch appeared on-screen as an actor.

Das Martyrium [Intrigue] (1920). Director: Paul Ludwig Stein; UFA.

Die geschlossene Kette [The closed chain] / *Intrigue* (U.S.-release title) (1920). Director: Paul Ludwig Stein; UFA.

Arme Violetta [The red peacock] (1920). Director: Paul Ludwig Stein; UFA.

Die Bergkatze [The mountain cat] / *The Wild Cat* (U.S. release title) (1921). Director: Ernst Lubitsch; UFA; costars: Victor Janson, Paul Heidemann. A German expressionist comedy and parody of the expressionist film genre.

Sappho / *Mad Love* (U.S.-release title) (1921). Director: Dimitri Buchowetzki; UFA; costars: Alfred Abel, Johannes Riemann.

Die Flamme / *Montmartre* (U.S.-release title) (1922). Director: Ernst Lubitsch; Ernst Lubitsch Film GmbH; costars: Alfred Abel, Hermann Thimig. Ernst Lubitsch's final German film.

Paramount Period

Bella Donna (1923). Director: George Fitzmaurice; Famous Players–Lasky / Paramount; costars: Conway Tearle, Conrad Nagel, Adolphe Menjou. Remake of the 1915 film starring Pauline Frederick.

The Cheat (1923). Director: George Fitzmaurice; Famous Players–Lasky / Paramount; costars: Jack Holt, Charles de Roche. Remake of the 1915 film starring Fannie Ward and Sessue Hayakawa.

Hollywood (1923). Director: James Cruze; Famous Players–Lasky / Paramount. Negri plays a cameo role in this film, which features guest appearances from many other Hollywood stars of the period.

The Spanish Dancer (1923). Director: Herbert Brenon; Famous Players–Lasky / Paramount; costars: Antonio Moreno, Wallace Beery, Adolphe Menjou.

Shadows of Paris (1924). Director: Herbert Brenon; Famous Players–Lasky / Paramount; costars: Charles de Roche, Adolphe Menjou, George O'Brien.

Men (1924). Director: Dimitri Buchowetzki; Famous Players–Lasky / Paramount.

Lily of the Dust (1924). Director: Dimitri Buchowetzki; Famous Players–Lasky / Paramount; costars: Ben Lyon, Noah Beery, Raymond Griffith.

Forbidden Paradise (1924). Director: Ernst Lubitsch; Famous Players–Lasky / Paramount; costars: Rod La Rocque, Adolphe Menjou, Pauline Starke, Clark Gable (in a bit role). The only American Lubitsch-Negri collaboration and their final film together.

East of Suez (1925). Director: Raoul Walsh; Famous Players–Lasky / Paramount; costars: Edmund Lowe, Noah Beery. Negri's only film directed by Raoul Walsh.

The Charmer (1925). Director: Sidney Olcott; Famous Players–Lasky / Paramount.

Flower of the Night (1925). Director: Paul Bern; Famous Players–Lasky / Paramount; costars: Warner Oland, Gustav von Seyffertitz.

A Woman of the World (1925). Director: Malcom St. Clair; Famous Players–

Lasky / Paramount; costars: Charles Emmet Mack, Holmes Herbert, Chester Conklin.

The Crown of Lies (1926). Director: Dimitri Buchowetzki; Famous Players–Lasky / Paramount.

Good and Naughty (1926). Director: Malcom St. Clair; Famous Players–Lasky / Paramount; costars: Ford Sterling, Miss Du Pont.

Hotel Imperial (1927). Director: Mauritz Stiller; Famous Players–Lasky / Paramount; costars: James Hall, George Siegmann, Max Davidson.

Barbed Wire (1927). Directors: Rowland V. Lee, Mauritz Stiller; Paramount; costars: Clive Brook, Einer Hanson, Gustav von Seyffertitz. Mauritz Stiller started the film but was replaced by Rowland V. Lee early on.

The Woman on Trial (1927). Director: Mauritz Stiller; Paramount.

The Secret Hour (1928). Director: Rowland V. Lee; Paramount.

Three Sinners (1928). Director: Rowland V. Lee; Paramount; costars: Warner Baxter, Paul Lukas, Olga Baclanova.

The Woman from Moscow (1928). Director: Ludwig Berger; Paramount; costars: Norman Kerry, Paul Lukas, Otto Matiesen. Silent film with soundtrack.

Loves of an Actress (1928). Director: Ludwig Berger; Paramount; costars: Nils Asther, Paul Lukas. Silent film with soundtrack.

International Period

Note: The international period also includes the German sound period.

The Woman He Scorned / The Way of Lost Souls / Street of Abandoned Children (1929). Director: Paul Czinner; Charles Whittaker Productions UK (distributed by Warners UK), United Kingdom; costars: Hans Rehmann, Warwick Ward. Silent film with soundtrack. Negri's final silent film.

A Woman Commands / Maria Draga (1932). Director: Paul L. Stein; RKO, United States; costars: Basil Rathbone, Roland Young, H. B. Warner. Negri's first sound film; features the songs "Paradise," "I Wanna Be Kissed," "Promise You Will Remember Me." "Paradise" was a major hit and went on to become a standard for many years; it was covered by Russ Colombo and Louis Prima, featured in the television show *Adventures in Paradise,* and used as soundtrack music for other films of the time.

Fanatisme (1934). Directors: Tony Lekain, Gaston Ravel; Pathé, France. Negri's only French film; features her singing three songs.

Mazurka (1935). Director: Willi Forst; Cine-Allianz/Tobis-Klangfilm, Germany; costars: Ingeborg Theek, Paul Hartmann, Albrecht Schoenhals. Features the songs "Je sens en moi," "Mazurka," and "Nur eine Stunde." Remade in 1937 by Warner Bros. as *Confession,* starring Kay Francis and directed by Joe May of Germany.

Moskau-Shanghai / Von Moskau der Shanghai / Der Weg nach Shanghai / Begenung in Shanghai / Zwischen Moskau und Shanghai / Moscow-Shanghai (1936). Director: Paul Wegener; UFA, Germany; costar: Gustav Diessl. Features the song "Mein Herz hat Heimweh . . ."

Madame Bovary (1937). Director: Gerhard Lamprecht; UFA, Germany. Negri's only German sound film to be shown in the United States.

Tango Notturno (1937). Director: Fritz Kirchoff; UFA, Germany; costar: Albrecht Schoenhals. Features the songs "Ich Hab an dich Gedacht" and "Kommt das Glück nicht heut? Dann kommt es Morgen."

Die fromme Lüge [The secret lie] (1937). Director: Nunzio Malasomma; UFA, Germany; costar: Hermann Braun.

Die Nacht der Entscheidung [The night of decision] (1938). Director: Nunzio Malasomma; UFA, Germany; costar: Iván Petrovich. Features the songs "Siehst du die Sterne am Himmel" and "Zeig' der Welt nicht dein Herz."

Final Films (United States)

Hi Diddle Diddle (1943). Director: Andrew L. Stone; Andrew L. Stone Productions (distributed by United Artists); costars: Adolphe Menjou, Martha Scott, Billie Burke, Dennis O'Keefe, June Havoc.

The Moon-Spinners (1964). Director: James Nielson; Walt Disney Productions; costars: Hayley Mills, Eli Wallach.

Discography

"Adieu" ("Farewell, My Gypsy Camp"). 1931. Small Queen's Hall, London. Accompanied by Boris Golovka and two others on guitar, with chorus. His Master's Voice OB-649, HMV B-3820.

"For That One Hour." c. early 1936. Berlin. English-language version of "Nur eine Stunde." From the film *Mazurka.* Parlophone R 2271.

"Ich hab an dich Gedacht." 1937. Berlin. Song from the film *Tango Notturno* (1937). Orchestra arranged by Hans-Otto Borgmann. Odéon P Be 11891, 0-4765.

"Ich möchte einmal nur mein ganzes Herz verschwenden." 1936. Berlin. Orchestra arranged by Hans-Otto Borgmann. Odéon P Be 11433, 0-4742.

"Je sens en moi." 1935. Berlin. Song from the film *Mazurka* (1935). Composed and arranged by Peter Kreuder. Odéon P Be 10937, 0-4723.

"Kommt das Glück nicht heut? Dann kommt es Morgen." 1937. Berlin. Song from the film *Tango Notturno* (1937). Orchestra arranged by Hans-Otto Borgmann. Odéon P Be 11892, 0-4765.

"Mein Herz hat Heimweh." 1936. Berlin. Song from the film *Moskau-Shanghai* (1936). Orchestra arranged by Hans-Otto Borgmann., Odéon P Be 11432-2, 0-4742.

"Mes nuits sont mortes." 1933. Paris. Ultraphone P 76523, AP 989.

"Nur eine Stunde." 1935. Berlin. Song from the film *Mazurka* (1935). Composed and arranged by Peter Kreuder. 128338. Odéon P Be 10938-3, 0-4723.

"Ochye Tchornia" [Black eyes]. 1931. Small Queen's Hall, London. Accompanied by Boris Golovka and two others on guitar, with chorus. His Master's Voice OB-647, HMV B-3820.

"Os sho tass." 1931. Small Queen's Hall, London. Accompanied by Boris Golovka and two others on guitar, with chorus. His Master's Voice OB-643 (not released).

"Paradis." 1934. French-language version of "Paradise"; A-side of single AP 989 Ultraphone P 76524, AP 989.

"Paradise." 1933. From the film *A Woman Commands* (1932).

"Siehst du die Sterne." 1938. Berlin. Song from the film *Die Nacht der Entscheidung* (1938). Orchestra arranged by Lothar Bruhne. Odéon P Be 12172, 0-288233.

"Stay Close to Me." c. early 1936. Berlin. English-language version of "Je sens en moi." Original version from the film *Mazurka* (1935). Parlophone R 2271, 128397.

"Sto nam gore?" [Why are you sorry?]. 1931. Small Queen's Hall, London. Accompanied by Boris Golovka and two others on guitar, with chorus. His Master's Voice OB-642, HMV EK-114.

"Two Guitars" (a.k.a. "Gypsy, Sing!"). 1931. Small Queen's Hall, London. Accompanied by Boris Golovka and two others on guitar, with chorus. Dedicated to Pola Negri by Boris Golovka. His Master's Voice OB-650, HMV EK-114.

"Ve chantasni" [The hour of longing]. 1931. Small Queen's Hall, London. Accompanied by Boris Golovka and two others on guitar, with chorus. His Master's Voice OB-641, HMV EK-114.

"Vergis deine Sehnsucht." 1936. Berlin. Orchestra arranged by W. Schmidt-Boelcke. Odéon P Be 11241, 0-4736.

"Wenn die Sonne hinter den Dachem versinkt." 1936. Berlin. Orchestra arranged by W. Schmidt-Boelcke. Odéon P Be 11242, 0-4736.

"Why Fall in Love?" 1931. Small Queen's Hall, London. Accompanied by Boris Golovka and two others on guitar, with chorus. His Master's Voice OB-648, HMV EK-115.

"Zeig der Welt nicht dein Herz." 1938. Berlin. Song from the film *Die Nacht der Entscheidung*. Orchestra arranged by Lothar Bruhne. Odéon P Be 12171, 0-288233.

Stage Works

Imperial Academy of Dance, Warsaw. 1911. Stage debut (dance). Pyotr Ilyich Tchaikovsky's *Swan Lake*. Negri's first public dance performance, in the chorus of baby swans.

Small Theater, Warsaw. 1912. Aleksander Fredro's *Śluby panieńskie*. Negri played the role of Aniela. It was revived in 1915.

Small Theater, Warsaw. October 1912. Theater debut (comedy). Molière's *L'école des femmes*. Negri made her theatrical stage debut before her graduation.

Small Theater, Warsaw. October 1912. Theater debut (drama). Maria Konopnicka's *Imagina*. An epic poem in praise of Polish nationalism.

National Theater, Warsaw. 1912. Ballet. Arthur Saint-Léons's *Coppélia*.

Casino Cinema, Łodź. 1913. The musical *Rozpasana*.

Small Theater, Warsaw. 1914. Henrik Ibsen's *The Wild Duck*. Negri played the role of Hedvig Ekdal.

Imperial Theater, Warsaw. 1914. Henrik Ibsen's *The Wild Duck*. Negri played the role of Hedvig Ekdal.

Casino Cinema, Łodź. December 31, 1914. Variety, dance. *New Year's Eve Ball*. Negri dances choreography from the play *Sumurun* (*One Arabian Night*).

Little Theater, Warsaw. 1915. Theater (drama). Bjornson's *Bankructwo*. Cast: Stefan Jaracz, Pola Negri, Bielecki, Zmijewska, Przystanski, Ryszkowski, Bromczowa.

Grand Theater, Warsaw. 1915. Variety show. Outdoor summer theater for the public.

Summer Theater in the Saxon Garden, Warsaw. 1915. Variety show.

Warsaw. February 2, 1915. *Niema z Portici* or *Die Stumme von Portici*.

Theater Nowosci, Warsaw. 1916. Drama, dance. Friedrich Freksa's *Sumurun* (*One Arabian Night*). Director: Ryszard Ordynski; cast: Stanislaw Kroke

Zawadzki, Wanda Osterwona, Waleria Gnatowska, Wlodyslaw Szczawinski, Juliusz Osterwa, Ryszard Ordynski, Pola Negri, Henryk Malkowski, Maryan Domoslowski, Michal Silvini, Edmund Jagielski.

Casino Cinema, Łodź. 1917. Variety, dance. *Dance of Passion.* Negri performed with Mr. Sobiszewski.

Rozmaitosci Theater, Warsaw. 1915–1917. Henrik Ibsen's *The Wild Duck* and other productions.

The Deutsches Theater, Berlin. 1917. Friedrich Freksa's *Sumurun (One Arabian Night).* Director: Max Reinhardt; cast: Ernst Lubitsch, Ryszard Ordynski, Pola Negri. This production was a great success and triumph for Reinhardt in Berlin and marks the first time Negri and Lubitsch worked together.

The Coliseum, London. February 1929. *Farewell to Love,* adapted by Max Frantel and Pierre Lagarde and produced by Norman Loring. Accompanied by the famous Gypsy Boris Golovka. Cast: Pola Negri, Frank Strickland, Richard Turner, Reginald Tate, Jose Padilla, Lydia Ferreira, Raymond Wilbert, Rigoletto Bros. & Co., Carr Brothers & Betty, Walter Williams, Bob Alden, Jenny Howard, Auntie, Los Olwars, Judy, The Cut Pup. Negri was assigned the same dressing room at the Coliseum as Sarah Bernhardt.

Schubert Organization, U.S. Tour. February 1932. George Jessel's Variety Revue. Cast: George Jessel, Pola Negri, Burns Allen, Marion Eddy, Russ Columbo, Aaron's Commanders, Mordecai Wells, and Taylor Albertina Rausch Dancing Stars.

Schubert Theater, New York. 1933. Variety show, *Trip to Petersburg.* Negri sang "Paradise" and performed a dramatic sketch.

U.S. Tour. 1932–1933. Variety show. Author-journalist Jack Lait wrote a sketch that Negri performed along with her song "Paradise," written by Nacio Herb Brown. She performed in theaters in New York, Boston, Chicago, Philadelphia, Atlanta, and New Orleans alongside George Jessel and Milton Berle.

La Scala, Berlin. 1936–1937. Written by S. S. Varady. *Hollywood.* Music by Peter Kreuder. Director: Eduard Duisberg; cast: Pola Negri, Harry Frank, Willy Schaeffers, Fritz Fischer, Albert Horrmann, Anne Schonstedt, Heinz Weidecker, Woldemar Runge.

Copley Plaza, Boston. 1945. Variety show. Negri performed her song "Paradise" and a dramatic sketch.

Hollywood Radio Theater, Los Angeles. 1943. Producer: C. P. Macgregor. Negri was involved in various radio dramatizations and broadcasts.

Nightclub tour, northeastern United States. 1945–1946. Variety show. Negri performed songs and sketches.

Notes

Introduction

1. "Pola Negri, Hollywood's Vamp," Combined News Services, August 3, 1987.

2. Marjorie Clapp, "Pola Negri: An Exclusive Interview," *San Antonio Light,* August 23, 1970.

3. Ibid.

4. Harry Carr, "The Mystery of Pola Negri," *Motion Picture,* April 1925.

1. Early Years in Poland

1. Pola Negri, "Pola Negri, Noted Screen Actress, Tells How Cossacks Looted and Burned Childhood Home," *Boston Globe,* October 15, 1922.

2. Pola Negri, "The Truth about Charlie Chaplin's Bride," *Picture Show,* March 10, 1923.

3. Pola Negri, "Rudy Valentino and I! My Great True Love Story," *True Story,* April 1932.

4. Lewis, interview.

5. Negri, *Memoirs of a Star.*

6. Stawski, *Pola Negri.*

7. Negri, *Memoirs of a Star.*

8. *Kurier Warszawski,* September 1912.

9. Pola Negri, "The Autobiography of Pola Negri, Part I," *Photoplay,* February 1924.

10. Negri, *Memoirs of a Star.*

11. Pola Negri, "Pola Negri Produced Her First Film Alone and under Great Difficulties," *Cleveland Plain Dealer Sunday Magazine,* November 5, 1922.

12. Ibid.

13. Eyman, interview.

14. Michal Oleszczyk, "Our Far-Flung Correspondents," *Chicago Sun-Times,* January 5, 2013.

2. The Move to Berlin

1. Friedrich, *Before the Deluge.*

2. Eisner, *The Haunted Screen.*

3. Pola Negri, "Kant and Schopenhauer Comfort Film Star in Her Hours of Sadness," *Cleveland Plain Dealer Sunday Magazine*, November 12, 1922.

4. Negri, *Memoirs of a Star*.

5. Slide, interview.

3. With Lubitsch in Germany

1. Negri, *Memoirs of a Star*.

2. Ibid.

3. *New York Times*, May 9, 1921.

4. "The Screen Hall of Fame: A Dozen Stars Name Their Favorite Role," *Motion Picture*, January 1927.

5. *New York Times*, May 9, 1921.

6. *Photoplay*, June 1921.

7. *Wid's Daily*, May 10, 1921.

8. Harriet Underhill, "On the Screen," *New York Tribune*, May 9, 1923.

9. Pola Negri, "The Autobiography of Pola Negri, Part II," *Photoplay*, March 1921.

10. Negri, *Memoirs of a Star*.

11. *New York Times*, December 6, 1920.

12. Eyman, *Ernst Lubitsch*.

13. *New York Times*, December 6, 1920.

14. *New York Daily News*, quoted in Zierold, *Sex Goddesses of the Silent Screen*.

15. Negri, "Autobiography, Part II."

16. Adele Whitely Fletcher, "Across the Silversheet," *Motion Picture*, February 1921.

17. Negri, *Memoirs of a Star*.

18. Lewis, interview.

19. Lewandowski, *Pola Negri w Sosnowcu*.

20. Negri, "Autobiography, Part II."

4. Postwar Berlin

1. Negri, *Memoirs of a Star*.

2. Ibid.

3. Pola Negri, "Pola Negri Writes Her Life Story for Movie Weekly Readers," *Movie Weekly*, September 16, 1924.

4. *Photoplay*, December 1921.

5. Adele Whitely Fletcher, "Across the Silversheet," *Motion Picture*, December 1921.

6. *Motion Picture Classic*, December 1921.

7. Herbert Howe, "The Real Pola Negri," *Photoplay*, November 1922.

8. Eyman, interview.

5. Switzerland to Paris to New York

1. Negri, *Memoirs of a Star*.

2. "Polish Film Star to Appear in Series of Paramount Pictures," *New York Times,* July 7, 1922.

3. Lewis, interview.

6. Coming to Hollywood

1. Negri, *Memoirs of a Star.*
2. Schönbrunn, interview.
3. Helen Klumph, "Now We Know about Pola," *Picture-Play,* December 1922.
4. Negri, *Memoirs of a Star.*
5. Slide, interview.
6. Lyles, interview.
7. Leider, interview.
8. Card, *Seductive Cinema.*
9. Pola Negri, "Love Was My Undoing," *American Weekly,* November 29, 1942.
10. Mary Jane Manners, "The Hollywood That Used to Be," *Silver Screen,* October 1943.
11. Ibid.
12. Basinger, interview.

7. Paramount Pictures, 1922

1. "Pola Negri in Bella Donna," 1923 theater poster.
2. *Time,* April 21, 1923.
3. *New York Times,* April 16, 1923.
4. *Film Daily,* March 19, 1923.
5. *Photoplay,* September 1923.
6. Helen Carlisle, "Why We Love Them: Pola Negri Tells Frankly of Her Leading Men as She Has Come to Know Them," *Movie Weekly,* February 21, 1925.
7. *Los Angeles Times,* July 18, 1923.
8. Ibid.
9. *New York Times,* January 22, 1922.
10. Slide, interview.
11. Lyles, interview.

8. Engagement to Chaplin

1. Chaplin, *My Trip Abroad.*
2. Negri, *Memoirs of a Star.*
3. Pola Negri, "Love Was My Undoing," *American Weekly,* November 29, 1942.
4. "Charlie, Pola to Go to Orient," *San Francisco Examiner,* January 30, 1923.
5. Slide, interview.
6. Alma Whitaker, "Heart and Mind in Grim Battle: A Penetrating Analysis of Romance between Pola Negri and Charlie Chaplin," *Los Angeles Times,* May 13, 1923.

7. "Pola Negri Is Happy as 'Love Spat' Ends," *New York Herald,* March 3, 1923.

8. Lewis, interview.

9. "Pola Says—I Have Finished with Love," *Pearson's Weekly,* February 14, 1931.

10. "Chaplin's Romance with Pola Is 'Definitely' Broken," *New York Herald,* July 29, 1923.

11. Grace Kingsley, "What America Has Done for Pola Negri," *Movie Weekly,* April 21, 1923.

12. "A Chat with Pola Negri," *New York Times,* March 22, 1925.

13. Negri, *Memoirs of a Star.*

9. Gloria Swanson

1. Ruth Biery, "Inside Politics of the Studios," *Photoplay,* August 1931.

2. Cal York, "Studio News and Gossip East and West," *Photoplay,* October 1925.

3. Nancy Pryor, "Pola Comes Back to Hollywood," *Motion Picture,* August 1931.

4. Chaplin, *My Autobiography.*

5. Basinger, *Silent Stars.*

6. Lyles, interview.

7. Ruth Biery, "Hollywood's Age of Fear," *Photoplay,* July 1931.

10. Paramount Pictures, 1923–1924

1. Grace Kingsley, "What America Has Done for Pola Negri," *Movie Weekly,* April 21, 1923.

2. Harry Carr, "The Mystery of Pola Negri," *Motion Picture,* April 1925.

3. Leider, *Dark Lover.*

4. Eyman, *Ernst Lubitsch.*

5. *Photoplay,* September 1923.

6. *Film Daily,* October 14, 1923.

7. *New York Times,* February 28, 1924.

8. Carr, "The Mystery of Pola Negri."

9. *New York Times,* May 5, 1924.

10. *Photoplay,* July 1924.

11. *Time,* May 12, 1924.

12. *New York Times,* August 25, 1924.

13. Ibid.

11. Forbidden Paradise

1. Negri, *Memoirs of a Star.*

2. Harry Carr, "The Mystery of Pola Negri," *Motion Picture,* April 1925.

3. Harry Carr, "Harry Carr's Page," *Los Angeles Times*, November 12, 1924.

4. Basinger, interview.

5. *Photoplay*, May 1924.

6. "Polish Star Gives Dynamic Trend to Czarina," *San Francisco Examiner*, November 11, 1924.

7. *Film Daily*, November 30, 1924.

8. Eunice Marshall, "The New Pola," *Screenland*, June 1924.

12. Becoming a Star

1. Helen Carlisle, "Why We Love Them: Pola Negri Tells Frankly of Her Leading Men as She Has Come to Know Them," *Movie Weekly*, February 21, 1925.

2. Ibid.

3. Ibid.

4. Ibid.

5. Ibid.

6. Ibid.

7. Ibid.

8. Pola Negri, "The Autobiography of Pola Negri, Part II," *Photoplay*, March 1924.

9. Negri, *Memoirs of a Star*.

10. Lewis, interview.

11. *Photoplay*, June 1925.

12. *New Yorker*, April 18, 1925.

13. Mordaunt Hall, "A Magnetic Pola," *New York Times*, October 19, 1925.

14. *Film Daily*, October 25, 1925.

15. *Time*, November 2, 1925.

16. "Pola Negri Says—I Have Finished with Love," *Pearson's Weekly*, February 14, 1931.

17. Mordaunt Hall, "The Screen," *New York Times*, December 14, 1925.

18. *Photoplay*, February 1926.

13. Finding Valentino

1. Leider, interview.

2. Leider, *Dark Lover*.

3. Leider, interview.

4. Negri, *Memoirs of a Star*.

5. Ibid.

6. Lewis, interview.

14. Losing Valentino

1. Lyles, interview.

2. Villecco, interview.

3. Morris, *Madam Valentino.*

4. Leider, interview.

5. *National Board of Review Magazine,* December 1926.

6. Oberfirst, *Rudolph Valentino.*

7. "Pink Powder Puffs," *Chicago Tribune,* July 18, 1926.

8. Botham and Donnelly, *Valentino.*

9. Herbert Howe, "The Prodigal Daughter Returns," *New Movie Magazine,* October 1931.

10. Leider, interview.

11. Corinne Rich, "Valentino's Last Words for Pola," *Los Angeles Examiner,* August 31, 1926.

12. Edwin Schallert, "Pola Ends an Eventful Chapter," *Picture Play,* October 1928.

13. Ibid.

15. Paramount Pictures, 1927

1. Lanza and Penna, *Russ Columbo and the Crooner Mystique.*

2. *Film Daily,* March 7, 1927.

3. Basinger, interview.

16. Princess Mdivani

1. Gasten, interview.

2. Negri, *La vie et le rêve au cinéma.*

17. Working in Europe

1. Negri, *Memoirs of a Star.*

2. "Aeronautics: British Tragedies," *Time,* May 18, 1931.

3. History of the London Coliseum, www.arthurlloyd.co.uk/LondonColiseum.htm.

4. "Pola Negri So Sad! Disappointing Stage Debut," *Evening Standard* (London), February 10, 1931.

5. "Pola Saved by Kiss: Audience Escapes Boredom by One Minute," *Daily Mail* (London), February 10, 1931.

6. "Wax Dummies and Pola Negri: Strange Music Hall Scene," *News Chronicle* (London), February 10, 1931.

7. *Motion Picture,* July 1931.

8. Ewart Hodgon, "Pola Negri," *Daily Express* (London), June 18, 1931.

9. Nancy Pryor, "Pola Comes Back to Hollywood," *Motion Picture,* August 1931.

10. Edwin Schallert, "Pola Ends an Eventful Chapter," *Picture Play,* October 1928.

11. "Pola Negri: Two Offers to Appear in Talkies," *Evening Standard* (London), March 6, 1931.

12. F. A. Beaumont, "Negri's Private Role as Fairy Godmother," *People,* January 25, 1931.

18. First Talkie

1. *Photoplay,* August 1931.

2. Nancy Pryor, "Pola Comes Back to Hollywood," *Motion Picture,* August 1931.

3. *Picture Play,* July 1931.

4. Herbert Howe, "The Prodigal Daughter Returns," *New Movie Magazine,* October 1931.

5. "Pola Negri Undergoes a Serious Operation," *New York Times,* December 16, 1931.

6. "Einstein Winks at Pola in Comment on Hitler Photos," *New York Times,* January 14, 1932.

7. *Photoplay,* February 1932.

8. *Time,* February 8, 1932.

9. Basinger, interview.

10. Lanza and Penna, *Russ Columbo and the Crooner Mystique.*

11. "Settlement Fails to Save New Play," *New York Times,* February 26, 1934.

19. Return to UFA

1. Lewis, interview.

2. "Files Liens on Pola Negri," *New York Times,* November 18, 1929.

3. Negri, *Memoirs of a Star.*

4. Sydney Carroll, "Mazurka," *London Sunday Times,* undated clipping.

5. Schoenhals and Born, *Immer zu zweit.*

6. "Reich Bans Pola Negri in Film," *New York Times,* February 1, 1935.

7. "Hitler Removes Ban on Pola Negri Film," *New York Times,* February 2, 1935.

8. Kreuder, *Nur Puppen haben keine Tränen.*

9. Lewis, interview.

10. Gasten, interview.

11. "Pola Negri Wins Suit," *New York Times,* July 16, 1939.

12. Basinger, *Silent Stars.*

20. Escape from Germany

1. *Time,* July 26, 1943.

2. Lewis, interview.

21. Life with Margaret West

1. Schönbrunn, interview.
2. Ibid.
3. Gonzales, interview.
4. Basinger, interview.
5. Schönbrunn, interview.
6. Gasten, interview.
7. Wallach, interview.
8. Mills, interview.
9. Ibid.
10. Wallach, interview.

22. Final Days

1. William Hall, *Evening News* (London), quoted in Negri, *Memoirs of a Star.*
2. Gonzales, interview.
3. Lewis, interview.
4. Basinger, interview.
5. Schönbrunn, interview.

Bibliography

Printed and Electronic Materials

Agate, James. *Around Cinemas*. London: Home & Van Thal, 1946.

Alexandria, Virginia. *The Jazz Age*. New York: Time-Life, 1998.

Anger, Kenneth. *Hollywood Babylon*. New York: Bantam Doubleday Dell, 1975.

Ankerich, Michael G. *Mae Murray: The Girl with the Bee-Stung Lips*. Lexington: University Press of Kentucky, 2013.

Barry, Iris. *Let's Go to the Movies*. New York: Payson & Clarke, 1926.

Barthes, Roland. *Mythen des Alltags*. Frankfurt, Germany: Suhrkamp Verlag, 1964.

Basinger, Jeanine. *Silent Stars*. New York: Alfred A. Knopf, 1999.

Beinhorn, Courtenay Wyche. "The Film Career of Pola Negri." Master's thesis, University of Texas at Austin, 1975.

Blum, Daniel. *A Pictorial History of the Silent Screen*. New York: G. P. Putnam's, 1953.

Bodeen, DeWitt, and Gene Ringgold. *Pola Negri*. New York: Screen Facts, 1961.

Botham, Noel, and Peter Donnelly. *Valentino: The Love God*. London: Everest Books, 1976.

Brooks, Alfred G., ed. *Max Reinhardt*. Catalogue of the Max Reinhardt Exhibition, New York Cultural Center, June 7–August 4, 1974. Binghamton, NY: Max Reinhardt Archive / State University at Binghamton, 1974.

Brownlee, Kevin. *Hollywood: The Pioneers*. London: William Collins, 1979.

———. *The Parade's Gone By*. Berkeley: University of California Press, 1968.

Calistro, Paddy, and Fred E. Basten. *The Hollywood Archive: The Hidden History of Hollywood in the Golden Age*. New York: Universe, 2000.

Card, James. *Seductive Cinema: The Art of Silent Film*. New York: Alfred A. Knopf, 1994.

Carter, Graydon, and David Friend, eds. *Vanity Fair's Hollywood*. New York: Viking, 2000.

Carter, Huntley. *The Theater of Max Reinhardt*. New York: Benjamin Bloom, 1914; reissued, 1964.

Cawthorne, Nigel. *Sex Lives of the Hollywood Idols*. London: Prion Books, 1997.

Chaplin, Charles. *My Autobiography.* Brooklyn, NY: Melville House, 2012.

——. *My Trip Abroad.* New York: Harper, 1922.

Clarke, David. *Location: Cornwall.* Ilkey, UK: Bossiney Books, 1990.

Corey, Melinda, and George Ochoa. *The American Film Institute.* London: Stonesong Press, 2002.

Crow, Cameron. *Conversations with Wilder.* New York: Bonzoi Books / Alfred A. Knopf, 1999.

Dyer, Richard. *Stars.* London: British Film Institute, 1998.

Edmonds, I. G., and Reiko Mimura. *Paramount Pictures and the People Who Made Them.* San Diego: A. S. Barnes, 1980.

Eisner, Lotte H. *The Haunted Screen: Expressionism in the German Cinema and the Influence of Max Reinhardt.* English translation of *L'écran demoniaque,* 1952 and 1965. Los Angeles: University of California Press, 1969.

Endres, Stacey, and Robert Cuschman. *Hollywood at Your Feet: The Story of the World-Famous Chinese Theatre.* Huntington Beach, CA: Pomegranate Press, 1992.

Everson, William K. *American Silent Film.* Cambridge, MA: Da Capo Press, 1998.

Eyman, Scott. *Ernst Lubitsch: Laughter in Paradise.* New York: Simon & Schuster, 1993.

Fowler, Guy. *A Woman Commands.* New York: Grosset & Dunlap, 1931.

Friedrich, Otto. *Before the Deluge: A Portrait of Berlin in the 1920s.* Harper Collins: New York, 1995.

Gasten, David. Pola Negri Appreciation Site, www.polanegri.com.

Golden, Eve. "The Opportunist: Pola Negri on Her (More or Less) Centenary." *Classic Images,* www.classicimages.com/1997/december97/negri.html, 1997.

Greene, Laurence. *The Era of Wonderful Nonsense: A Casebook of the Twenties.* Indianapolis: Bobbs Merrill, 1939.

Griffith, Richard, and Arthur Mayer. *The Movies.* New York: Simon & Schuster, 1957.

Guiles, Fred Lawrence. *Marion Davies.* New York: McGraw-Hill, 1972.

Hake, Sabine. *Passions and Deceptions: The Early Films of Ernst Lubitsch.* Princeton, NJ: Princeton University Press, 1992.

Hallett, Hilary A. *Go West, Young Women! The Rise of Early Hollywood.* Berkeley: University of California Press, 2013.

Hichens, Robert. *Bella Donna.* New York: A. L. Burt, 1909.

Holman, Russel. *The Cheat.* Edited by Pola Negri. Based on the story by Hector Turnball. New York: Grosset & Dunlap, 1923.

Hugo, Victor. *The Spanish Dancer.* Trans. Henry L. Williams. Based on a stage play by Adolph d'Ennery and P. S. P. Dumanoir. New York: Grosset & Dunlap, 1901.

Hull, David Stewart. *Film in the Third Reich*. New York: Simon & Schuster, 1973.

Jackson, Denny. "Pola Negri: A Vamp and a Lady." GeoCities, www.geocities.com/Hollywood/Hills/2440/negri.html, 1998.

Jacobs, Lewis. *The Rise of the American Film*. New York: Teachers College Press, 1968.

Jewell, Richard B., and Vernon Harbin. *The RKO Story*. New York: Arlington House, 1982.

Jewsbury, Lewis, and Neil Hackett. *Civilization Past and Present*. Vol. 2. New York: Harper Collins, 1992.

Keylin, Arleen, and Suri Fleischer. *Hollywood Album*. New York: Arno Press, 1977.

Kotowski, Mariusz. *Pola Negri: Life Is a Dream in Cinema*. Bright Shining City Productions, 2006. A documentary film.

Kreimeier, Klaus. *The UFA Story: A Story of Germany's Greatest Film Company, 1918–1945*. Berkeley: University of California Press, 1999.

Kreuder, Peter. *Nur Puppen haben keine Tränen*. Munich: Percha, 1971. Reprint, Munich: Dtv, 2003.

Lamparski, Richard. *Whatever Became Of?* New York: Crown, 1967.

Lanza, Joseph, and Dennis Penna. *Russ Columbo and the Crooner Mystique*. Los Angeles: Feral House, 2002.

Lasky, Jesse L., Jr. *Whatever Happened to Hollywood?* New York: Funk & Wagnalls, 1975.

Legenda Kina: Pola Negri: A Cinema Legend. Łódź, Poland: Muzeum Kinematografii w Lodzi, 2008.

Legenda Kina: Pola Negri: Eine Kinilegende. Łódź, Poland: Muzeum Kinematografii w Lodzi, 2007.

Leider, Emily W. *Dark Lover: The Life and Death of Rudolph Valentino*. New York: Farrar, Straus and Giroux, 2003.

Lewandowski, Jan F. *Pola Negri w Sosnowcu*. Katowice: Gnome Wydawnictwa Naukowe, Art ystyczne, 2002.

Lynn, Kenneth S. *Charlie Chaplin and His Times*. New York: Simon & Schuster, 1997.

McKay, John P., Bennett D. Hill, and John Buckler. *A History of World Societies*. Princeton, NJ: Houghton-Mifflin, 1996.

Monush, Barry. *The Encyclopedia of Hollywood Film Actors*. New York: Screen World, 2003.

Morris, Lloyd. *Not So Long Ago*. New York: Random House, 1949.

Morris, Michael. *Madam Valentino: The Many Lives of Natacha Rambova*. New York: Abbeville Press, 1991.

Munden, Kenneth W., exec. ed. *The American Film Institute Catalogue of Mo-*

Bibliography

tion Pictures Produced in the United States: Feature Films, 1921–30. New York: R. R. Bowker, 1971.

Negri, Pola. *La vie et le rêve au cinéma.* Edited by Albin Michel. Paris: Albin Michel, 1928.

———. *Memoirs of a Star.* New York: Doubleday, 1970.

Nowakowski, Jerzy. *Boska Pola i inni.* Warsaw: TO MY, 2005.

Oberfirst, Robert. *Rudolph Valentino: The Man behind the Myth.* New York: Citadel Press, 1962.

Parish, James Robert. *The Hollywood Scandals.* New York: McGraw-Hill, 2004.

Pratt, George C. *Spellbound in Darkness: A History of the Silent Film.* Greenwich, CT: New York Graphic Society, 1973.

Robinson, David. *Chaplin: His Life and Art.* New York: Da Capo Press, 1994.

———. *Hollywood in the Twenties.* International Film Guide Series, no. 3. New York: Paperback Library Edition, 1970.

Rotha, Paul. *The Film till Now.* New York: Funk & Wagnalls, 1949.

Sayler, Oliver M., ed. *Max Reinhardt and His Theatre.* New York: Brentano's, 1924.

Schoenhals, Albrecht, and Anneliese Born. *Immer zu zweit: Erinnerunge.* Wiesbaden: Limes, 1977.

Siegel, Scott, and Barbara Sigel. *The Encyclopedia of Hollywood.* New York: Facts on File, 1990.

Slide, Anthony. *Silent Players: A Biographical and Autobiographical Study of 100 Silent Film Actors and Actresses.* Lexington: University Press of Kentucky, 2002.

Stawski, Aleksander. *Pola Negri: Ksienzna Mdivani Krolowa ekranu.* Warsaw, 1928.

Swanson, Gloria. *Swanson on Swanson.* New York: Random House, 1980.

Taylor, John Russell, ed. *Graham Greene on Film: Collected Film Criticism, 1935–40.* New York: Simon & Schuster, 1972.

Thomson, David. *A Celebration.* New York: Doubleday, 2001.

———. *Cinema Year by Year.* New York: Penguin, 2003.

Vance, Jeffrey. *Chaplin: Genius of the Cinema.* New York: Harry Abrams, 2003.

Villecco, Tony. *Silent Stars Speak.* Jefferson, NC: McFarland, 2001.

Weber, Eugene. *Europe since 1715.* New York: W. W. Norton, 1972.

Weinberg, Herman. *The Lubitsch Touch.* New York: E. P. Dutton, 1968.

Wiesława, Czapińska. *Pola Negri—Polska królowa Hollywood.* Warsaw: Philip Wilson, 1996.

Wolfenstein, Martha, and Nathan Leites. *Movies: A Psychological Study.* New York: Hafner, 1971.

Zierold, Norman. *Sex Goddesses of the Silent Screen.* Chicago: Henry Regnery, 1973.

Interviews

Note: These interviews were conducted by the author for his documentary film *Pola Negri: Life Is a Dream in Cinema* (Bright Shining City Productions, 2006).

Basinger, Jeanine, author, professor of film studies at Wesleyan University, and founder and curator of the Cinema Archives at Wesleyan University. Wesleyan, Connecticut, October 2004.

Eyman, Scott, author and film historian. Los Angeles, April 2005.

Gasten, David, writer. Denver, August 2004.

Gonzales, Brother Alexis, professor, Loyola University, New Orleans, March 2005.

Leider, Emily, author. San Francisco, August 2004.

Lewis, Alfred Allan, author. Miami, August 2004.

Lyles, A. C., producer at Paramount Pictures, 1957–1980. Paramount Studios, Los Angeles, April 2005.

Mills, Hayley, actress. New York, July 2004.

Schönbrunn, George, close friend of Pola Negri's. Los Angeles, April 2003.

Slide, Anthony, author. Los Angeles, April 2005.

Villecco, Tony, author. New York, October 2004.

Wallach, Eli, actor. New York, August 2004.

Index

Acker, Jean, 123, 145

American moviemaking: description of the studio system in, 58; early larger-than-life film personalities, 67–68; Hays Office, 57, 60; hazards of, 63; impact of cinematography on the appearance of actresses, 66; impact of controlled lighting on, 63, 66; impact of *Madame Du Barry* on, 34–35; Negri and the advent of talking pictures, 164–66; Negri on happy endings in movies, 111–12; Negri's first talking picture, 167–68; Negri's transition to, 55–56, 57–59, 60–62; public attention to stars in the 1920s, 105–6; the "vamp" image, 77, 85. *See also* Hollywood; moviemaking; Paramount Pictures; United Artists

Arbuckle, Fatty, 56, 72

Arlen, Michael, 127

Associated First National Pictures, 34

ballet, 7–11

Banky, Vilma, 127

Bara, Theda, 77, 85

Barbed Wire (1927), 150, 151–53, 157

Barrymore, John, 150

Basinger, Jeanine, 62, 86, 101, 154, 170, 189

Bayes, Nora, 112

Beery, Noah, 96

Belasco, David, 74

Bella Donna (1923), 63, 64–65, 89, 110

Bella Donna (Hichens), 55

Bergère, Ouida, 78, 168

Berle, Milton, 170

Berlin: Negri's flight from, 182; Negri's life in the postwar years, 37–41; Negri's return to in the 1930s, 173–82; in World War I, 27

Bernhardt, Sarah, 50, 164

"Black Eyes" (song), 164

Blumenthal, Ben, 34, 48–49, 50–51, 53

Bow, Clara, 67, 106, 158

Brahm, Otto, 17

Brenon, Herbert, 90, 91–92

Brook, Clive, 152

Brown, Nacio Herb, 169

Browne, Porter Emerson, 85

Buchowetzki, Dimitri, 94–95, 96

Camille (1921), 123

Capitol Theater (New York), 34

Card, James, 60

Carmen (1918), 25–27

Carr, Harry, 4, 94, 100, 101

Carroll, Sydney, 175

Chaliapin, Feodor, 10–11, 120

Chałupec, Barbara Apolonia. *See* Negri, Pola

Chałupec, Eleonora: appearance and personality, 6; death of, 188; death of Jerzy, 38; in France, 113, 162, 166; Jerzy's arrest and imprisonment, 7, 8–9; Jerzy's separation from, 27–28; in Los Angeles, 188; marriage to Jerzy, 5; Negri's marriage to Serge Mdivani and, 156, 157; Negri's relationship with, 113; visit to Negri in Hollywood, 133, 134

235

Screen Classics

Screen Classics is a series of critical biographies, film histories, and analytical studies focusing on neglected filmmakers and important screen artists and subjects, from the era of silent cinema to the golden age of Hollywood to the international generation of today. Books in the Screen Classics series are intended for scholars and general readers alike. The contributing authors are established figures in their respective fields. This series also serves the purpose of advancing scholarship on film personalities and themes with ties to Kentucky.

Series Editor

Patrick McGilligan

Books in the Series

Mae Murray: The Girl with the Bee-Stung Lips
Michael G. Ankerich

Hedy Lamarr: The Most Beautiful Woman in Film
Ruth Barton

Von Sternberg
John Baxter

Hitchcock's Partner in Suspense: The Life of Screenwriter Charles Bennett
Charles Bennett, edited by John Charles Bennett

The Marxist and the Movies: A Biography of Paul Jarrico
Larry Ceplair

Warren Oates: A Wild Life
Susan Compo

Jack Nicholson: The Early Years
Robert Crane and Christopher Fryer

Being Hal Ashby: Life of a Hollywood Rebel
Nick Dawson

Intrepid Laughter: Preston Sturges and the Movies
Andrew Dickos

John Gilbert: The Last of the Silent Film Stars
Eve Golden

Pola Negri: Hollywood's First Femme Fatale
Mariusz Kotowski

Mamoulian: Life on Stage and Screen
David Luhrssen

Maureen O'Hara: The Biography
Aubrey Malone

My Life as a Mankiewicz: An Insider's Journey through Hollywood
Tom Mankiewicz and Robert Crane

Hawks on Hawks
Joseph McBride

William Wyler: The Life and Films of Hollywood's Most Celebrated Director
Gabriel Miller

Raoul Walsh: The True Adventures of Hollywood's Legendary Director
Marilyn Ann Moss

Some Like It Wilder: The Life and Controversial Films of Billy Wilder
Gene D. Phillips

Ann Dvorak: Hollywood's Forgotten Rebel
Christina Rice

Arthur Penn: American Director
Nat Segaloff

Claude Rains: An Actor's Voice
David J. Skal with Jessica Rains

Buzz: The Life and Art of Busby Berkeley
Jeffrey Spivak

Victor Fleming: An American Movie Master
Michael Sragow

Thomas Ince: Hollywood's Independent Pioneer
Brian Taves

Carl Theodor Dreyer and Ordet: *My Summer with the Danish Filmmaker*
Jan Wahl